EMPIRE IN GREEN
AND GOLD

Books by Charles Morrow Wilson

EMPIRE IN GREEN AND GOLD

OIL ACROSS THE WORLD

AMBASSADORS IN WHITE

CENTRAL AMERICA: CHALLENGE AND OPPORTUNITY

MIDDLE AMERICA

A MAN'S REACH

ROOTS OF AMERICA

BACKWOODS AMERICA

MERIWETHER LEWIS OF LEWIS AND CLARK

TREES AND TEST TUBES

CORNBREAD AND CREEK WATER

AROOSTOOK

CHARLES MORROW WILSON

EMPIRE

IN GREEN
AND GOLD

THE STORY OF
THE AMERICAN BANANA TRADE

HENRY HOLT AND COMPANY

To the banana men with whom I have worked and played in the tropics and out, during nine busy, frequently happy, and always adventurous years.

CONTENTS

EMPIRE IN GREEN AND GOLD

"FRUIT OF THE WISE MEN"

ALFREDO CERRARES was a Carib, a "black Indian." His working equipment included a stubby canoe or *cayuco* hewn from a ceiba log, two patched canvas sails, and a double-bladed paddle. But he had other possessions almost as important to his station—a homemade water jug fashioned from the butt of a banana stalk; a solitary gold tooth; a battered derby; and a ragged pair of white duck breeches, the legs of which had been hacked off about eight inches above the knees—to assure sufficient ventilation.

Alfredo was nimble and handsomely muscled. For years he had been a fisherman in Almirante Bay of Panama, but before the turn of the last century he had become known as the best boatman on the dangerous south pass. That was why the banana *hombres* had chosen him to carry messages down the rugged and storm-beaten coast front between the banana headquarters at Limon in Costa Rica and the banana headquarters at Bocas del Toro, Panama—a seventy-five-mile run among surf-smashed reefs and treacherous inlets. He knew that the slips of paper he carried in a rubber belt tied around his neck were important because they gave the instructions for cutting the fruit for the big steamships which two or three times every month nosed into Almirante Bay from the outer channels.

Each time he started his run the banana men at Limon paid him twenty-five American gold dollars, whereupon the Carib boatman would slip the beautiful golden disks into the pouch about his neck, massage his one lustrous tooth, remove his breeches, hop into his six-foot *cayuco*, and paddle out to sea. When the weather was calm he could make the run in thirty hours, setting the yard-square mainsail and paddling furiously through the blistering day and chilly night, dipping among flying fishes, pushing on without food or rest until he shoved his *cayuco* into the green-shadowed Bocas inlet.

This was Alfredo's supreme moment. He would pull on his breeches and trot up the beach to the thatch-roofed "boss house." There he would remove the money belt from his neck, lift out the all-important scrap of paper, and deliver it with silent eloquence to the "boss man." Occasionally the boss would glower as he read the message and swear loudly. More frequently he would scowl, then grin broadly, and begin to whoop in a jargon of Spanish and English. Men would emerge from adjacent patches of shade; banana reapers and mule men would appear from numerous hidden corrals.

Soon hundreds of sleepy mules and half-naked men would be on the trails to the outlying crescent of banana fields, where hundreds of other workmen were waiting to meet them. Into the receivers of dozens of wooden-box telephones, gun-toting *Yanquis* were shouting orders, and within the hour the full colony would be cutting fruit in anticipation of the arrival of the steamship. And all because Alfredo, now the richer by twenty-five gold dollars, had paddled and sailed the final seventy-five perilous miles to deliver a message which originated in Boston and was sent by land telegraph wires to Galveston, Texas, thence by land and sea cable across Mexico, down the west coast of Central America to a frontier port in Nicaragua where the land wires of two national telegraph-telephone systems relayed the information to the banana company wires at Limon. Eventually the word came to Alfredo, who brought the message in his *cayuco* to Bocas del Toro, "The Mouth of the Bull."

Alfredo lived dangerously and proudly for several years. He became the richest man in his village. He built a manaca shack at least twice as big as any other, and inasmuch as he now earned more in a week as a message runner than he had previously made in many years as a fisherman, he bought gaudy red shirts and straw hats for his sons. When his aging woman had grown unreasonably fat from rich eating, he took another wife. Next he built a shrine in front of his thatched home and invited a local medicine man to lodge with his family, bless his home, and pray for safety on his voyages.

But one day during the late summer hurricane season of 1902, Alfredo failed to appear at Bocas with the scrap of paper. Another Carib runner was sent to look for him. Several days later the runner found Alfredo's overturned *cayuco* high on the beach and half filled with sand. Some distance beyond the boat the runner found Alfredo's body, the money belt still tied around his neck, the gold pieces and the precious cutting order sealed safely inside the pouch.

Since the time of Alfredo and his *cayuco* many other banana messengers have made the Limon-Bocas run. It is not nearly so dangerous now, for radios, telephones, and telegraph stations are quite common around Almirante Bay. They are quite common, for that matter, throughout the banana lands of Central America. But the banana trade continues to be a hazardous one. Although the immediate physical risks may not be so great as they were thirty or forty years ago, they have not been entirely eliminated. Dysentery, malaria, and numerous varieties of tropical disease remain. The death rate among the citizens of Latin America as a whole is twice that of the citizens of the United States. And the death rate among the inhabitants of the banana reservoir—the low coastal lands of Central America—though drastically reduced by costly sanitary and medical works, can and does flare fiercely if the medical and sanitary protection is ever neglected.

But apart from physical risk there are other circumstances that make the banana trade hazardous. The crop is perennially unpredictable. An investment of one million dollars may return a profit of twenty-five or possibly fifty percent, or it may return the investor a worthless plot of flooded or blighted jungle acreage and a bankruptcy loss. It is just this element of risk that makes banana growing a pioneering agriculture. It was born in an era of frontiers. It developed as an extension—psychological if not geographical—of the pioneering advance toward the western boundaries of the United States.

The frontier is no theorist's dream. It was and is a way of thinking and working made possible by the existence of free, or practically free, land for easy taking. But the development of the banana frontiers proved to be markedly different from the quickly exploited frontiers of the American West. In the United States, foreign capital investments, unofficial approval of fraud and speculation, and a line of government services which followed in the immediate rear of the first settlers made the task of the Western pioneers far easier than that of the Central American frontiersmen.

The banana pioneers found to their amazement that the ways of the banana lowlands were entirely different. They knew that bananas grow quickly. They were dismayed to find that the fruit sometimes dies even more quickly. They discovered how difficult it is to clear the jungle edge and how easily the jungle takes back all that man plants. As the trade grew, the early pioneers began to realize that much would have to be done before they could expect any agricultural benefit from the land. Labor forces would have to be assembled, swamps would have to be drained, and at least the structure of a functioning community would have to be established in a lawless, pestilence-ridden, and almost uninhabited territory.

They were faced with the problem of establishing a trade in forbidding jungle valleys which white men had shunned for centuries and which Indians had avoided for even more centuries. "Out West" or "down South" in our own country were millions of acres of comparatively tillable land where a man could stake a homestead or buy a quarter-section for a few dollars, build himself and his family a log shack, and, by using his own brawn, craftsmanship, and energy, clear a first few acres, plant a first crop, and expand and develop larger fields. If his first selection was in error he could abandon it and take another. Good land was plentiful. He was never obliged to conquer the desert, the swamps, and the unfertile mountainsides. But the tropical valley havens offered no such advantage.

Frontiersmen in the United States took relatively good health for granted as more or less "the usual thing." In the lowland tropics, disease and sickness were normal and good health the exception.

Roads, trails, ferries, and railroads linked United States frontiers with settled communities. But Central American jungles made almost all types of communication hazardous. Building roads and railroads was enormously difficult. Trails and footpaths were sucked down by the jungle in a few days or weeks. Port sites were few, and those few were isolated from the more populous inland areas. Before 1885 Central America had no regular shipping service.

In the colonization of the American West, small cities of the plains grew, surface ores were easily mined, ranches and boom towns gave way before an advancing industrialization. Soon the frontier became a pattern of organized settlements and eventually a cultivated and prosperous community of cities, towns, and farms.

No large areas of tropical America were new in the sense that the United States West was new. During the sixteenth, seventeenth, and eighteenth centuries—generations before the million square miles of the Louisiana Territory became a part of the United States—practically all the lands of the tropical American mainlands and the Caribbean islands had been picked over and accepted or rejected for what the Indians, conquistadors, and other settlers had considered to be good reasons. Nearly all the potential banana lands of the tropical mainlands had been rejected by these early adventurers. Like the principal Indian nations before them, the white settlers, whether they had come for conquest or for peaceful activity, had taken to the inland areas—the high valleys, mesas, steppes, and mountainsides. In these sites they built their cities, capitals, and principal settlements. Long before the banana trade was born, the major highlands of Central America and its adjoining tropics had ceased to be frontiers.

But the Central American lowlands are today and will be tomorrow self-perpetuating frontiers. The jungle is forever making forays into its former possessions. Its growth is as inevitable as the death which lurks within its borders. Although it has lately become a proving ground for aviation, for socialized medicine, and for pathological research, the Central American jungle remains an eternal frontier.

How can man secure his position in the verdant but overwhelming tropics? In the world at large, moral and social codes are more clearly defined, though perhaps no more effectively enforced, than they were a century ago. But along the banana frontier the trade is often forced to administer justice, provide for the general welfare, and promote social reform, in addition to managing the most difficult of the world's agricultures.

Less than one-twentieth of one percent of the tillable soil of the American tropics is suited to the growing of bananas. It is clear to all persons familiar with Caribbean lands that Central American nations cannot possibly endure as "banana republics." It is impossible to maintain one crop superlatively well when all other crops are dying or dead. The banana industry cannot survive in a mire of poverty, political corruption, and human degradation.

The solution which the trade is proposing, and to some extent has already accomplished, involves the establishment of scores of subsistence crops which can be grown profitably by citizens of Middle America. Another decade may see at least one hundred acres in other crops for every acre of banana planting. This is not merely a matter of capital earning for the banana companies. It is a matter of basic survival.

The problems of transportation and marketing have always been troublesome. Even when the banana pioneers succeeded in raising the fruit, there remained the problem of a road to market. The difficulties began with collecting the cargoes of green bananas. Half a century ago most banana loads were gathered from jungle-edge or river-bank clearings among the Honduran coastal valleys between Ceiba and Old Tela. "Honduras" is a Spanish-Indian word meaning depths, or deep waters. But whatever harbor conditions may have been at an earlier time, the Honduran coast in 1870 had no deepwater ports. Nevertheless, at least five New Orleans shippers were calling for banana cargoes and collecting the heavy green harvests from such loading points as Micos Lagoon, La Ceiba, Cuero, Salada, Bonito, Rio Viejo, and Old Tela, none of which could be reached directly by any seagoing ship.

To prepare for the loading of a ship the banana buyers stationed an agent in the territory, usually a bewhiskered, per-

spiring *tropico* with a manaca shack and something resembling
a salary—or a subagent to whom the shippers paid a meager
commission for fruit delivered to shipside. Lacking an agent,
the shippers nailed a bulletin board to the trunk of a coconut
palm tree, where the *avisos*, or cutting orders, were posted.
The *avisos* were carried by runners like Alfredo. By sea, La
Ceiba is about forty-five miles from Micos Lagoon, but the
coast line is so ragged and meandering that runners who followed it were obliged to sprint and dogtrot sixty or seventy
miles between the two principal banana loading stations.

During the 1870's and '80's most bananas were grown by
local farmers or fever-ridden immigrants who worked small
plantings in clearings near the mouths of rivers or creeks and
sold fruit to a generally erratic clientele of shipmasters and
produce firms. The rivers provided some measure of the drainage that banana plants urgently require and some degree of
accessibility to the sea front. Since most of the banana plantings were little more than garden size, the task of collecting
even a thousand-bunch cargo required that *avisos* or verbal
notices be delivered to at least a dozen, sometimes to as many
as fifty, growers. At the most distant destination the runner
would deliver one or more *avisos*. Then he would start back
along the line, trotting stubbornly and without rest, delivering his messages to the agent or subagent at each point, or
tacking the *avisos* on the prescribed coconut trees.

The runners, little-honored Mercuries of the original American banana frontier who ran through storm and darkness, had
to be trustworthy and incredibly hardy. They had to make
the round trip of approximately 120 miles in thirty-six hours.
They sprinted or slogged along the beaches, through thorny,
mosquito-infested swamps and jungle edges, taking only short
rests, sometimes gulping a meal of *frijoles* or *tortillas* en route.

There were two kinds of *avisos*. One called for *corte libre*
—open cut—an invitation for any farmer to reap and deliver
bananas, usually by mule pack or bull cart, to the nearest

seacoast point or river's mouth. The other specified *corte limitada*—a limited cutting—and was directed to those growers who held contracts with the buyer. When markets were strong and ships were plentiful, the "open cut" *avisos* were in order. When ship tonnage was short and New Orleans markets were overcrowded, only the contract harvests could be accommodated. The "gulls," or occasional buyers, recruited banana cargoes on "open cut," usually paying rock-bottom prices in *Yanqui* money or barter.

Most banana ships were casual tramp freighters, many of them Norwegian craft, that ferried about any available cargo. Banana running called for laborious and sometimes perilous routines. For example, a ship would put in at La Ceiba to take aboard the local banana gang and stower forces. The ship would then raise anchor and sail for Old Tela, the lower headquarters for taking on banana cargo. There the lighters—wooden rafts buoyed at the corners with empty barrels or casks—were brought astern and towed twelve miles across the bay to Micos Lagoon Bar, where hundreds of bunches of bananas had been unloaded from mules, oxcarts, or the sturdy shoulders and heads of men and women. Since there were no piers or wharves and the waters were much too shallow to permit the ship to beach, the green bunches had to be carried through the surf and held high to keep the fruit from being sloshed with salt water.

Carrying the green, newly harvested bananas through rough surf was dangerous work. Stripped to loincloths and clamping their teeth on the slips of paper or tokens paid for each bunch of bananas loaded, the Carib waders—men, women, boys, and girls—splashed into the surf to place the heavy bunches on the lighters.

Each lighter was manned by a crew of at least five men, including two pole men on each side and a man in the bow to handle the anchor and catch the towline from the ship's boat which circled languidly just outside the breakers. As soon as a lighter was loaded with stacks of green bananas, the crew of the ship's boat would push their craft between the breakers, maneuvering deftly to avoid being caught broadside, then throw their line to the lighter, and tow it to the mother ship.

Meanwhile, stages, or floating platforms, had been lowered at the sides of the mother ship. The lighter crew, standing warily on their wobbly platform, would toss the bunches of fruit across to the ship's stage, where men waited to pick up the bunches and pass them on to the handlers who, in turn, would pass them on to a handlers' receiving line aboard ship. This work would continue until all the fruit cargo was stowed in holds or on deck.

The operation was far from safe. The lighters would surge violently on the breakers. But in spite of battering eight-foot waves, a lighter load of 300 or more bunches would often be put aboard ship without a single bunch being spilled or smashed.

At other points along the coast Caribs and other citizen farmers would paddle up to the steamship in their log canoes, also loaded with green bananas for delivery to shipside. These seagoing farmers frequently transacted their business and collected their pay in money or barter over the rail.

Then the cargo ship, still carrying its force of banana stevedores, toiled back to Tela, where the same routine was repeated and the lighters were anchored near the mouths of the smaller streams. Finally, after four or five laborious days of putting in and taking on, the ship would meet her cargo quota, pay off and discharge her sweating mob of stevedores, and head north for New Orleans.

On the sea, as in the surf, frontier banana transport was rough. Consider, for example, the run from Belize via the "inside route" south. There were, fortunately, a few capable pilots available—men familiar with the ways of their particular span of coast.

Immediately east of British Honduras is English Cay, an island about a quarter of a mile long and eighty yards wide. A somewhat inaccurate census once put the population at ten, and among those ten were the brothers Bill and Ed Gill, who piloted ships along the tedious way down to Puerto Barrios in Guatemala. Their father, old Bill Gill, from the Maine fishing coast down Rockland way, had settled on this sliver of earth about 1835 and in 1840, at the ripe age of twenty-one, began piloting.

After fifty-one years of steering ships, the senior Gill retired, "still a young man," and left the piloting to his two sons. Perhaps better than any other men, Bill and Ed Gill and their father knew the early history of Caribbean shipping. The boys recall that the sailing schooners running out of New Orleans prior to 1870 normally kept far out to sea, skirting and dodging the reef-strewn coast lines, awaiting wind and weather suitable for their dashes to points of the coast where they could barter mildewed merchandise for ripe coconuts and green bananas. With the brimy modesty of old-school Maine shipping men, the Gills were not backward about revealing that no Gill had ever wrecked a ship or left a ship aground. But they gave no guarantees against spilling deck cargo into the sea.

In the days of sailing ships, the eighty-two-mile passage from the East Snake to Belize, which even a slow steamer now makes in six hours, took a seaworthy schooner about eleven days. But repeatedly the Gills "blowed 'em acrost"— and entirely without the use of compass bearings or sextant angles. For the Gills knew by sight or in pitch darkness every shoal, drift, reef, and bar for 400 miles. They did, that is, until after the turn of the century when, according to the Gills, Caribbean weather "commenced to change."

In their own way the Gills had a great deal to do with opening the coastal runs from Central America. Ed and young Bill remember how harassed crews, delayed by storms or calms, used to work all day and all night dumping overripe bananas into the sea and stowing newly harvested fruit. They remember, too, how the ship decks used to be piled high with bananas—"stowed and throwed into every place you could see or think of—over and under the winches, covered with oil and dirt, sloshed by salt spray, and without a scrap of dunnage or any sort of protection." More often than not, the early banana ships were laden with deck cargoes piled so high that crews would swear they couldn't put to sea. But invariably they did. On boarding their charges, the Gills were accustomed to climb and slide over mountains of bananas and finally, on reaching the wheel, to find even that most sacred nautical shrine surrounded by still more hillocks of bananas.

One unusually rough morning, Ed Gill took over a steamship piled to the bridge with bananas. Ed piloted her "somethin' beautiful." But the sea was choppy with half a gale running. When Ed let her have a mere thirteen-degree list, the ship rolled her entire deck load—more than a thousand bunches —"square into the sea." Ed recalls that the captain was considerably upset on seeing so many precious bananas lost to the dolphins. "He commenced to storm and cuss, so I quiets him with a friendly punch in the belly. 'This here's a parable,' I says—'a parable to foretell the day when there'll be so blamed many bernaners you can fill up the whole Caribbean with 'em and still have plenty left to fill up all the pushcarts from Canal Street to Beacon Hill. That,' I says, 'is the parable and omen— the handwritin' on the sea.' "

There are about twenty-seven species or subspecies of bananas. Among the better known edible bananas are the Cavendish, a small, dry, yellow banana most common in the Guianas and Brazil, and the plantain, or starchy, green-skinned cooking banana. There are also the dwarf bananas—"lady fingers," which one can frequently buy in the Caribbean countries but rarely in the United States. And there is, finally, the

Gros Michel, the sweet, yellow fruit, which now accounts for more than ninety-nine percent of the banana imports into the United States and has become the standard commercial banana in Canada, the British Isles, and most of Europe.

To a considerable extent, the story of the banana is the story of tropical man. According to Dr. Herbert Spinden, the distinguished anthropologist long associated with the Peabody Museum of Harvard, "the first home of the edible banana was, in all probability, the humid tropical region of southern Asia . . . [which] includes northeastern India, Burma, Cambodia, and parts of southern China, as well as the large islands of Sumatra, Java, Borneo, the Philippines, and Formosa. Here the seedless varieties of the true domestic banana are commonly found growing wild, although perhaps they have merely escaped from cultivation."

It is probable that bananas were carried far into the Pacific by the first migration of the Polynesians about the time of Christ. Certainly many of the early explorers reported finding the plants in Hawaii and on Easter Island, this latter a dot of earth nearly 2000 miles from the nearest inhabited land.

The first clear references to the banana, Dr. Spinden points out, are found in Greek, Roman, and Arabian authors, who designated it as a remarkable fruit tree of India. Ancient Chinese manuscripts also mention bananas. Linnaeus, the famous Swedish botanist, called the banana *musa sapientum*—fruit of the wise men—because Pliny had said that certain sages of India lived on it. At the same time Linnaeus named the closely related plantain *musa paradisiaca*, out of deference to a medieval legend which said that this green starchy banana, and not the apple, was the forbidden fruit of Paradise. The name *musa* is from the Arabs who—and again we quote Spinden—"probably introduced the plantain into the Holy Land and northern Egypt, having obtained it in India." One of the earliest Arabic references to the fruit appears in the work of Masudi, a poet who died in A.D. 956. He extols a dish called

kataif, an Arabian delicacy popular in Damascus, Constanti-
nople, and Cairo. This was a confection of almonds, honey,
bananas, and nut oil.

There is reason to believe that the Arabs introduced bananas
into Africa by way of their tradings with Morocco and the
Sudan, and their ivory and slave trade in Central Africa. In
any event, the banana was well established in West Africa
when the Portuguese traders arrived there several decades
before the time of Columbus.

The name "banana" originated in West Africa. By the end
of the sixteenth century it had come into rather general use
—perhaps, as Spinden suggests, because the Portuguese carried
the plants very nearly around the equator—west to Brazil and
east to the Moluccas, one of their first colonies. Oviedo, after
visiting the West Indies and Central America, wrote the first
natural history of the New World. In this work he says that
Friar Thomas de Berlanga brought a fruit, which is obviously
the true banana, from the Canary Islands to Santo Domingo
in 1516.*

"There is a fruit here," Oviedo wrote, "which is called
'Platanos' but in truth they are not . . . nor did they used to
be in the Indies but were brought hither. . . . One hears
on all sides that this special kind was brought from the Island
of Gran Canaria in the year 1516 by the Reverend Father
Friar Thomas de Berlanga of the Order of Predicadores, to
this city of Santo Domingo, whence they spread to the other
settlements of this Island and to all other islands peopled by
Christians. And they have even been carried to the mainland,
and in every port they have flourished. . . ."

The Gros Michel banana originated in the Americas. It
was the product of a graft from parent stocks of Old World
origin. It was introduced into Jamaica about 1836 by Jean
François Pouyat, a French botanist and chemist who owned a
plantation, "Belle Air," in St. Andrew. On his return from a

---

* *Historia General de Natural de Indias,* Vol. 1, pp. 290-293.

visit to Martinique, Pouyat planted the rhizomes of this banana on his estate. At first known as the "Banana-Pouyat," it was later renamed the "Martinique" and, still later, the "Gros Michel." It is quite likely that the tens of millions of banana plants now cultivated in Jamaica, Central America, and elsewhere around the Caribbean, came originally from this single plant of M. Pouyat.

But bananas, of whatever variety, were about as important to our great-grandfathers as guanabanas, mangosteens, or similarly attractive but "bizarre" tropical fruits are to us today. Perhaps not one *Norteamericano* in ten thousand had ever seen or tasted a banana in 1870, and even to seaport residents bananas were strange and unfamiliar items. The United States' annual imports of bananas in the 1870's could be counted by the thousands of bunches.

During the 1880's, demands for the fruit increased. In spite of mechanical hazards both to life and cargo, the early steamships were drastically cutting voyage times, and the tropical sources of supply were now much closer to the major seaports of New Orleans, Tampa, Charleston, Baltimore, Philadelphia, New York, and Boston. New Orleans was a year-round banana port; but since bananas freeze and are spoiled in winter, the season on the East Coast was limited to spring, summer, and early autumn. Nevertheless, the annual tallies of banana imports were climbing from hundreds of thousands into the millions.

In 1884 banana imports into the United States reached the astounding total of 10 million bunches, but in succeeding years there was a great fluctuation in imports. Hurricanes, shipwrecks, glutted markets, droughts, and floods made the trade unstable and unpredictable. In spite of this, the trade continued to grow, and by 1885 it faced a problem which to some extent still remains unsolved—the problem of a steady source of supply.

The small island of Jamaica, where most of the early tropical pioneers had settled, could not continue indefinitely to supply the increasing quantity of bananas being sold to United States markets. Many tropical agriculturists believed that the rich alluvial valleys of Central America's Caribbean front were the best potential sources of supply to be found anywhere in the American tropics, or perhaps anywhere in the world. At that time, one could see a few clearings of banana fields scattered along these shore lines of Central America, but most of the bearing plants were growing on river banks, where the channels provided natural drainage. Other small plantings of bananas grew on turtleback islands or farther slopes of the valleys. Practically all the plantings were in small, isolated plots surrounded by swamps and jungles that bred nothing but pestilence and misery.

If the banana trade was to succeed it would have to make its own land and to create land values where values had not existed before and otherwise probably would never have existed. Central America simply had no developed lands upon which a great banana industry could be founded. The agricultural pioneers were forced to make suitable lands from jungle and swamp. The challenge was inescapable. And the proof of their success is that today at least ninety percent of all bananas in international trade are grown on such reclaimed lands.

Growing the crop efficiently and in dependable volume called for concentrations of suitable lands: blocks of thousands—still better, tens of thousands—of acres that were fertile, drainable, and reasonably accessible to port sites and possible railroad sites. Lands had to be cleared of jungle growth. The necessary work forces had to be brought together and provided with homes, stores, churches, and schools, and, most important of all, with hospitals, doctors, and a basic system of sanitation to protect them from the ravages of disease. Without this protection the whole venture would have been but a temporary stand against certain death.

The annual death rate in the sweltering Central American port towns of 1885 was estimated at 150 per thousand people. In the lowland interior the death rates were probably higher. Yellow fever was endemic throughout most of the Caribbean lands. Malaria was everywhere. So were malignant dysenteries and many other microorganic enemies of man.

Banana harvests are bulky, heavy, and extremely perishable. An average yearly harvest from one rather good acre of wheat weighs about 1300 pounds; from an average acre of corn, about 2800 pounds; but from a fairly productive acre of bananas, at least 18,000 pounds. Wheat or corn, harvestable only once a year, can be stored indefinitely and marketed at the convenience of the grower. But the efficient harvesting of bananas requires that the fruit be cut frequently throughout the year and shipped to markets punctually. The necessary ships, railroads, and other carriers are enormously expensive, and regular cargoes are essential to a functioning transportation system.

A working routine of shipping was just as important to banana agriculture as a reliable source of supply. As early as 1870 there were in Boston and New York, as well as in New Orleans, at least a few shipping men who agreed with pilot Ed Gill of English Cay and the upper Central American coast that banana history must be written on the sea.

One of the most determined of these believers was a schooner master from Wellfleet on Cape Cod. His name was Lorenzo Dow Baker.

CHAPTER TWO

CAPE COD SKIPPER

CAPTAIN LORENZO DOW BAKER spoke loudly. On land or sea, in the crow's-nest or on the foredeck of his schooner, he was accustomed to address his men in a deep and vibrant bellow. As he grew older his hearing became impaired (probably from overdoses of quinine), and the deafer he got, the louder he shouted. He talked loudly and he prayed even more loudly. The captain was a devout Wesleyan, who read his Bible daily and led his crew in worship.

Tall and not particularly robust, Lorenzo Baker sailed bravely and well, and true to the best Yankee sea tradition he remained an almost incorrigible individualist. He worked for himself. He owned, wholly or partly, all the ships he sailed, and if the ships happened to be barnacled and leaky, as several of them were, Captain Baker accepted the responsibilities and consequences with Wesleyan patience and forbearance.

He habitually recruited his own cargoes and hired his own crews, put them aboard, and paid them off. He provisioned and rigged his ships and personally inspected every man, cargo ton, pork side, biscuit, or hawser coil that went aboard. That was old-style Cape Cod shipping, and Lorenzo Dow Baker was every inch and ounce a Cape Cod salt. His nose was hooked and rather large. His sideburns had turned gray before he reached forty, but his features remained youthful. He rarely scowled and rarely laughed. His thin lips were set in a sort of permanent beginning of a smile.

Captain Baker's master's license recorded that he was born on Boundbrook Island, Wellfleet, Massachusetts, "on or about" July 4, 1840. He was fourteen when he first went to sea in a Cape Cod fishing schooner, and for fifteen years thereafter he sailed on fishing boats, collecting wages in "shares of fish catch," and thriftily saving his small earnings. At twenty-three he was part owner of a 30-ton mackerel seiner. In 1870, when he was thirty, Baker became master and principal owner of an overage fishing schooner, the *Telegraph*, an 85-tonner, three-masted and stanchly built, for her log indicated that she and her crew had survived many a hurricane.

The first record of the *Telegraph* under Baker proprietorship tells that her master sailed her from New York on Monday, April 20, 1870, with a party of ten prospecting gold miners and about four tons of machinery and "work luggage" for Ciudad Bolivar, about 300 miles up the Orinoco River in Venezuela. For an aging pea-shell of a schooner, this was a long, dangerous voyage. But the reward for the proposed journey to Ciudad Bolivar was tempting—$8500 in gold, which was at least $500 more than Lorenzo had paid for a major interest in the schooner. Moreover, the miners were willing to take chances, and so was the youthful bewhiskered skipper, who hired a Yankee crew of eleven and stowed aboard cured meats, sea biscuits, flour and beans, and two dozen hogsheads of fresh water before setting sail.

It was a hard voyage. After ten days the *Telegraph* was in the Caribbean and the hurricane belt. But with trust in God

and good seamanship they sailed on. By the middle of May
the *Telegraph* was toiling up the Orinoco, relying heavily on
towlines. Early in June she completed the river journey and
discharged passengers and equipment. Lorenzo Baker collected his pay in French and Spanish gold—then the best
accredited moneys of the Caribbean area—and headed the
Telegraph, still leaking badly, downstream for a return voyage, putting in at Port Antonio, Jamaica, for repairs and cargo.

The calking took about ten days, and during that time, after
much argument and haggling, the young skipper acquired a
low-pay ballast of Jamaican bamboo and a few bales of
ginger and allspice. But he stood by to take on a more profitable cargo. On the Antonio pier he saw fat green bunches of
bananas wrapped in straw.

Lorenzo Baker had previously eaten the ripe fruit and had
liked it. The dock merchant told him that the green bananas
would stand fourteen days of shipping and offered them at
a shilling a bunch. The young skipper recognized a fair challenge to his seamanship. If he could push his ship to a market
within two weeks, he might sell the fruit for a comfortable
profit. If he should hit storms or calms he would lose the lot.
But the young man from Wellfleet on Cape Cod was veteran
of a gambling trade. He bought 160 bunches at a shilling a
bunch and stowed them on the deck. The return voyage was
blessed with fair weather and favorable winds. After eleven
days at sea, the *Telegraph* "came to anchor at Jersey City, all
well." Baker promptly sold the yellow bananas at a profit of
two dollars a bunch.

He decided to gamble further with the peculiar fruit of the
hot tropics. First, however, he sailed home to Cape Cod and
after eight months of coastwise fishing and freighting he again
set sail in March, 1871, from Provincetown. He headed for
Jamaica, this time to bring back a full cargo of coconuts and
bananas. After five stormy weeks at sea the *Telegraph* again

drew into Port Antonio in such bad shape that it took four weeks to calk and repair her.

Here are daily entries of the log of the voyage:

May 8th, 1871. Finished taking in coconuts—whole number on board 35,200. Took in 400 bunches of bananas.

May 9th. Clear and pleasant. Took in some bananas.

May 10th. Clear and pleasant. Took in some fruit.

May 11th. At 4 A.M. Pilot came on board took vessel arount to the East Harbor. Took in some fruit and at 11 A.M. got under-weigh and proceeded to sea at noon.

After a tempestuous return voyage the schooner arrived at Boston. The log continues:

May 28th. At 8 P.M. passed Boston light. At 9 P.M. came to anchor at Quarantine.

May 29th. At 6 A.M. got underweigh and came to the City and hauled alongside Long Wharf. Pumps duly attended and so ends sea log.

This was the first large cargo of bananas sold in Boston. Lorenzo Dow Baker was definitely in the business. He continued to "sail bananas" during the summer months, when the delicate cargo could not be spoiled by freezing.

As banana running began to show signs of greater volume and profits, Captain Baker docked his schooner and spent several weeks visiting coastal farms of Jamaica, where he urged the islanders to grow more bananas and with greater care, so that more of the fruit might be sold in the United States. Jamaican bananas were still a casual, local crop, grown and reaped principally for local markets. But Baker believed the situation could be changed. In time it was changed, largely by the persistence of the bewhiskered Yankee schooner man, who confessed an intense personal liking for "the dadblamed silly fruit" that his Cape Cod neighbors referred to as "monkey food."

Young Captain Baker sailed back to Boston and shipped out

again as skipper of the *Eunice P. Newcomb*, a sturdy 109-ton wood-built schooner which Donald McKay's yards in East Boston had built for rough weather and hard wear. Once more Lorenzo Baker was part owner. And once more he proposed to sail bananas from Jamaica in the summer, to fish off the Maine banks in the winter, and, markets permitting, to dredge oysters around Chesapeake Bay in the spring. But the schooner paid best with bananas. In her lower hold and 'tween decks, the *Newcomb* could carry between 1800 and 2000 bunches, cut prematurely, or "thin," and carefully selected to minimize losses from ripening en route. Except in calms or troublesome head winds Captain Baker kept reasonably well to summer schedule, with the result that about three-fourths of the banana cargoes were landed in marketable condition. That called for good fruit, excellent seamanship, and a great deal of courage, particularly in the face of the tropical hurricanes that periodically disturb the late summer calm of the Caribbean.

At the Boston piers Lorenzo Baker had become acquainted with a sleepy-voiced young man named Andrew Preston. In 1871 young Preston was twenty-three and the all-round handy man for a staid Boston commission firm, Seaverns and Company, a partnership of Henry Seaverns and Lincoln Morrison, old-line and wholly respectable produce caterers. The partnership lasted twenty-seven years, and Andrew Preston worked for the firm nineteen of those years.

The two partners liked Andrew Preston, called him Andy, and, in the solid tradition of early Boston, made certain that he was not overpaid or too much pampered. The soft-spoken, diligent young man had come to work for them in 1866. Andy was then eighteen and already seasoned to hard work and hard times. He had spent his boyhood on his father's farm near the Massachusetts village of Beverly Farms. Farming was hard in New England in those times, and when Henry Seaverns offered Preston three dollars weekly—working hours 7:00

A.M. to 6:00 P.M.—Andrew took the city job, which paid in a week as much hard money as a good farm hand could earn in a month.

The new employee made the most of his chance to learn the trade of "perishables." He began as Seavern's janitor, clerk, shed handler, and sorter. Soon he assumed the additional duties of buyer, seller, and bookkeeper. He met the farm wagons and freight wagons which came lumbering and clattering to the warehouse doors. He maintained the firm's reputation for buying square and selling square—and for diligently selling all produce bought. In the summer he met the incoming fruit schooners and bought lots of pineapples, citrus fruits, and coconuts at shipside. Still a mere "clark," he was acting on his own enterprise when, on a July morning in 1871, he bought part of Captain Baker's deck cargo of the exotic fruit called bananas. Seaverns and Company had never dealt in bananas, but shortly thereafter the firm was advertising by hand posters "Fine Tasteful Yellow Bananas Fruit on Direct Import from The Antilles. . . ." Many years later Andrew Preston summarized the situation with Coolidge-like brevity: "I saw 'em, I bought 'em, and I sold 'em."

Like Lorenzo Baker's, Andrew Preston's conversion to the banana trade was thorough. He liked bananas. He declared that full-ripe bananas, either reds or yellows, were just about the most delicious food he had ever tasted, excepting, of course, Hubbard squash spread with sweet butter and baked slowly.

Boston was the least promising of United States banana ports. The sources of supply were from 1400 to 2000 miles away and, to make the worst of a bad situation, all Boston shipping had stubbornly refused to admit that steamships might someday replace the sailing schooners. Furthermore, the Boston market was notoriously conservative, and Boston eating habits next to unalterable.

The Yankee-bred Andrew Preston was nevertheless proving that bananas, however exotic and perishable, were salable in the Hub City. He had also learned that the demand for the fruit could be increased by the traditional Yankee fondness for peddled merchandise. He recognized the banana as the peddler's dream. Yankee peddling of the 1870's was preponderantly a vocation of back packs or hand baskets. Andrew Preston watched happily as the peddlers loaded their fat wooden baskets and set out afoot, not to return until the last banana had been sold.

Both Andrew Preston and Captain Baker were enthusiastic about the marketability of the unfamiliar Central American fruit—so enthusiastic that they were among the first to turn their attention to practical procedures for the cultivation and importation of the bananas. They were, however, not the first to recognize the commercial possibilities in such procedures. One of the first accredited port records of bananas imported into the United States is dated June 6, 1843, but for several decades thereafter the banana trade remained comparatively inactive.

The late William H. Bennett, a shipping reporter who wrote of an earlier inter-American trade, said that an unnamed skipper of an unnamed merchantman first brought Caribbean-grown bananas to our shores in 1690. This shipment probably came from Panama, and it is said to have been delivered at Salem, where the Puritans boiled the bananas with pork to complement a boiled New England dinner. The citizens reported with great indignation that the bananas tasted like soap.

It is also quite probable that occasional shipments of bananas reached New Orleans before 1803, the date of the Louisiana Purchase, although there are no authentic records of such imports. In 1883 the *Fruit and Produce Gazette*, an early periodical of the fruit trade, reported that the three-masted schooner *Reynard*, sailing out of Havana, delivered to the New York water front in July, 1804, a first shipment of thirty bunches of fat red bananas. Favorable winds and weather had permitted this shipment to reach market suitably ripe.

In May, 1843, John Pearsall, a New York commission dealer, imported and sold at "honest auction" 300 bunches of "Cuban reds." In 1845 the same dealer imported two more small cargoes of red bananas, but by 1850 clipper schooners had begun to bring much larger cargoes of Cuban bananas to New York, Philadelphia, and occasionally Baltimore. These cargoes included both yellow and red bananas, and when delivered in edible condition they were sold at prices ranging from ten to twenty-five cents a "finger," or individual banana.

Usually the independent shipmasters sought the bananas in Cuba or other tropical ports as deck cargo; bartered for the fruit with whisky, rum, cheap jewelry, whips, or firearms; and haggled for the lowest price or best swap. They knew that no matter how favorable the terms of purchase were, the trade remained a wild gamble, for even when the fruit was entirely green at the time it was laid on deck, it was likely that overripe bananas would have to be pitched overboard before the ship reached a market port. If the shipments arrived at port in fairly good condition, prospective buyers went to the wharves or the ships and picked over the fruit. They bought small quantities, usually five to twenty bunches at a time. The early comers sometimes got a bargain, but the late comers got only "shatters and leavin's."

Schooner loads of yellow bananas were arriving in New Orleans during the latter years of the Civil War, even while the foremost port of the Confederacy was theoretically under Union blockade. Most of those bananas were from shore-line Honduras or the Bay Islands off the Honduran coast. The importers and distributors were, for the most part, Italian immigrants. Among them were such tropical trade frontiersmen as Salvatore Oteri and D. Cifalu, and later the three Vaccaro brothers of New Orleans, who eventually founded the Standard Fruit Company.

As American shipping began its recovery from the ruinous consequences of the Civil War, the first continuing banana trade was opened between Panama and New York. Its entrepreneur was Carl Augustus Frank, a German-born ship's steward on an early Pacific Mail ship which ran from New York to Colon, on the Isthmus. Frank, who preferred to be addressed as C. Augustus Frank, had noticed occasional native plantings of bananas along the right of way of the Panama Railroad. An experienced cook, and a reveler in good eating, he liked bananas and presently demonstrated that most of his ship's passengers also liked them.

During long and humid port calls at Colon, then a principal Colombian port, Frank had plenty of time to go ashore and study the tropical fruit. He saw how banana plants were raised —that banana farming was a mere matter of digging up the rhizome, or heavy bulbous root of a mature plant; chopping it into "bits" or seed stocks, leaving each a good eye, as with seed potatoes; planting the bits; and returning ten to fourteen months later to harvest the heavy fruit. He noted, too, that the natives invariably cut the fruit green and ripened it in the cool shade. Frank wondered if a model ripening room, where the green fruit could be ripened gradually by means of ventilation and controlled temperatures, would not be a better system. He further surmised that if the fruit was cut sufficiently thin (unripe) and protected from wind and salt spray, it could be carried on long ocean voyages and eventually sold in cool and distant markets. The pattern was set for the basic routine of the banana trade.

During June, 1864, Frank ventured into the malarial hinterlands of Colon, bought six dozen bunches of green bananas, loaded them on his ship, and, after an eleven-day voyage, unloaded the fruit and sold it on New York piers at a net profit of approximately 1000 percent. Frank was delighted. He quit his job as ship's steward and determined to give all his time to importing bananas from Colon to New York. He chose the commission firm of Napier, at 229 Fulton Street, to sell the fruit, returned to Colombia's province of Panama, and supervised the clearing and planting of one of the first banana farms.

The following year, Carl's brother Otto became the New York salesman and the Franks began shipping bananas all summer long, taking available stowage space on practically any steamship or steam-sail craft. Storm losses were frequent, the spoilage rate was high, and the shipment would often arrive in New York dead ripe, whereupon brother Otto would scurry frantically to sell the fruit before it was too late. But the Franks persevered. In May, 1870, a month before Captain Lorenzo Baker sighted the Jersey coast with his first deck cargo of Jamaica bananas, New York already had the banana firm of Frank Brothers, with Carl and Otto as proprietors.

During that summer the Franks sold in New York three steamship cargoes of bananas, totaling about 3000 bunches. Two years later, the Franks attempted to ship bananas inland by railroad and to sell them in towns as far west as St. Louis. That venture failed. Usually the bananas were ripe on arrival at New York and rotten when they reached Cincinnati or St. Louis. But even this failure was an indication of the shape of trade to come.

The year 1875 marked the beginning of a bitter commercial feud between the Panama Railroad and the Pacific Mail shipping lines. Eagerly the Frank brothers set out to benefit by the feud. As freight rates were slashed, they raised their tonnage of banana imports and chartered three ships of their own. For three successive summers they enjoyed an almost complete monopoly of the New York banana trade.

But there was threat of competition from the Northeast. After ten years of good work, Andrew Preston, in 1876, was acting manager of Seaverns and Company. Life was good to the young man from Beverly Farms, though his salary remained distinctly modest.

Captain Lorenzo Baker was a prominent and prosperous shipping man in 1876 and a minor partner of a newly founded Boston firm, the Standard Steam Navigation Company.

In the same year bananas appeared at the Philadelphia Centennial Exposition of American Independence; bananas wrapped in tin foil were sold to the free-spending crowds at ten cents apiece. They were bought eagerly, and many fairgoers became acquainted with the exotic tropical fruit for the first time.

In 1877, Lorenzo Baker took himself, his wife, Susan, and his two-year-old son, Lorenzo Dow, Junior, to live in Jamaica, one of the first commercial banana strongholds of the hemisphere. Baker had observed that a man could not keep on shipping and selling bananas unless somebody raised the dadblamed things. And he was confident that Jamaica was the best place to raise them.

Captain Baker regretted leaving the Cape, though he planned to return on two or three runs a year. To be doubly sure of that, he made a down payment on a thousand sandy acres on Cape Cod and listed himself as a major partner in the Standard Steam Navigation Company, operators of wholly steamless sailing schooners, including Lorenzo Baker's newest, the *Eunice P. Newcomb*, which he owned in partnership with his good Cape Cod friend, Captain Jesse B. Freeman, president of the company. Fearful of homesickness in such faraway territory, Captain Lorenzo persuaded four associates to accompany him to Jamaica—a Wellfleet neighbor boy named Amos Simons; his barrister brother-in-law, Ed Hopkins, from Boston; his nephew, Jim Atwood, a tall strapping Cape Codder who at twenty-three was already skipper of a fishing schooner; and young Tim Clark, a boy bookkeeper, to serve as cashier. Baker explained his choice of Clark this way: "Timmy looks so dadblamed sad, he makes a body feel right happy by contrast . . . besides which mighty few folks would have the heart to ask him for money."

One pleasant May morning, Captain Baker loaded family, friends, crew, and provisions on the *Eunice P. Newcomb* at Boston and sailed away to Port Antonio, Jamaica—an artist's dream of a seaport. There he bought a home and set up the office of the L. D. Baker Company, General Shipping. His plan was to buy and sell tropical cargoes of coconuts, oranges, ginger, spices, pineapples, and sisal on commission and to serve as an agent for various ship lines that were plying to and from the island. But the principal objective of the L. D. Baker Company was an island-wide banana trade.

After settling at Port Antonio, Baker continued his pilgrimages among the coastal farms, persuading or trying to persuade the better planters and farmers to grow more and better bananas for export. Since Jamaica was suffering grievously from an overdependence on sugar, the Yankee shipping man found several willing converts. By the end of the year he had contracted to purchase all exportable fruit from about 2000 acres of good banana plantings.

Jamaicans, women as well as men, were then, as they are now, among the world's best banana farmers. The Jamaicans were, in addition, magnificent port workers and stevedores. Baker banked heavily on these virtues of Jamaican citizens, and many years later, when the island's government presented him with a huge silver loving cup that described him as "Godfather of the Jamaican Banana Trade and Foremost Friend of Jamaica," the captain replied that it was due "to God and the people of Jamaica."

Slowly and steadily Lorenzo Baker was laying plans for a banana trade with Boston. Aided by the diligent and persuasive selling efforts of Andrew W. Preston, he was likewise helping to open much of the Caribbean to banana shippers. With good seamanship and stowage, Jamaica bananas, cut

green and thin, could be carried to Boston in sixteen to seventeen days of sailing time and occasionally—when the winds
were exactly right—in fourteen days. Perhaps twenty days
after harvest the fruit would still be at least partly salable on
arrival at Boston, even though it was yellow ripe.

Lorenzo Baker had long since learned the hard way that
if the schooners were delayed by calms or headwinds the fruit
would reach port too ripe for profits. But he had also proved
that when the fruit is carefully cut and sorted and loaded on
stanch ships driven by capable skippers who could forecast
wind and weather with "fair truthfulness," at least two cargoes
out of three could be successfully sold by Andrew Preston,
duly assisted in Boston by several dozen determined peddlers
who were waiting with their baskets and handcarts. The percentage of profit on a single cargo was so high at that time
that the successful handling of two out of three cargoes netted
the importer a substantial profit.

Meanwhile Baker considered the newer developments of
merchant shipping. Though devoted to sailing ships, he could
not completely overlook the already evident supremacy of
steamships. In most of the nations of America, 1870 ushered
in a decade of steam power. Throughout much of the United
States and the British Isles, and in many sections of western
Europe, steam railroads were beginning to bind together cities
and nations.

But the change-over from sail to steam was neither spontaneous nor effortless. Sailing men, zealous and proud of their
great craft, resented the appearance of puffing stacks and
scalding vapors. Shipowners dreaded the costs and worries of
remodeling sailing ships and refitting them with steam equipment. British shipyards had promptly taken the lead in building steamships, and British shipping interests were using steam
to secure the lifelines of an expanding empire and to increase
their already enormous interests in the China-seas trade, the
far capes, and other distant shipping lanes that had once dealt

handsome profits to Yankee clippers, Scandinavian sailing craft, and other bold contenders.

The shipping world was learning that steam meant greater speed, more ton-miles per hour, and therefore more power and profit on the seas and at least a measure of protection from hurricanes, trade winds, monsoons, and calms—also that the steamships could make profitable the sea transport of perishable and semiperishable cargoes. Bananas were but one small entry in the new lists of transocean merchandise.

Citizens in dozens of ports eagerly expected their towns to become world metropolises, now that shipping lanes were being so miraculously lengthened by steam. Prophets of shipping were discussing grandiloquently the new sea frontiers and the new shipping lanes which were being opened by steam power.

Citizens of New Orleans were especially enthusiastic. During 1877, Signor Salvatore Oteri, then known as New Orleans' banana king, had bought the first steam-propelled vessel ever used exclusively for shipping bananas. It was a tug—*E. B. Ward*. Three weeks after launching, this first banana steamship vanished at sea, presumably a hurricane casualty. But New Orleans' traders were not easily discouraged. They had one of the first stakes in the banana trade, and the French Quarter banana crowd was determined to keep abreast of the latest developments.

Those were also Lorenzo Baker's sentiments. In 1877, after the summer cargoes to Boston had been delivered, he had the *Eunice P. Newcomb* loaded with good green Jamaica fruit and in late December sailed her to New Orleans. Luckily for the Cape Codder, there were no other banana ships in port that week, a happy circumstance that enabled him to sell the cargo at a good profit while invading cherished rebel territory. Back at Port Antonio, the captain joined his office force in a buttered-rum toast to the Deep South: "I liked all I got at

New Orleans except the Confederate money they wanted to give me and I didn't take. . . ."

The sailing man from Wellfleet continued to study the advantages of steam navigation. In 1877, the L. D. Baker Company had opened a receiving office in Boston, and at Port Antonio it had become Jamaican agent for the Atlas Steamship Line and its fleet of *A* ships—the *Atlas, Andes, Alps, Adirondack, Attros,* and many others—British-owned ships flying the flag of Spain as they carried cargoes from the Americas. All Atlas ships were powered by steam. Other steamships were beginning to carry Jamaican bananas to New York. Captain Baker noticed that the steamships were cutting previous sailing times in half and stretching the New York and Boston banana-trade seasons by at least two months.

On the Jamaica-to-Boston run two round-trip schooner voyages per season were a rather good average. For sailing schooners, port repairs and overhaul were usually necessary after each trip, and late-summer layovers were necessary if the hurricanes were to be avoided. In winter, late fall, or early spring even a brief norther or easter could chill and blacken a banana cargo in the time it took to chew a three-inch sea biscuit, and nothing could prevent the damage.

But Lorenzo Baker wanted to remain a sailing man, and the Standard Steam Navigation Company, of which Baker, his handsome and aging Cape Cod friend, Jesse B. Freeman, and the eloquent Boston financier, Thomas Mandell Hart, were principal owners, remained with sailing craft for three more years, principally because, as Baker put it, "We all liked to sail." Somewhat sadly, "Cap'n Lorry," as his intimates knew him, turned over command of the *Eunice P. Newcomb* to twenty-eight-year-old Captain William Anderson, a squat, ferocious-looking Yankee salt who was mentioned respectfully as one of the greatest sailing men ever to come out of New England. Still under forty, Lorenzo Baker gave up his position as shipmaster and became instead a supervisor of ships and cargoes. He knew that the banana trade was "taking" and that steamships were responsible for its growth.

Late in 1879, after a lengthy examination of conscience, Boston's Standard Steam Navigation Company voted to build a "grander" ship for the Jamaica banana trade—an "ocean racer" of 500 tons. She was christened the *Jesse H. Freeman*, in honor of the Cape Cod skipper who was president of Standard Steam. Four years after her keel was laid, the *Freeman* was launched at Bath, Maine, by Goss and Sawyer, the famous builders of clipper ships. By the oddest of coincidences she turned out to be another dadblamed sailing ship— a splendid three-master with a 32-foot beam and 180-foot over-all length. But careful observers noticed that her mizzen mast was also a smokestack and that her waist was fitted with an auxiliary steam engine. Nevertheless, the *Freeman* went out under sail. Under full sail before a fair breeze her speed was eleven knots, which cut the voyage from Jamaica to Boston from sixteen or seventeen days to nine or ten.

On her first voyage, while the ship was under full sail, the crew started the auxiliary steam engine. It promptly broke a shaft. Captain Baker shouted that this was what he had dadblamed well expected and ordered that the boiler fire be extinguished. But when the *Freeman* swept into the Antonio harbor Lorenzo Baker was proud. Earlier schooners had carried maximum loads of 1800 to 2000 bunches of bananas. The *Freeman* loaded a cargo of 12,000 bunches, and she could make four round-trip voyages a summer instead of the usual two. For four profitable years the sail-and-steam ship carried bananas from Jamaica during the warm-weather months and general cargo between Boston and Halifax in winter. When she began to wear out, the Standard Steam Navigation Company sold her to a whaling company and shortly thereafter she met the fate of many a whaling ship. Frozen in a North Pacific ice pack, the *Freeman* caught fire and burned to the water.

Meanwhile Baker and his associates were building a ship even larger than the *Freeman*. This was a three-masted schooner appropriately christened the *L. D. Baker*. Like the *Freeman's*, her mizzen mast was also her stack. She carried auxiliary engines geared for a speed of ten knots, but the chief engineer was skeptical about this. He explained, "She made ten knots as quick as she could." With favorable winds the *Baker* could make the Boston-Jamaica run in eight days. The ship's cargo capacity was 18,000 to 20,000 bunches—by far the biggest of her day. She was equipped with ventilators to preserve the valuable cargoes of bananas.

But the *Baker* established precedences in other ways. She had accommodations for ten passengers, and she was a year-round banana ship. Eight round-trip voyages a year was her goal, and for the first three years she met this goal with such regularity that Lorenzo Baker recorded: "She kept Andy Preston so busy selling bananas that his pants never got shiny behind, but he wore out a pair of shoes every two weeks."

At the beginning of her fourth year in service, on a July night off Nantucket Shoals, the *L. D. Baker* met tragedy. An anonymous passenger wrote to the *Boston Transcript*:

Flames burst from the wood-finished house above the engine-room amidships. There was a strong west wind, and the starboard lifeboat immediately caught fire. The port lifeboat was swung out, and the one woman passenger and a few other passengers were put aboard. Because of the location of the fire, the engineroom could not be reached nor the engines shut off. The rolling ship was continuing under full headway, there was a heavy sea, and as soon as the lifeboat touched water . . . it capsized.

The first mate, Henry Paine, a tall rangy man from down on the Cape, was able to right the boat, bail it out with a half-barrel which had held ship's biscuits, and get the others aboard. . . . Fifteen men had been left aboard the ship, five of them sailors held forward by the fire. The ten aft launched a liferaft, which was damaged in the process and sprung a leak. It supported, however, nine of the ten survivors in the water, clinging to its sides, until Paine, following the wake of the ship in his lifeboat, picked them up. The burned foremast fell overside but was held to the ship by the wire rigging. The five sailors clung to this spar in the water.

The red light in the sky was sighted by the whaling schooner *Franklin* of New Bedford, which reached the sinking ship at about daylight, rescued four of the five sailors only an hour before the *Baker* went down, and, following the ship's wake, picked up the survivors in the lifeboats. . . . It would be . . . fine to write that Henry Paine was rewarded and decorated for his heroism, but there is no such record. He shipped as mate on a ship for South America and was lost at sea. . . .

In those days ship's mail was no speedier than ship's cargo. It was early August when Captain Lorenzo D. Baker, at Port Antonio, learned of the end of his nautical namesake, the *L. D. Baker*. According to the late Tim Clark, who used to keep the books, Cap'n Lorenzo read the letter twice and for a time sat in dazed silence. Then he got up, strode to the window, and looked out to sea. In all the harbor only one sail was showing, and that one was ragged and mildewed.

That was the end of the *L. D. Baker* and of an epoch of sails and wooden ships. The tropical pioneers realized that the new banana ships would have to be built of iron and propelled by steam.

Steam was already powering the important merchant fleets. On land, steam was powering shops and factories, and railroads were also adding to the industrial development of cities, farms, and nations. In spite of his love for sail, Captain Lorenzo Dow Baker was doing more than any other man to demonstrate that steamships were deciding the present and indicating the future of the banana trade.

CHAPTER THREE

KEITH OF THE AMERICAS

ONE SULTRY SUMMER DAY in 1871 a slight young man slogged along the mud beaches of Padre Island, a few miles offshore from Corpus Christi, Texas. This young man, Minor Cooper Keith, was the island's principal citizen. He was resident executioner to a large flock of fierce hogs, which he fed on fish seined from convenient creeks and shore lines and on beef also raised on the grassy island. Texas cattle markets were so overcrowded with livestock that the twenty-two-year-old hermit made no effort to sell the beef from the 3000 longhorns which he and his father had bought almost as an afterthought when they had leased the island as a lumber property. The cost of ferrying live animals to the jammed stockyards of the Texas mainland persuaded the island rancher to slaughter the animals on the island, sell the hides and tallow, and feed the beef to swine. The swine he slaughtered and sold, for in the tropics to the south there was an increasing demand for salt-cured smoked bacon and hams.

The mail sloop from the mainland was one of Keith's few

contacts with the world beyond his island. When, on this particular day in 1871, the sloop brought him a letter, he opened it eagerly and found it to be a message from Henry Keith, his older brother. It suggested that young Minor might find railroad building more profitable and no less adventurous than butchering Texas longhorns or shooting wild boar.

Grass and wild fruits grew so abundantly on Padre Island that the cattle and hogs could fend for themselves and enjoy far better life expectancies without the presence of an energetic young man with a strongly developed profit motive. A careful appraisal of the situation convinced young Keith that he had been on the island long enough. He left Padre Island and made his way to Brownsville on the mainland. He had liked the island—its seclusion, its white fogs, its swarms of wild mallards. But he left as he had come, in happy anticipation of still better adventures—this time farther to the south.

Minor Keith knew that he had railroading blood in his veins, inherited from his maternal uncle, Henry Meiggs, who had drifted from lumber selling in Brooklyn to the gold rush of '49, to California politics, then to inter-American railroad building and inter-American politics, with never a dull moment and rarely a peaceful one.

The Keiths took kinship seriously. Minor, the second of the five sons of Minor Hubbell Keith and Emily Meiggs, was born in 1848 in a squat stone house on Delancey Street, where myrtles bloomed on the forty-by-forty lawn and rambler roses covered the front windows. Minor's older brother, Henry Meiggs Keith, was named for his mother's brother Henry, the family's most fabulous member. Uncle Henry was brother Henry's godfather and took him away on trails of high adventure when young Henry was only sixteen.

Little Minor Keith was the recipient of no such honors. He did, however, have an adventurer's spirit, an exceptional energy, and a talent for making friends. He was an undersized child and never grew taller than five feet eight even when

he arched his shoulders. During his early teens Minor worked
in his father's lumberyard. Once he stacked a mountain of
boards in a particularly original design which promptly
tumbled over onto the street, spilling Minor and several
thousand board feet into the thick of a Saturday's traffic,
thereby, so the police complaint read, "impeding a public
right-of-way and destroying the back end of Schmuck's
Bakery Wagon."

When Minor was fifteen his father quit the lumber business
for an imaginative but unsuccessful fling in real estate, and
temporarily Minor got a job at three dollars a week (hours:
8:00 A.M. to 7:00 P.M.), first as a cash boy and later as a clerk
in a lower-Broadway haberdashery shop.

The year was 1863. The Civil War seemed to be turning
in favor of the North; Abraham Lincoln was being derided by
the Eastern newspapers; returning soldiers in shabby uniforms
were swarming through the streets of New York and Brooklyn begging for jobs or handouts of food. Washington was a
madhouse of fiercely battling political factions. The prestige
of the United States in matters of international commerce
and finance was vanishing. The times were generally bad—
both north and south of the Rio Grande.

The Latin American desires for national sovereignty were
being encouraged by British credit firms. British credit was
by far the world's strongest, and the British government was
solidly behind any British banking interest in a position to
export capital. Railroads were a favorite loan risk. Already
there were extensive British-financed ventures into railroad
building in Latin America, particularly in Peru, Chile, the
Plata lands, and the West Indies. British banks were extending
shipping-line credit to both coasts of South America and to
the Amazon.

The British were also interested in Central America—
especially in its mildly flavored highland coffees and the
lowland indigo, which was still important to the English dye

trade and to textile manufacturers. Both the Caribbean and Pacific coasts of Central America were dotted with British-owned trade and commission houses, which frequently served as local bankers as well as general merchants, lending money to the coffee or indigo planters and equipping and financing the exploiters of jungle mahogany and other desirable jungle harvests. There were in 1865 at least thirty important frontier commissary firms in Central America, practically all of them British owned.

These commissaries were almost indispensable to the growth of Middle America. In the normal course of credits and fore-closures, they came to own tens of thousands of acres of the Central American lands. In time the coastal commissaries became banking firms, for whom many an early Central American *presidente* or soldier-of-fortune dictator readily signed, frequently with an X, practically any kind of English-written credit document that was set before him. Central America required credit. Strengthened by the world's first effective system of centralized deposit banking, England had consolidated its position as the foremost lending nation, whereas the United States and most European countries were conspicuously credit poor.

During the 1830's, the short-lived United States of Central America had been obliged to borrow public funds from English banks. President Morazan, for example, on behalf of the new confederation welcomed a pooled loan from London banks totaling 7 million dollars at six percent interest and a twenty-eight percent discount, even though barely one-ninth of the face value of the loan was actually advanced. When the Central American federation was disestablished, the loans were divided among the five countries which had comprised the union. Thereafter Central American finance became primarily a railroad finance and the Central American governments met their obligations regularly.

Above all other physical properties Central America wanted

railroads. But many personal, mechanical, and topographical obstacles had to be surmounted before the wish could be realized. The necessary materials had to be imported from mills and ports thousands of miles distant. The supply of qualified contractors was small, and remote creditor countries, lacking technical advisers and experienced civil engineers, were at the mercy of the contractors, too many of whom, according to Mr. Lee Christmas, one of the early Central American railroad pioneers, "started off as damned scoundrels and right away got a little wusser."

Railroad building in the tropics involved incredible difficulties of terrain. The inland mountains are high and precipitous; the valleys are forever threatened by violent floods; rivers are swift; and the volume of rainfall—in some places totaling 200 inches a year—is five times the average in verdant temperate climates. Moreover, the lowland jungles are formidable; natural seaports are scarce; and the lowlands are breeding grounds for fever, malaria, dysentery, and many other diseases.

Mr. Lee Christmas, a *Yanqui* locomotive engineer who came to Central America as a soldier of fortune, an *hombre* who frequently liked to pause and meditate between drinks or bursts of fire, often reflected that although all Central America wanted railroads in the worst way, nobody had clearly decided what would keep the railroads going once they were built. Railroads cannot survive without cargo, and Central America's proposed railroads, all of which were projected as starting inland from the sea, had no adequate source of freight. The highland coffee fincas could provide loads during part of the year when and if the railroads could be built through to the highlands. But the low coastal lands had no resources of any sort. It was plain that if railroads were to succeed in Central America, somebody would have to find or develop a large and continuing freight.

In 1865, at the age of seventeen, Minor Keith decided that

he had had his fill of the haberdashery business. He quit and spent several months with his father surveying timber in the Maine woods. Returning to Brooklyn, he celebrated his eighteenth birthday by taking over and reopening a small lumberyard which had been abandoned by his famous Uncle Henry Meiggs. After two more years of stacking, sorting, and selling boards, Minor was again in a foot-loose mood, even though the lumberyard was yielding a gross profit of nearly $3000 a year. There were three younger Keith boys ready to take over the lumberyard and, besides, Minor Cooper Keith sought adventures more in the tradition of his distinguished Uncle Henry Meiggs who was building railways in faraway Peru.

Uncle Henry was the daring kind. Until 1848, the year of young Minor's birth, he had also kept a lumberyard, lived in another squat Brooklyn house decorated with climbing roses, voted the straight Whig ticket, and attended the Wesleyan church. Then news of the great California gold rush reached Uncle Henry. Almost overnight he left his lumberyard and planing mill in custody of Minor's father, filled his house with roomers, and became a forty-niner.

En route to California, Henry Meiggs went by ship to Colon (then Aspinwall, Colombia), survived the dangerous portage of the Isthmus, and eventually reached San Francisco. There he opened a trading post, apparently having lost his enthusiasm for panning the hot sands of the desert. He opened other trading posts in the dry valleys near by and then plunged into San Francisco politics, borrowed money, established more stores, bought larger tracts of land, gambled wildly, and became a principal real estate speculator in the roaring and tumultuous El Dorado of the Pacific coast.

But Uncle Henry soon went broke. He managed, however, to hold out enough bullion to pay for his passage to some distant point, and in about 1853 he appeared at Santiago de Chile, where he introduced himself as a contracting engineer.

Like many another *turista*, he employed to the best possible advantage the few Spanish words he knew. When next heard from, Uncle Henry was taking contracts for building the pioneer Chilean Railway from Santiago to Valparaiso.

When the job was finished, with the help of much audacity, political horse trading, British-made materials, British bank loans, and the grace of God, Henry Meiggs, whom the warmhearted South Americans had renamed "Don Enrique," set out for Peru, "just to look at the scenery." Uncle Henry liked the scenery—especially the mountainous deposits of guano on the Chincha Islands off the upper Peruvian coast. He saw an opportunity to establish an immensely profitable fertilizer industry, and he immediately went off on another spree of constructive opportunism. He made friends and built political fences at Lima and set himself up as a lawful partner of the Peruvian government in developing and exploiting the guano mounds of the Chinchas. He sought and obtained British bank loans to finance the venture, which was almost instantly successful.

Promptly Don Enrique began to build more railroads, at first to carry the guano to the coast, and later, his enthusiasm getting the better of him, to link high, stately Lima and other cities of the Peruvian Andes with the sea. In accomplishing this the venturesome gentleman recruited some twenty transient engineers from the United States and Great Britain. He made the proper political friendships and solicited enormously large loans on the strength of guano and other specific resources of Peru, to which railroads are indispensable. The government of Peru underwrote most of the loans and Henry Meiggs got railroad building contracts to the tune of more than 125 million dollars. With the money he built railroads that even today would present fantastically difficult problems of construction. Meiggs built high, looping trestles, bored tunnels through snow-capped mountains, and carved roadbeds out of the sheerest rock cliffs. In the Peruvian Andes the Orozo Line, one of the most breath-taking of the Meiggs creations, exhibits a structural ingenuity which railroad experts maintain is still unsurpassed anywhere on earth.

The former lumberyard proprietor also proved the indispensable economy of railways. During the first two decades the Meiggs Railways earned some half a billion dollars from guano alone, and the path was cleared for an even greater wealth from the resources of the Andes. With the same recklessness with which he had planned railroad tunnels and mountainside loops, Meiggs plunged into Peruvian politics, social orders, and wage structures. With good reason the railroading and financial worlds were astonished and flabbergasted. In Manhattan, Cornelius Vanderbilt referred to Meiggs as a pretender, an opportunist, and an ignoramus. The London engineering journals noted crossly that the "Andean railway genius" lacked formal schooling in physics, mathematics, or investment finance. But London banks were competing with one another to grant him additional loans, and the fame of Don Enrique began to spread throughout the Americas and much of the world.

Uncle Henry did not hesitate to point out that not one of the railways then under construction in the United States faced structural difficulties that could hold a candle to those of the Peruvian Andes. Or that Meiggs railroads were paying their way—in sharp contrast to the new transcontinental lines of the United States, which were drawing fat federal bounties in lands, cash, and favors, while indulging in a great deal of fraudulent promotion and stock watering.

Henry Meiggs had a true Brooklyn flare for self-expression. He accepted his honors unembarrassedly and gave free drinks to anyone who would listen to the story of his life. It was not at all surprising that when Tomas Guardia assumed the presidency of Costa Rica he petitioned Don Enrique Meiggs to accept a contract to build the national railway of Costa Rica.

President Guardia's representative overtook Señor Meiggs

in Lima late in 1870. Don Enrique gestured grandiloquently. He did not know Costa Rica. He had never attempted to build railroads through watery swamps. He realized that construction problems in wet country would be difficult and unusual. But surely not impossible. No, Señor—not impossible to Henry Meiggs, or indeed to his next of kin.

The miracle man from Brooklyn called in his twenty-three-year-old nephew, Henry Meiggs Keith. Here was the man to build Costa Rica's railroad! They talked terms. Don Enrique was purposely obscure. He was willing to begin a road from a suitable Caribbean outlet to San José for 75,000 pounds British sterling. Young Henry Meiggs Keith would be in charge. President Guardia's man signed the contract for Costa Rica.

Since there was no dependable shipping service along the Caribbean coast of Central America, Henry Meiggs agreed to dispatch his own 2100-ton steamship, which he had named the *Henry Meiggs,* around the Cape to attend to the necessary transport of materials. Henry Keith wrote a letter to his brother Minor, who by that time had given up the Brooklyn lumberyard in favor of the lumber claim on Padre Island. The letter suggested that the brothers meet at Puntarenas, on the Pacific shore of Costa Rica, about the first of the following December. That would give Minor time enough to close out his island, return to Brooklyn to see the folks, and travel by ship from New York to the Isthmus, then by Panama Railway to the Pacific and by schooner from Panama City to Puntarenas. It would be Minor's job to manage the railroad's commissary. At least this was the plan in April, 1871.

Late in December, 1871, Henry and Minor Keith met in the palm-shaded Pacific port of Puntarenas. Each bought two mules, one to ride and one to carry luggage, and the party set out along the winding, flower-bordered road to San José, the capital. The coffee harvest season was drawing to a close, and the rough trail was jammed with slow-moving caravans of coffee carts drawn by drowsy oxen. The carts were two-wheeled conveyances with solid wooden wheels painted extravagantly with intricate designs in blue, gold, lavender, and red. Some of the oxen wore bright ribbons about their necks or horns, and many of the cart shelves were studded with tinkling copper bells. The vehicles were piled high with creamy brown coffee beans. Most of the ox drivers were men, colorfully dressed; some of them carried mandolins and strummed and sang as they tramped the grassy trails.

This was the introduction of the Keith brothers to the *Costaricensa*, a proud and beautiful people. Minor Keith saw the immaculate roadside shrines and the gay wayside camps of the coffee pilgrims, and from the hillsides he looked down on the bright green coffee groves. He was fascinated by the cottages with their thick white walls, blue doors, and blue shutters.

After a week of pack riding the Keith brothers arrived on the high, verdant plateau of San José. It was Christmas week, and thousands of Costa Ricans had come to their capital for the masses and the festivals. The plazas were ablaze with bands and processions. Doorways, balconies, and patios were crowded with bright flowers. Street peddlers carried silver baskets piled high with orchids and hibiscus. Minor Keith strolled alone through the tile-roofed city, listened to the bands, watched the youths and girls promenading—with their chaperones—in the plazas. The Brooklyn boy knew he was in paradise, and he decided that he would never leave Costa Rica.

Shortly before New Year's Day, the Keith brothers bought supplies for another muleback journey and rode away to the north and east toward the jungle-rimmed seacoast where the railroad was to begin.

But before leaving San José the brothers called on General Tomas Guardia, the president-general. The president was somewhat astonished at the youth of his railroad builders—

Minor was twenty-three and Henry twenty-five. The president was more impressed when Henry explained that his younger brother would be in charge of feeding and sheltering the work force and managing a chain of commissaries and countryside stores which their uncle, Henry Meiggs, had decided to finance with a working capital of $200,000. The president knew that there were no cleared spaces in which to build stores and no people to patronize them, but he said little. He did, however, assign the Keith boys an Indian guide and suggested that they buy an extra string of mules for replacements. He also reminded them politely of an ancient Costa Rican proverb that a man is a hero the first time he travels to the Caribbean sea front, whereas if he goes a second time he is a plain damned fool.

Nevertheless, the Keith boys set out, following the highland roads which tapered off into rough gully trails, then into bush-grown jungles. Through a completely rainy week they rode on (defying the rumor that travelers in the rainy season invariably die of fevers) until they came to a dark, reef-strewn seacoast. This was Puerto Limon.

But it was not the sort of *puerto* they had hoped to find. The president's first survey party had allegedly found a lemon tree growing in the thorn bush behind the sand banks. That discovery established the name. Beyond the coast were unmeasured miles of swamp. The sunlight beat fiercely on the open coast, and waves of mosquitoes droned seaward from the vast crescent of jungle.

A line of frayed tents had been pitched at the edge of the water, and Henry Meiggs's first shipment of laborers, some three hundred Jamaica Negroes, were building rows of palm shacks near by. The shacks had neither floors nor windows. Ragged holes served as front doors. The cost of such housing had been computed at one dollar per person and five dollars for a family, however large.

The Keith boys released their mules, took over a leaky

tent, and appraised the situation. There was plainly no point in establishing commissaries until more people arrived. The jungle lands had no inhabitants; not even the poorest Indians would live there. The Jamaicans were hacking away with axes and machetes at a tempo that suggested that several centuries would be required to clear brush from the first mile of right of way. The first drainage ditches poured jungle seepage into the camp instead of the sea, as had been the original plan.

Minor Keith groaned. He was supposed to be the camp mess manager, but there was no refrigeration and no fresh meats, vegetables, fruit, or milk. He opened the boxes of dried fruit. The contents were moldy. The barrels of smoked bacon, flour, and dried beans had been eaten through by weevils and borers. There was no doctor and there were no medical supplies. Occasionally Carib fishermen brought in canoe loads of fish, but these were usually spoiled. Some of the Jamaicans had brought chickens with them, but these disappeared quickly. Several wildcats had been seen with telltale circles of feathers about their mouths.

Adding to the difficulties, the coastal jungle seemed to be growing back faster than the Jamaicans could chop it down. So Minor became personnel head as well as mess manager.

As soon as he had recovered from his first siege of fever, and Uncle Henry's ship, the *Meiggs*, had edged gingerly among the reefs to land emergency supplies, Minor went aboard and headed for New Orleans, where he hoped to recruit an additional labor force.

From San Francisco, where he was temporarily incapacitated by heart disease, Uncle Henry Meiggs had communicated with about twenty railroaders, principally civil engineers and labor foremen, and asked them to stand by for his nephew's arrival at New Orleans. Since the times were desperately hard, and the southern ports were faced with unemployment problems, Uncle Henry figured that labor could be recruited without shanghaiing. To make doubly sure, he ran a brief advertisement in New Orleans papers: "Wanted for steady work; young men, preferably single, with a liking for travel. $1 per day; food, lodging and ship fare free. Call Mr. ——." Mr. ——, a member of the police department, was professionally desirous of exporting as many tough characters as he could.

After a fortnight of recruiting, Minor had persuaded about 700 men to climb aboard the *Meiggs*. Among the 700 were the twenty railroaders, whom he immediately made foremen. The rest, so the New Orleans chief of police reported, included many of the toughest characters ever brought together anywhere. By provident forethought Minor had put aboard some forty barrels of whisky, several cases of bolo knives, and several dozen pistols for himself and his new foremen.

The ship pulled out for Havana and, reaching there, took on cargoes of sugar, rice, beans, and other food staples. During this service stop twenty-five or thirty of the recruits slipped off the ship and did not return. Minor counted the rest, noticed that they were not altogether happy, and distributed pistols among his foremen. Heading for Belize, the final port of call, the ship plowed into a hurricane. She floundered far off course and scraped a coral reef some ninety miles north of Belize and about sixteen miles off the coast of Yucatan. Now the trouble began.

The captain was drunk. Young Minor Keith squared his shoulders, took several deep breaths, and assumed command of the ship. He patted an oversized revolver as he talked with the mates and made plans to pull the ship off the reef. The crew clamored for whisky. Keith poured each man a dram, then stationed foremen with drawn pistols to guard the barrels.

Next morning, when the storm abated, mass desertion was in the air. When the crew began heading for the lifeboats Minor took out his pistol and yelled for his foremen. With their help, the beardless and self-appointed skipper checked the riot. Then Minor began a desperate attempt to free the ship from the reef. He had the foremen put squads to work shifting cargo. He ordered that deck cargo be thrown overboard and directed crews to shift cargo from the bow holds to the stern. Finally, with enormous effort, stimulated by a flourishing of firearms on the part of the foremen, they raced the engines to top speed and pulled the ship off the reef. To the astonishment of all ship men aboard, the ship still floated. She limped on to Belize, and, while the foremen stood guard against further desertions, Minor Keith hired ship carpenters to make temporary repairs. After another week the weary *Meiggs* reached a point near the coral-ringed inlet beyond which lay Puerto Limon.

It had been raining at Limon, and the townsite was submerged. The rain continued for nine months. Total precipitation for the year 1872 reached the almost incredible figure of 254 inches—twenty-one feet on the level.

Mosquitoes droned out of the swamps. Many of the workers had contracted fevers before landing. At least half of those who had survived the voyage were sick within a week. Since medical men had not yet learned the prevention, cure, or even the diagnosis of common malaria or yellow fever, the diseases were termed simply "tropical fevers." Men shivered, burned, moaned, and vomited. Scores of them died. The one accepted therapeutic was strong whisky. The Keith brothers had imported plenty of whisky and very soon practically all white men in the camp were requiring it in the worst way and almost continuously.

When Henry and Minor led out the first location crews they found barely half of their prospective workers able to work, or even to walk. Within a week men were dying, and within a fortnight the proposed work camp was conspicuously a sick camp. Even the Keith brothers contracted the fever, but they kept at work—"cured themselves," as Minor later explained.

When the *Meiggs* again pulled in with a first cargo of English-made steel rails and white-oak ties from the States, the work force had dwindled to about a hundred white men and two hundred Negroes. More than three hundred of the New Orleans gang had died. Only nine of the railroad men survived, but true to the best American railroading tradition, they swore, drank, whooped, and worked, despite hell, high water, or yellow fever. They put the Negroes to digging drains and shaping grades with picks and shovels. Goading strings of mules, with merciless whips, they "snaked through" oak ties and steel rails—and before the year's end they had put down nearly four miles of track. By this time less than a hundred white men were alive. The Jamaicans, however, had been little affected by the fevers.

The Keith boys, now about as ragged and bearded as their confederates, again took stock of the situation. Henry Meiggs's original contract had expired. Uncle Henry was sick, but Costa Rica was willing to back the Keith boys in building the railroad. Yet Costa Rica could not supply labor for the swamps, for every Costa Rican, with excellent reason, believed the coastal jungle land to be synonymous with certain and painful death.

The Keith brothers had to look elsewhere for labor. They thought of Italy, a great portion of which is warm and swampy. Perhaps the citizens were acclimated to the fevers. Millions of Italians, moreover, were emigrating to other countries—into the slums of New York, New Orleans, and Chicago; to the Balkan frontiers; into Brazil and Argentina; and into far-scattered labor colonies where man power was needed—the Suez Canal sites, the lower Mississippi flood plains, and along the African Congo.

In Mexico City the Keith boys made arrangements with the Italian government for recruiting labor from South Italy, where their promise of a dollar a day with free lodging, food, and transportation seemed fabulous. About 200 Italians, ages sixteen to sixty, were landed at Limon in 1873. The first group promptly stampeded into the rancid jungles. About sixty died before the renegades could be lured back to work, and even after they were stationed in the nearer highlands the Italians continued to die of the fevers. Barely one hundred of the immigrants survived. Thereafter the Keiths relied principally on the Jamaicans, without whom there probably would never have been a Panama Canal, a Costa Rican railroad, or a Caribbean banana industry.

The problems of Costa Rican railroad construction were exceeded only by the multiplying troubles in railroad finance. The first 75,000 pounds sterling pledged to Henry Meiggs was quickly spent. In 1871 President-General Guardia had traveled to London to negotiate a million-pound loan. When sold, the paper netted Costa Rica only 556,000 pounds, which was less than half the cost of the completed railroad according to the highly optimistic estimates of the Keiths. The following year General Guardia's government negotiated an additional loan of 2,400,000 pounds sterling and received some eighty percent of the face value. But the instant the bonds were placed on an open market, they began to tumble in price. Cagily the interested London banking group encouraged patriotic Costa Ricans, particularly those who were earning money from their London sales of highland coffee, to buy up the Costa Rican paper. Believing this of benefit to their country and the all-important railway, the patriots bought more of the paper than they could afford. Exchange prices of the paper continued to fall. Soon the cash assets and national credit of Costa Rica were all but destroyed.

But the railroad moved ahead without any assurance of present money or future freight. There was no guano in the Costa Rican swamps, and no gold or silver or dyewood. The murderous onslaught of malaria and rain continued. But the Keiths and their helpers continued to build the railroad. More Jamaicans arrived—plodding, good-natured black men who swung picks and shovels, sloshed through water frequently neck deep, swung axes to fell the barricades of mangroves, slept on wet earth, ate deplorable food uncomplainingly. While white men died of fevers, the Jamaicans worked on. A meandering roadbed was shoving into the jungle. The first four miles of rails were laid and, as the workers pushed·on, death and swarms of small black buzzards followed the roadbed.

Someone has said that a man died for every rail laid down. During the first three years and twenty miles, at least 4000 deaths from malaria, yellow fever, and other diseases were recorded. It is possible that many more deaths were not recorded.

But the work went on. Lean and bearded railroad builders came to join the venture. Immigrants from many lands joined the work crews from Canada, Holland, and Sweden, from Syria, Turkey, India, and Egypt. But for every white man or brown man, there were at least twelve Jamaicans.

Henry became desperately sick and Minor put him aboard a tramp steamship to New York. Within a month Henry was back, still sick but determined to keep working. Old Jack Marti, who tended the Fourth of July Bar, Limon's first saloon, diagnosed Henry's ailment as yellow jack. Apparently the bartender was right. Henry collapsed at the Toro Amarillo camp and died within a short time.

Henry had been buried only a fortnight when another Keith came to replace him—the younger brother, Charlie. The severest of Keith critics could never say the brothers had led men into dangers which they themselves avoided. Henry's death, which left Minor in complete command, was not the last of the Keith casualties.

The railroad stretched inland—twenty miles, thirty, and finally, about sixty miles from Limon. There the job was hopelessly blocked at the edge of the Toro Amarillo, a river that was forever changing its course abruptly and destructively. Minor Keith abandoned the last twenty miles of railway and with the help of his engineers began to survey a new route, by way of the Rio Sucio and thence through the foothills to San José.

By that time the money was gone. Tomas Guardia and Costa Rica were still for the railroad. The government created a special issue of privileged bills—*billetes privilegiados* —at twelve percent interest. These were legal tender only for paying custom dues. Keith used the *billetes* to borrow cash from loan sharks, who habitually demanded an annual interest of twenty-four percent with collateral of twice the loans in *billetes*. It was obviously a deplorable system of finance. But Keith had a railroad to build.

After six years of work, deaths from fever decreased as the ratio of Jamaicans to white men increased. But there was still no money. Minor Keith was unable to meet the pay rolls. His force of 1500 Jamaicans went nine months without a payday. Yet they worked on. Minor Keith had become a leader the hard way.

Food supplies and building materials were exhausted. The *Meiggs* was dry-docked after a losing bout with a hurricane. Only chartered ships, most of them ancient and rusty tubs, were available for bringing in construction supplies. Their crews did not understand English, and many of the captains spoke only Swedish or Norwegian. But Minor Keith observed that all could understand him when he said he had no money. Furthermore, the ship masters knew the nautical hazards of Puerto Limon. Its shores were fringed with dangerous coral reefs, and its low green hills were notoriously deceptive landmarks for navigators. Altogether, the ship men feared Limon as they feared the plaguing fevers they knew to be associated with it.

Minor Keith, who had now begun to think like an engineer, believed that the tiny island called La Uvita, just opposite Limon, might offer a natural breakwater, and that if a sea

wall were built, the hills leveled off, the treacherous coral
covered over with earth from the hills, and the townsite
drained and equipped with a sewage and water system, Limon
could be made a real port. He had everything but the money.

Once more the young man from Brooklyn began to search
for a paying cargo for the railroad which, still nowhere near
the upland coffee farms, now plainly had to earn its own way
to completion. For months Minor had been wondering about
a rather remarkable fruit called banana. He did not particularly like the fruit, and he noticed that few Costa Ricans ate
it. But his Jamaican laborers were fond of bananas, a staple
food of their home island. Moreover, word had got around
that the Frank brothers were growing bananas alongside the
Panama Railway tracks, exporting them from Colon to New
York, and, oddly enough, actually selling them.

Minor Keith was confident that the valley lands back of
Limon would grow the bulky lowland crop. The valley of
the Matinas and Zent rivers, and the Santa Clara plains, all
more or less accessible to the new railroad, might therefore
supply banana freight. So Minor made a trip to Colon,
Panama, and looked up Carl Augustus Frank. Frank agreed
to sell young Mr. Keith a few hundred rhizomes or root bits
for experimental planting in Costa Rica.

A month or so later the roots arrived at Limon and Minor
Keith and his Jamaicans planted them in a sheltered valley.
They watched day by day as the giant leaves and pithy stalks
grew rapidly. Later in the year Minor arranged with the
Frank brothers to make joint-account shipments of bananas
to New Orleans aboard the *Meiggs*. It was part of the agreement that Minor Keith would be reimbursed for the actual
cost of shipping fruit and that profits, if any, would be divided
equally between him and the Franks. Keith made a first trial
shipment of 250 bunches to New Orleans in 1874 as deck
cargo of the hard-used *Meiggs*.

Net profits amounted to almost one dollar a bunch. Immensely pleased, Minor Keith resolved to plant more bananas in the fertile Zent valley near the headless railroad so that the first small harvests could be carried to Limon by handcar.

Meanwhile, Keith looked about for other means of earning in the tropics. He began to open the chain of commissaries which his Uncle Henry had planned. The first store in the chain was a palm-thatched shack near Limon. Rice, beans, flour, cured pork, cheap ready-made clothes for men, and gaudy bolt cloth for women were its principal stocks. But this first store did not prosper. Its sole customers were Keith employees, and since Don Minor was rarely able to pay his employees, they rarely had money with which to buy merchandise.

Appreciating this dilemma, Minor resolved to open a store where there were people with at least some money. Late in 1873 he opened a store at Bluefields, Nicaragua, in a rough board shack which he had crowded with dried beans, sodden blocks of brown sugar, bolts of calico, kegs of cheap liquor, and a great deal of miscellaneous hardware, much of which had been gathered at New Orleans auction sales and shipped south as ballast. Then Keith tried to find an honest *hombre* to manage the store. His first manager promptly vanished with the cash drawer.

Minor next met a professedly reformed beachcomber named Newcomb Brown, who suffered from an incurable kidney disease and had therefore renounced sin, joined three churches, and gone on a diet of green coconut juice and pious thoughts. Newcomb Brown said he was living every day as if it were his last, which any day might well have been, since, as Mr. Brown frequently stated, "My kidney is gone, my stummick is gone, my lungs and heart is gone, and all I got left is Christian principles."

When Mr. Brown opened the store for Minor Keith he sought his customers' good will by giving away all the hard liquor. When all the liquor was drunk, a somewhat besotted clientele lingered around the doorway. They explained in warm confidence that they had no money and never seriously expected to have any, but they had live turtles, captured alligators, pellas of wild rubber, sarsaparilla, tortoise shells, and monkeys which they were perfectly willing to barter for merchandise.

The sanctimonious Mr. Brown, who did not have much longer to live anyway, accepted the barter in lieu of cash. When Minor Keith returned to see how the store was getting along he found the rear of the premises alive with reptiles, the shelves and kegs empty of merchandise, and the entire premises pervaded with the appalling stench of dead turtles and raw rubber. A line of scantily garbed Indian women waited hopefully with additional barter goods. Mr. Newcomb Brown had last been seen heading toward the beach carrying a heavy oaken keg on one shoulder, the last cannister of rum on the other. He was wearing no trousers and his shirt front bulged with a pocket-sized Bible, Mr. Keith's money bag, and several green coconuts.

At twenty-five, Minor Keith was clearly a man buffeted by adversity. He resolved to establish more stores—a coastwise line of trading posts to stretch from Belize southward to Costa Rica. He would dispatch Jamaicans to build the shacks and sheds at least within sight of possible seaports. He would make his brother Charlie overseer of the stores and scrape together every dollar he could find to invest in merchandise. Instead of trying to predict the fluctuations of Latin American currencies, he decided to trade in barter goods, salable in New Orleans for comparatively sound United States dollars. His plan called for leasing one or more steamships and for the storage, grading, and selling of native produce in large quantities.

Minor Keith was becoming acquainted with soldiers of fortune and the criminal refugees to the Spanish Main—those nameless men best influenced by pistols, profanity, and cash rewards. As a pioneer proprietor of trading posts, Don Minor, unlike his British competitors, could neither lend money nor give credit. But he was confident that he could trust his younger brother, that he could use what he had learned of tropical psychology, and that in one way or another he could produce the cargo and money needed to complete the railroad.

Having thus made a rather precarious start as a storekeeper and banana planter, he went back to Costa Rica and the railroad.

The railroad was then pushing through the Reventazon Valley some forty miles from Limon, toward Cartago, one of Costa Rica's oldest and richest highland towns.

The location engineers were shooting ahead. Minor Keith later recalled watching old Sam Norris as he stood behind his transit and peered through the telescope . . .

As I watched he whistled, untied a huge red bandana handkerchief which he wore around his neck, waved it frantically a few times and then threw it on the ground with considerable violence along with his Stetson. Then he stamped on the handkerchief and hat, grinding them both into the dirt. I asked what was wrong.

He said, "Oh! there's nothing really wrong. I was just signaling my foreman. I don't understand any Spanish and he only *sabes* a little English, so we have arranged a signal code. One long whistle means cut to the right, two means cut to the left, three means that the line is right and four long blasts is to tell the gang to come to dinner."

"That's all very well, but it doesn't explain your removing your hat and handkerchief and stamping all over them."

"Oh, that's a supplementary signal," Sam explained. "When I go through those motions it means that everything has all gone to hell, the work is all wrong, and that Cinforiano is to bring in the gang to get their time checks."

It was December again—Costa Rica's season of flowers. The year was 1882. Nearing thirty-four, Keith was still a bachelor, and a bachelor in Costa Rica is conspicuous—particularly so when the man is distinguished, wealthy, and physically sound. Minor Keith had become a Costa Rican institution, a tested and accredited representative of the nation, its leading rail-road builder, and, practically speaking, a lawful partner in the Costa Rican state.

In banking circles, Minor Keith's wealth was a debatable subject. He had come to Costa Rica in 1872, presumably with a little money of his own and grandiloquent though extremely abstract promises from his Uncle Henry Meiggs. But in 1882 Minor's personal finances were interwoven with the public treasury of Costa Rica. Moreover, by means of a system of credit and I.O.U. swapping which would have driven a certified public accountant to despair, Minor Keith now owned and operated a chain of seven frontier commissaries. He was leasing two aged steamships at charter fees of $3000 a month and conducting an international barter trade valued at a quarter-million dollars a year.

In Costa Rica's Zent Valley he was planting farm after farm of bananas. He had also acquired title to 10,000 acres of jungle lands for additional banana farms near Bluefields, Nicaragua, and 10,000 more acres around Almirante Bay, on the Caribbean side of Panama. In South America he had gained ownership of 15,000 acres of valley lands near Santa Marta, Colombia.

In each of these tracts he was directing the clearing and planting of banana farms to supplement the monthly shipments of the fruit which his leaky boats already carried from Limon to New Orleans. His Colombian venture, like his merchandising and banana-growing experiments in Central America, were backed by London-chartered limited-liability corporations of which Minor Keith was the principal owner.

Late in 1881 he had made the first full-cargo shipment of bananas from Limon to New Orleans. Keith-grown bananas were then being shipped to market at the rate of 2500 stems a month. Though the shipments were weak and irregular, banana farms were already feeding the far-scattered Keith enterprises, insofar as they were being fed, and banana farms were the green hope of the still struggling railroad.

Nobody could doubt Minor Keith's courage or his ardor for developing Central America. But people could and did doubt his possession of hard jingling money. In lower Central America one still hears stories of Minor Keith as a "miracle man"—how he once rode away penniless to meet a pay roll, his money bag stuffed with banana leaves and during his ride he stumbled upon a cache of United States greenbacks which had been stolen from his paymaster more than a year before. Señor Keith quietly picked up the money, met the pay roll, and treated each of the workmen to a dram of good whisky before he gulped an entire bottle, without once lifting it from his lips.

There are stories, too, of how Minor Keith, while borrowing money from illiterate Syrian usurers, substituted for his usual *billetes* slips of paper bearing the admonition in English, "Learn to trust a Christian gentleman." But even if money was not always available, the Keith enterprises were multiplying and Costa Rica's railroad, which had been started two years before the first steel rail was laid in Mexico, was pushing stubbornly toward the highlands.

Late in 1881, Minor's younger brother, Charlie, had died, presumably of yellow fever. Like his elder brother, Henry, Charles Keith died at twenty-seven. For a rainy fortnight, Minor had been almost paralyzed with grief; then he had returned to work with a frenzied determination to carry on. A month later, John, the youngest of the brothers, joined Minor in the jungle.

A decade before, when he first arrived in Costa Rica, Minor Keith had confided to his brother Henry that he planned to marry a Costa Rican girl. Now that he was thirty-four and alone, and since it was again Costa Rica's season of flowers, he planned a holiday pilgrimage to San José before taking off on a credit-hunting journey to London. He knew that during the Christmas season San José's plazas would be bright with flowers and resounding with band music, and that observant female chaperones, clad in discreet black, would keep sharp eyes on the promenading maidens and self-conscious swains. The Costa Rican from Brooklyn was in a holiday mood.

But the holiday was interrupted. Once more Minor Keith found himself in a railroading quandary and once more the problem was one of labor supply. Ferdinand de Lesseps and his Inter-Oceanic Canal Company were undertaking to build a great canal across the Isthmus of Panama. Their venture was supported by a canal-building concession granted by Colombia; by the right to use the Panama Railway, then the only completed rail line in Central America; and by one of the most audacious stock-promotion campaigns in world history.

During his distinguished work at Suez, de Lesseps had learned the seriousness of tropical fevers and the difficulties of holding labor forces. So he began the Panama venture with a bold bid for all available workers, particularly Jamaicans, and offered instead of a specified daily wage, such as Keith was paying, an alluring contract or task wage, whereby practically any unskilled laborer could earn five to seven dollars a day in gold. Minor Keith could not compete with such an offer. Temporarily he and Costa Rica were unable to meet common labor pay rolls of one dollar a day. The de Lesseps wage system would have instantly whisked away the whole card-castle structure of Costa Rican railway finance.

For several months Señor Keith had watched the Jamaican labor forces drifting toward the swampy isthmus, and for some time he had been pondering other possible sources of labor. He would not rely on Italy or the rowdy docks of New Orleans. Perhaps he would be obliged to draw on the admittedly inferior Negro labor of the Barbados and other islands of the West Indies. But first he resolved to search again for native Central American workers. He remembered the sturdy black Caribs whom he had often met in the jungle fronts of Honduras and Nicaragua. So he boarded a tramp steamer bound for the Honduran coast, landed by rowboat off a sand-blocked inlet which was soon to become Puerto Castilla, and set out on muleback with a Carib guide.

After some time the two rode into the Indian village of Santa Fé, a community of perhaps a thousand people. The squared houses with their neatly thatched roofs were arranged in well-ordered streets.

The village *alcalde*, black as a well-polished kitchen stove, greeted them, bowed magnificently, and asked Keith and the interpreter into his home. The mayor's home was built of stucco and contained only one room. A small hole in the wall served as a combination window and smoke vent for a cooking fire that smoldered in a far corner. In the center of the room there was a table, made of a sort of bamboo, and the table was set with gourd bowls and plates hand-carved from dark, heavy mahogany.

On another wall hung a board studded with sharp rocks— a primitive washboard which the natives used for shredding coconuts. Across from it was a smooth stone mortar for grinding corn. High above the open fire were clusters of drying fish and corn ears. Beyond the table was a pile of coconuts and wild tangerines. The household *purone*, an earthen water cooler fashioned from red clay, was set against the far wall. Across the pole rafters overhead were stowed extra masts and patched sails for the *cayucos* used for fishing voyages.

The *alcalde* listened solemnly as Minor Keith's interpreter spoke. . . . Men to work; to dig earth; to fell trees and lay sticks of heavy iron. Men to dig trenches so that the waters might move away. Men to work in the giant fields. . . . Without replying, the village leader strolled out of the door and a moment later returned carrying a fat green turtle. Behind the

mayor a line of laughing black-brown children, all naked
except for the bright bandanna handkerchiefs tied around their
heads, danced and shouted. The *alcalde* introduced his merry
offspring with a flourish of his hand, then beheaded the turtle
and placed it on the corner fire. Now he addressed his guest
through the interpreter.

The *alcalde* of Santa Fé was honored by the coming of the
distinguished visitor. The Carib men of the village were
honored to be asked to go and work in the far strange lands
where it was desired to lay down the heavy iron sticks. But
the men of Santa Fé village were fishermen and boatmen by
trade. They had been so since time began. They will remain
so until time ended. The women and children tilled garden
fields of corn and squash, gathered the coconuts from near-by
groves, and mended the sails for *cayucos*. Thus the village
had lived always and would continue to live.

The *alcalde* apologized for the absence of his men. The day
before a giant boat had scraped upon the coral beach and the
people aboard had come ashore before the breakers began to
smash their giant canoe to pieces. Among the passengers was
a most beautiful *doña* who spoke in a strange tongue and was
followed about by another of her kind.

Minor Keith remembered that one of his chartered ships,
the *König*, had only a short time before left Belize for the
Keith commissary at Bluefields. He was sure that the wrecked
ship was indeed the *König*. After the formalities preliminary
to a Carib meal, Don Minor took a polite bite of his serving of
fat, rawish turtle, crunched a hard twist of the cassave tube,
and directed his interpreter to bargain with the village chief
to take him by *cayuco* to the scene of the wreck. He also
asked if it were possible to overtake the shipwrecked passengers, who evidently had hired passage on the Carib dugout
canoes to the port of Old Castilla.

The host agreed to provide transportation to the port and

after much polite hesitation accepted as a friendly gift the two mules which Keith had brought from Castilla.

After a plunging, salt-sprayed journey in sailing canoes, the party reached the decrepit port to which the ship's survivors had been brought. There Keith learned that the wrecked ship was indeed his own *König*, loaded in great part with Keith merchandise, and that both the ship and its principal cargo had been lost. Among the survivors was the beautiful *doña* whom the Carib chief had described earlier. Her name was Cristina Castro. In San José, many years before, Minor had met the young lady's distinguished father, a former president of Costa Rica.

There was nothing to do but wait at port for the next ship. Among the survivors of the *König* were six Chinese seamen, the Swedish captain and the mate, a missionary from Northampton, and two suspicious-looking characters from New Orleans' *Vieux Carré*. Far more interesting to Señor Keith was the Señorita Cristina Castro. Somewhat less interesting was her chaperone and aunt, Tía Maria Montealgre, also of San José, Cartago, and the Costa Rican aristocracy.

Minor Keith gave money to the Carib boatmen and prepared to wait as comfortably as possible. In the most proper Costa Rican manner he paid his respects to Tía Maria. In his Sunday-best Spanish he chivalrously said that if a shipwreck were required for him to make the acquaintance of so charming a lady as Tía Maria, he could but be thankful for the storm and the shipwreck. Señorita Cristina laughed heartily. Her eyes sparkled and her laughter, according to Minor, was like a bird song in a Long Island pasture. Tía Maria smiled, too. So did Keith. In less elegant Spanish he asked what he might do for the fair ones.

The señorita, still laughing, answered in English. She said that every Costa Rican knew of Minor Keith, the friend and builder of Costa Rica. She and her aunt wanted above all else to get back home to San José before Christmas. They were returning from a Christmas shopping tour in New Orleans. They had taken passage on the *König* en route to Colon; from there had planned to travel by Isthmus railroad to Panama City and thence by Pacific Mail boat to Puntarenas. But now they were shipwrecked. All their Christmas presents and practically all their other belongings were lost at sea. They wanted to get on to San José. But first, gracious señor, they needed to eat. For two days they had eaten nothing but sea biscuits and coconut juice.

Minor Keith understood. He said that he would tramp the countryside and find something edible. He promised also to find them a shelter if there were any. Soon an Atlas steamer would be calling for coconut cargo. They could all ride down to Limon with the coconuts. From Limon Señorita and Tía Maria could travel by handcar on the new railroad as far as it went, then by mule train to Cartago and San José.

By nightfall Minor had returned with a freshly caught mackerel and bags full of oranges and rice. He had hired an Indian woman as a servant and had been promised quarters for the distinguished ladies in a private home. Moreover, he had searched the water front for rain capes for protection against the daily afternoon downpours. But the village, which accepted the daily downpour as one of the dull routines of providence, had no raincoats. After prolonged search, Minor found in the back of an old store two straw-yellow linen dusters which had been manufactured in the States. The dusters would be better than no coats at all, so he carried them to Cristina and Tía Maria. The women were somewhat startled to discover on the back of each garment the inscription, Goetz: Complete Embalming and Undertaking Service.

Eleven days later, the barnacled steamer *Andes*, rusty veteran of the coconut runs, anchored at Old Castilla and, after the pilgrims from the *König* climbed aboard, set out for Costa Rica. During the voyage, Minor Keith told Cristina the entire story of his life and for good measure added an outline of his future plans. He would complete Costa Rica's railway, then build a magnificent chain of railroads from Mexico City south to the Isthmus. He would build fleets of trading ships and bring trade and a better life to all of the Caribbean coast. Cristina proved her genius as a listener. She said, smiling, that she adored listening to Minor Keith, since there was no other way to pass the time.

After three days of heavy seas the *Andes* cleared the wet green capes of Costa Rica. At the port of Limon, Keith pointed out to the passengers the beginning of Costa Rica's railroad. Debarking from the ship with Cristina and Tía Maria, Keith ordered that a string of mules should be ready at the other end of the railroad. Then he called for three handcars, the hand-propelled teeter-totter type on which sturdy Jamaicans worked the platform hand bars. Minor rode the first car so that he could inspect the tracks, Cristina's car came next; Tía Maria's was last.

It was an exciting journey. Only ten feet above sea level at Limon, the rails led through newly cleared banana farms and climbed toward Moin Junction, three and a half miles inland. There the road branched, and there Minor Keith christened the right-hand fork (the twenty-mile roadbed from Moin to Estrada) the Castro Line.

From the junction the rails again dropped to sea level and for eight miles followed the shore of the Caribbean. Here vast palm-dotted sand beaches separated the blue Caribbean and its rolling, white-capped breakers from the deep green of the jungle beyond. At Swamp Mouth, the railroad turned sharply from the sea front and plunged into the jungle through miles of leafy tunnels into which even the brightest sunlight seldom penetrated. Keith had lost most of his men here. West of Estrada the new railroad bridged the torrents of the Matina River, then made for an eight-mile straightway into the dozing village of Madre de Dios.

The new rails led on across the Pacuare River and up to

the grand junction, Siquirres, thirty-seven miles inland, and there began the long hard climb into the fabulously beautiful highlands. In 1882 the newly laid rails went only to the east bank of the River Reventazon.

Keith and his party ferried the river in a leaky rowboat. At La Junta, saddle mules, pack mules, and a Negro guide were waiting for them. Thus equipped, they began the pilgrimage into the mountains, keeping to a brushy trail that followed the general course of the Reventazon through boulder-littered gorges and dense forest and around innumerable sharp turns.

As they climbed up to mile-high El Alto and so on to Cartago and its succession of coffee lands that were again gay with ripe red berries, Minor Keith and Cristina Castro rode side by side. Tía Maria looked on in affable silence, thankful that Doña Cristina had at least one more Christmas to spend at home as a child.

In San José the spell continued. Oleanders and blood-red hibiscus bloomed in the gay blue doorways of the town. Dwarf palms raised feathery fronds, and wild orchids were peddled in the market places. Cascades of red and purple bougainvillea spilled over walls and verandas. The sunshine was bright. Bands played, and lovers strolled in the plazas.

After a great deal of pleading on Keith's part, Señorita Cristina and Tía Maria agreed to walk once through the Central Plaza with him. This was more telling than a full-page notice of engagement published in all the local *diarios*. The distinguished builder of the Nacional was wooing the daughter of a Costa Rican president. Minor Keith was thankful for the shipwreck and thankful to be alive and no older than thirty-four.

When the holidays were ended and the many happy farewells were done, the marriage banns of Cristina Castro and Minor Keith were announced at the cathedral. Minor strolled again through the plazas and attended the final concerts and the miracle play in the company of Cristina and Tía Maria, and then made ready for his great journey to England.

Keith's luck seemed to be changing. Don Tomas Guardia, Costa Rica's long-time president, was dead. But immediately the Don's brother-in-law, General Prospero Fernandez, had stepped into the presidency. The general called in Minor Keith and presented a plan to restore the credit of Costa Rica and transact loans that would complete the railroad up the Reventazon to Cartago and San José. Don Prospero also approved a contract whereby Costa Rica gave Minor Keith the power to renegotiate its defaulted foreign debt.

The young man from Brooklyn kissed his fiancée good-by and proceeded at his own expense to London. It was a long and involved errand. Señor Keith went ahead stubbornly, first to negotiate loans that would help restore Costa Rica's credit. From the London banking house of C. de Murrieta, he obtained for Costa Rica a loan of about 6 million dollars to complete the railroad.

In London, he also attended to some of the expanding personal enterprises of Minor Keith. He set up formal accounts and published stock certificates for his British-incorporated Tropical Trading and Transport Company, and the Colombia Land Company. He described plans for a railway through Guatemala and for new and bigger banana plantings in Nicaragua, Panama, Guatemala, and Honduras as well as Costa Rica—future Keith plantations that would supply freight for future Keith railroads. In London he talked with the wealthy fruiterers of Covent Gardens and boldly promised to export Central American bananas to England to supplement the small shipments London was then receiving from the Canary Islands. He also made the acquaintance of Sir Arthur Forwood, principal owner of the Atlas Steamship Line and with him effected what Sir Arthur termed a joint-account trade, according to which Keith's Costa Rican bananas would be grown, harvested, drawn by rail, and delivered to Atlas ships at Limon without charge, then shipped to New Orleans, also without charge, and there sold, with profits to be divided equally between Keith and Arthur Forwood. This was a hard bargain for Minor Keith. But it would help the railroads.

Six months passed before the *Yanqui* with an empire mainly on paper could break away from London. Then, in September, he returned to San José with trunks full of gifts and many gilt-edged papers. He had also bought a huge South African diamond for his betrothed, and, for himself, a London-tailored cutaway, Prince Albert style, with stiff tails that tickled the backs of his knees when he walked.

On October 31, 1883, the Eve of the Feast of All Souls (in Brooklyn it was just Halloween), Cristina Castro, of Costa Rica, and Minor Cooper Keith, of Brooklyn, Costa Rica, and the American tropics at large, were joined in marriage. Cristina confided to Tía Maria and others that she was the happiest girl in all Costa Rica. Minor Keith was sure that he was the happiest man anywhere.

CHAPTER FOUR

BOSTON FRUIT COMPANY

MINOR KEITH had launched a banana trade primarily to develop his railroad interests in Central America. Captain Lorenzo Baker had seen bananas as a profitable cargo for his Yankee ships. Andrew Preston was most interested in bananas as a salable produce. For all three, bananas were a means of earning profits at a time when profit-making was generally regarded as a praiseworthy occupation and failure to earn profits, under ordinary circumstances, a sign of incompetence or laziness.

All three men had begun as poor boys—Lorenzo Baker as an apprentice sailor at fourteen; Andrew Preston as a produce-dealer's handy boy at eighteen; Minor Keith as a lumberyard helper at thirteen. None had more than five years of common schooling. All were strong young men making ready to run what they knew would prove to be a long and strenuous race.

Andrew Preston and Lorenzo Baker were convinced in 1885 that it was high time Boston had an accredited banana-selling firm. This conviction was shared by several of their friends, particularly by Captain Baker's associates in the Boston Standard Steam Navigation Company.

In spite of heavy losses of fruit from spoilage and freezing, which seemed unavoidable, and the usual marine hazards to sailing craft and undependable steamships, Baker and Preston had done much to prove that bananas could be made, as Andrew Preston said, "a respectable merchandise." They had studied the procedure of the trade and decided that Jamaica would probably be the best continuing source of supply.

Captain Baker knew that island well. He had made friends among the planters. Rumor had it that the Yankee skipper planned to buy several banana farms on the island. As a shipping man, Lorenzo Baker did not pretend to be an agronomist. But he had noticed that in Jamaica bananas seemed to grow almost everywhere, on hillsides as well as in the valleys. He had also learned that the principal planters of the island were tired of their dependence on sugar as a money crop. Even at a shilling a bunch, bananas were usually more profitable than sugar at forty dollars a ton. Jamaican citizens seemed to understand particularly well the processes of banana agriculture. Jamaica's Negro peasantry were beginning to grow the strange fruit on their tiny hillside fields. That gave some measure of insurance against the domination of the island's banana supply by corporation farmers with Downing Street connections.

Andrew Preston's approach to the problem of establishing a banana-selling firm was influenced by considerations of marketing. He had already succeeded in selling bananas profitably. At thirty-seven, he was being pointed out as one of the best produce dealers of Greater Boston. Because of its great distance from the banana lands, the Boston market was rarely flooded with direct imports of the fruit. Moreover, Boston and its factory suburbs were growing. Factory workers were eager buyers of bananas, so long as the fruit was cheap. Andrew Preston proposed to keep it cheap. He had no ambition to start a big company, but he did want to "interest" Boston shippers, bankers, and merchants in a banana firm.

Such a firm, he thought, should limit its enterprises to selling the fruit, and Baker, Freeman, and their associates could continue their general shipping activities. Andrew Preston sought only enough capital for a modest and independent commission firm, with some degree of protection against abrupt losses. He promised: "We'll feel our way—chew fine and spit careful. . . ."

After a year of quiet soliciting and explaining, Andrew Preston, with Captain Baker's aid, put together an organization with the same precise care with which an old-style Yankee carpenter would build a milk house.

The Boston Fruit Company, destined to grow into the biggest tropical farm and shipping company in the world, began, as Andrew Preston put it, as "just a small firm of good people."

It was an informal partnership, with a paid-in capital of $15,000, well divided among twelve New Englanders:

Captain Jesse H. Freeman	1¼ shares	$1,875
Captain Lorenzo D. Baker	1 share	1,500
Lamont G. Burnham	1 share	1,500
Thomas Mandell Hart	1 share	1,500
W. F. Robinson	1 share	1,500
O. S. Crowell	1 share	1,500
A. S. Messner	1 share	1,500
Thomas B. Griffiths	1 share	1,500
John F. Crocker and Elric Elridge	1 share	1,500
Andrew W. Preston	½ share	750
E. E. Locke	¼ share	375
Total		$15,000

It was a hand-over-and-shake proposition. All partners agreed that no dividends were to be paid or claimed during the first five years. Andrew Preston, who had invested the best part of a year's income in his $750 half-share, became manager of the Boston office at a salary "no greater than previously received" from Seaverns and Company.

The shipping men, Freeman, Baker, Hart, and Crowell—all partners in the Standard Steam Navigation Company—were the principal owners. Andrew Preston placed an order for the printing of letterheads, sales sheets, and receipt forms and set up a one-room office down the lane from Seaverns and Company. Tall, meditative Captain Jesse H. Freeman, largest shareholder by $375, became president of the new Boston Fruit. Captain Lorenzo Baker assumed the significant title of tropical manager, a position which is to the banana business what the Prince of Wales used to be to the British Empire.

Then the first members of the Boston banana partnership began to take a long, hard look at the banana trade of 1885. Both Lorenzo Baker and Andrew Preston had previously heard of the astounding "tropical plunger," Minor Cooper Keith. Captain Baker's agency had several times been allied with banana importers in New York, Philadelphia, and Baltimore, and he had sailed at least one banana cargo right into New Orleans, the banana capital of the world. During 1885 at least sixty individuals or firms were bringing bananas into United States ports. New Orleans, whose principal banana supply now came from Central America, was far in the lead and benefited by minimum shipping distances and mild winters, which permitted the trade to continue throughout the year. The banana supply of the Eastern seaboard, such as it was, had come mainly from Jamaica, Cuba, and the Panama province of Colombia. The East Coast importing season was from May to November.

In New Orleans, New York, and Philadelphia competition was keen, especially during the summer. There was still no effective inland distribution of the fruit. One steamship load or two schooner loads in the same week could glut a port.

Because of such conditions the trade was rough and commercial casualties were high. The year Boston Fruit was established at least seven importers, six of them substantially bigger than the new Boston firm, had failed. In the struggle against crowded markets practically all the importers were at the mercy of the brokers or jobbers—who could, and all too frequently did, stand by until the bananas were ripe before buying them for ridiculously low prices. There was, moreover, no co-ordination or planning among banana importers. Ports deluged with the fruit for a few days would have none at all the following week, and one port often would be flooded with fruit while ports near by would have less than a dozen bunches.

In Manhattan, John Pearsall, one of New York's first banana importers, had gone bankrupt in 1875 when he left 3000 bunches of overripe "Cuban reds" on Bowery side streets for anybody to carry away. But shortly thereafter the impetuous Mr. Pearsall found a partner named Gomez and the two made a sudden comeback by raising their New York imports to half a million bunches a year and launching banana farms near Banes in Cuba and along the wild frontiers of what is now called the Dominican Republic.

Also in New York, Edgar Tilton, sole survivor of the wrecked Frank Brothers partnership, was fighting to recover the remnants of the Frank banana farms in Panama and to retain his place in the bedlam that was the New York fruit trade. In 1880 an English firm, Hoadly and Company, opened warehouses in New York. This firm had contracted to market bananas that were being planted in Costa Rica by Minor Keith. A number of banana importers were uncomfortably aware that Minor Keith's Colombia Land Company, Ltd., was also planting large acreages of bananas on the South American mainland beyond the port of Santa Marta. Since his planting costs were reportedly less than $15 an acre, importers were nervously suspecting that Keith was maneuvering into a position to deluge all the ports with bananas. Jitters were common to the banana trade. Brief obituaries appeared regularly in the New York business papers.

But for almost every casualty there appeared a new and eager replacement. Rich Philadelphia's interest in the rowdy game was stirred. The Tropical Fruit Company and the Merchants Fruit Company started boldly and failed suddenly. In 1885 there appeared in Philadelphia the H. V. Howes and Company, a partnership which chartered two schooners to import bananas directly from Bluefields, Nicaragua. That firm also failed. Two years earlier, Henry Brothers, a partnership of Joseph and Samuel Henry, had begun in near-by Baltimore with a capital of $150,000—ten times the original capital of Boston Fruit. Their import volumes climbed to what was then an all-time high—one million bunches a year. After two successful years, the Henry Brothers experimented with loading bananas in Jamaica and "topping off" the cargoes with pineapples from the Bahamas. The delay involved by the latter mission caused the combined cargo to reach home port completely spoiled. This venture bankrupted the Henry Brothers.

Another banana firm appeared in Baltimore in 1886. It began as J. E. Bell and Company, a partnership of James E. Bell and Cecil B. Buckman. With an initial stake of $25,000 the two partners bought a small, aging steamer, the *Acadia*. Their ship was promptly lost at sea and the firm failed. But Cecil Buckman soon reappeared and founded his own company to ship and sell bananas from Jamaica. In time he became one of the outstanding men in the banana trade.

In New Orleans, trading in tropical fruit had become a major commercial enterprise. Such first venturers as Joe and Mike Machecca and the C. A. Fish Company (1881-1886), a partnership of Luigi del Orte and S. L. Vaccaro, were fighting the increasing opposition of formidable competitors. The Southern Pacific Steamship Company was importing from coastal Nicaragua nearly a million bunches a year. In 1885 J. L. Phipps and Company also opened in New Orleans to sell

Minor Keith's Colombia-grown bananas, which were climbing toward a high of a million and a half bunches yearly. Soon to appear (in 1888) was the New Orleans Royal Mail and Central American Steamship Company with a capitalization of $300,000 (twenty times that of Boston Fruit), five midget steamships, and plans to carry from the banana coasts of British Honduras and Honduras at least one and a half million bunches a year.

Many New Orleans banana ships were being lost at sea, and many more were arriving at port disastrously late. Prices had dropped until bananas were being described locally as a food fit only for Republicans and carpetbaggers. Red and yellow bananas, green fruit, and overripes were mingled at shipside auction. The only grades listed were straights and culls, and these terms were almost interchangeable. When fruit was comparatively salable, practically all bananas were called straights or first class. When the market was glutted, all bananas were culls.

As the New Orleans banana flood grew deeper, despairing importers began to load trainloads of the fruit for dispatch to interior cities. They damned the fraudulence of inland buyers when the shipments were returned. There was no inspection of car loadings. Too frequently railroad cars loaded at the ports would show good fruit only at the loading doors, while the rest of the contents would be "ripes," "shatters," or worse. One old New Orleans banana man remembers the classic instruction of an early dock foreman to his loading crew: "After you sons of bitches have banged in what needs to be got rid of, recollect to stack some good fruit in fronta the car door! We got to keep the customers happy for anyhow the first five bunches!"

Shippers cheated brokers and brokers cheated shippers. The trade became more and more unscrupulous. Old-timers tell of Cap'n Slumpy Gus, for example, who approached quarantine with a schooner load of dead-ripe bananas. Cap'n Gus had

a sick man aboard and he suspected that the crewman had
yellow fever. He knew that the quarantine officer would see
the man and hold the ship for "inspection"—perhaps for several days or even a week. During that time all the bananas
would rot. So the old skipper picked up the sick man and
threw him overboard, sailed through quarantine, and sold the
cargo.

Captain Lorenzo Baker paid another brief but observant
visit to New Orleans in 1885. The Cape Cod skipper said that
he would be dadblamed if the Boston banana trade ever went
the way the New Orleans trade was going. Andrew Preston,
who in due time came to know all the piers and many of the
bars of old New Orleans, seconded Captain Baker. Andrew's
mother had said that the best way to keep a house clean was
never to let it get dirty, and her son had applied the maxim
to produce selling.

As Lorenzo Baker succeeded in buying and shipping to
Boston more and more thousands of bunches of Jamaican
bananas, Andrew Preston kept selling them as they came. He
said that he let the fruit prove its own grade. "When it's ripe
I call it ripe. When it's cull I sell for cull. When it's straight
it gets straight prices. We got good bananas. . . ."

During its first year Boston Fruit received and sold about
150,000 bunches of bananas. Andrew Preston considered plans
to extend the trade territory to additional towns and cities of
near-by New England, but Boston Fruit was "chewing fine
and spitting careful." Andrew Preston could afford to be self-
belittling. His organization was earning solidly in Boston while
the great majority of banana companies outside of Boston were
losing.

Boston Fruit's first year was profitable; its second year was
even more successful. During 1886 the imports ran to almost
a third of a million bunches, and by the end of the year, and

without any dividend obligations to its founding partners, the firm showed cash resources of $200,000. In twenty-three brief months the $15,000 nest egg had hatched thirteenfold, and during the summer of 1886 it had doubled by the month. The banana lottery was paying off.

Luck was a substantial factor. There had been no bad storms or hurricanes to destroy the Jamaican crops. Thanks in large part to Captain Lorenzo Baker, there had been no losses at sea. The quality of fruit handled was outstandingly good. And Andrew Preston had sold it well. But luck, too, had been with the Boston partnership which had started with barely enough capital to stock an average country store and in two years had grown into what young Mr. Preston termed a "considerable banana firm."

The delighted partners agreed to an interim reorganization to put the bounteous earnings to work. The leadership remained the same. In Jamaica, Lorenzo Baker proceeded to buy four banana plantations for Boston Fruit—about 1300 acres, capable of producing at least 150,000 bunches yearly. With that move Boston's banana traders became banana farmers.

Arguing that banana shipping, like banana selling, was in need of improvement, Andrew Preston voted for purchase of a steamship, even though he knew that both of his superiors were incorrigible sailing men. Speaking respectfully and as a landlubber, he pointed out that the real measure of Boston Fruit's success or failure was in the precise number of bunches of fruit that could be sold at Boston in the course of a four- or five-month season—that speed at sea meant money in the bank.

In 1888 this argument became more forceful and pertinent. After two fat years, Boston Fruit had suffered a lean year. Cargoes had arrived too late and too ripe. New York traders had invaded the Hub territory with heavy rail shipments of bananas. Andrew Preston admitted that in 1887 he had been obliged to spend good money for red ink, but in 1888

Boston Fruit was given the opportunity to lease a steamship for the Jamaica-Boston run. She was the big new *Marmion*, and she stowed and decked 20,000 fifty-pound bunches of bananas and boasted a steady speed of ten knots. This was a large ship in 1888—200 feet long and with a displacement of 777 tons.

After several trial runs on charter, Boston Fruit bought the *Marmion* for $65,000, a sum which had to be borrowed. Captain William Anderson, who became master of the new ship, in later years used to recite the following dialogue which was spoken in Andrew Preston's office at least once weekly for many months after the purchase:

CAPTAIN FREEMAN: Preston, do you know what we've done?

PRESTON: We've bought a steamship for sixty-five thousand dollars.

CAPTAIN FREEMAN: All borrowed money!

PRESTON: Yes, sir; and it's the best purchase the company ever made.

After a period of thoughtful silence the captain would walk out.

Mr. Thomas M. Hart, one of the partners in Boston Fruit, was aboard the ship en route to Jamaica immediately after his firm had bought the doughty little ship. She rode smack into a hurricane, which Mr. Hart described:

No ship like those of Columbus could have lived through that night, and even the *Alvo* of the Atlas Line, a vessel nearly four times the size of the *Marmion*, was lost with all on board within a few miles of us.

During the early afternoon the wind had completely died out . . . and a long heavy swell from the southeast had long before the sunset begun to make the empty ship roll about like a drunken seaman. To those experienced in West Indian waters the unnatural calm and the rising sea were clear indication of an approaching hurricane with evidence . . . that we were in the dangerous semicircle of the storm. . . . Under these conditions there is nothing to do but keep the vessel's nose to the storm and trust to God, your engines—maybe supplemented with a sea-anchor—and the staunchness of the craft.

That any vessel built by man could have stood the turmoil of that night I would not have believed had I not experienced it. I was the only passenger. The strongest man could not have held himself in his berth. Either standing or half crouching, holding tightly on to something, or lying flat on the cabin floor or deck with arms and legs braced, was all that prevented broken bones.

No part of the decks was free from breaking seas and swashing water—the noise was one vast unearthly shriek. So awful was the night that it had a grandeur all its own. . . . I believe no man on board had the slightest belief—hardly hoped—that we would ever see another day. . . . Three times that night two of the officers and the one passenger, clinging to ropes in lee of the forward deckhouse, were confident . . . that the sternpost and the after-part of the ship had given up the struggle against the sea and racing screw. . . . Yet the vessel hung together. . . .*

Like scores of banana ships that followed her, the *Marmion* rode out that and many other storms to bring home cargoes of tropical fruit.

Respectfully reminding his partners that "you can't take out without putting in," Andrew Preston urged that another $75,000 be spent for reconditioning the *Marmion* and that plans be drawn up for two more steamships to be designed exclusively for the banana trade. Captain Freeman doubted the wisdom of these proposals, but Lorenzo Baker, who again looked to sea from his palm-shaded office in Port Antonio, scribbled his cautious approval, adding the reminder that three steamships, together with other cargo space already obtained, would be delivering to Boston at least 75,000 bunches of ba-nanas a month during almost half the year. That would be too dadblamed many bananas for Boston to eat. It would be like

* *Personal Reminiscences of the Caribbean Sea and the Spanish Main,* Francis Russell Hart, 1914, The Devinne Press, Boston.

feeding a sardine on cod heads. Part of the haulage would have to be sold elsewhere. That meant swinging into other banana ports. It also meant rough-and-tumble competition.

Andrew Preston agreed. Soon afterward he revealed that Boston Fruit would take for long lease two new steamships in building at the yards of Workman and Clark at Belfast—ships equipped with reciprocating triple-expansion engines to attain a speed, then spectacular, of twelve and a half knots.

The new ships were named *Ethelred* and *Ethelwold*, and they were painted white—partly to reduce the radiation from the fierce tropical sun, partly because the Yankee Preston considered white "real pretty." Both were single stackers with quarters for crews of twenty men and half a dozen passengers. They were streamlined ships, each 208 feet long, with a 28-foot beam and capacity for 20,000 bunches of Jamaican bananas. In 1890 the new twin ships, flying the Stars and Stripes, put to sea and quickly proved to be the fastest and most dependable craft on the Caribbean. Within another two years the "Boston Twins" were invading Philadelphia and Baltimore with banana cargoes.

In March, 1890, the partners of Boston Fruit had further plans to announce. Their five trial years were completed. Boston Fruit was ahead of its East Coast competitors. It was time for a division of earnings and another careful examination of the tropical fruit trade. After five experimental years Boston Fruit was the most successful (though by no means the largest) banana-selling firm in the United States. The original investment of $15,000 had grown to $531,000 as of March 1, 1890—a capital gain of approximately 3600 percent during a period in which most banana importers had lost money. Andrew Preston said it was all due to "tolerable management and tremendous good luck."

Early in 1890, Captain Jesse H. Freeman, Boston Fruit's largest stockholder, died and, since Captain Baker was in Jamaica, the Boston manager became the *de facto* chief of all operations for the company. The young man from Beverly Farms had grown a vigorous walrus mustache and, though he still disliked using the "spluttery blamed nuisances" called telephones, Andrew Preston regarded with mingled amazement and respect the new mechanical age which the telephone symbolized. He felt a pardonable Yankee pride in the growth of Boston, and he welcomed the arrival of immigrants as a potential source of good banana customers. He had begun to speak of his helpers as "my boys." He had a good wife and a happy home, and his daughter Bessie, already in her teens, was in Andrew Preston's own words "most as pretty as her mother and a blame sight prettier than her dad." He had lately celebrated his twentieth wedding anniversary. Now that he could afford it, Mr. Preston was building a new and bigger home at Swampscott. He was no longer just another poor produce handler. He had learned his trade and he was, practically speaking, head man of what even the *Boston Transcript* described as "one of the better of the newer companies of Boston."

On September 20, 1890, the Boston Fruit Company was formally incorporated under the laws of Massachusetts. Of the $531,000 in capital assets, $500,000 became the capital stock of the new company, and $31,000 its "working surplus." Some of the original partners sold their interests in the new corporation, and in the reorganization Lorenzo Dow Baker was made president and tropical manager. Andrew Preston remained Boston manager.

Busy and prosperous years followed. Baker was hiring more and more spry young men "that ain't afraid of work." There were many such youths in and around the Hub City and still more in what Captain Baker rather disdainfully called "the suburbs of the universe."

The team of Baker and Preston continued to sell bananas— at such a rate that they had to increase their Jamaica plantings to 3100 acres, an area which by 1892 was yielding nearly a quarter of a million bunches a year. They had managed to stretch Boston's banana season to eight months of the year. Even so, the Boston market began to show symptoms of saturation. It was time to seek other banana market ports. Rich and conservative Philadelphia seemed to be a good choice. So Andrew Preston went to Philadelphia to take a look at the Quaker City competition. It looked tough. Near-by Baltimore seemed less formidable. There the soft-spoken Bostonian met Cecil Buckman, and a few days later Baltimore newspapers announced the birth of the Buckman Fruit Company of Baltimore, with a paid-in capital of $50,000, of which Boston Fruit had contributed fifty-two percent. Late the following year Philadelphia newspapers mentioned the founding of the Quaker City Fruit Company, also capitalized at $50,000, of which the Boston Fruit Company had subscribed exactly half.

Three years later there appeared in New York the reorganized American Fruit Company. Boston Fruit had bought forty-eight percent of the $50,000 stock. Two years after this, Boston Fruit acquired a six-percent interest in the $560,000 capital stock of the Banes Fruit Company, a firm which raised bananas and shipped cargoes from Banes, Cuba, to New York. The expanding Boston organization then purchased twenty percent of the Sama Fruit Company and an equal share in the Dumois Fruit Company. Both companies were capitalized at $150,000 to import and sell West Indian bananas in New York.

But, in spite of its growth during the 1890's, Boston Fruit was not a big company, even by local commercial definition, and it held an important place only in Boston, which was fourth among banana-market ports. The firm of Baker and Preston had no monopoly of Boston's banana trade. At least four smaller firms were busily selling "summer bananas" in the Hub City. Yet Boston Fruit kept its local leadership and

The Bowen, banana queen of the 1880's.
(Courtesy of United Fruit Company)

The Jesse B. Freeman, early carrier of bananas.
(Courtesy of United Fruit Company)

The Brookline, a pioneer in the banana trade.
(Courtesy of United Fruit Company)

The Bound Brook, stalwart banana carrier of the 80's and 90's.
(Courtesy of United Fruit Company)

Village church in a banana country.
(Photograph by Giles G. Healey)

Indian worship at the Cathedral of Chichicastenango.
(Photograph by Giles G. Healey)

Mountain lake in Guatemala. *(Photograph by Giles G. Healy)*

Irrigated banana cultivation. *(Middle America Information Bureau)*

Guatemalan Indian family. *(Photograph by Giles G. Healey)*

Harvesting bananas in Costa Rica. *(Photograph by Charles Morrow Wilson)*

A banana railroad. *(Photograph by Iris Woolcock)*

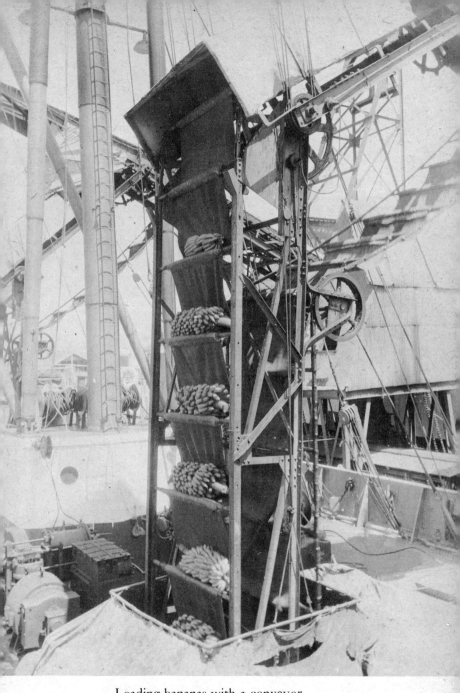

Loading bananas with a conveyor.
(Middle America Information Bureau)

Pineapples—a companion crop to bananas.
(*Photograph by Charles Morrow Wilson*)

Native marimba orchestra of the banana countries.
(Photograph by Iris Woolcock)

A Costa Rican family picking over coffee beans.
(Middle America Information Bureau)

Six-month-old banana plantings. *(Photograph by Iris Woolcock)*

An Indian village. *(Photograph by Giles G. Healey)*

Loading bananas. *(Courtesy of United Fruit Company)*

Young Guatemalans. *(Photograph by Giles G. Healey)*

Banana transport in the Canary Islands.
(*Photograph by Charles Morrow Wilson*)

Central American Indian children.
(*Photographs by Giles G. Healey*)

Lake Atitlán, Guatemala. (*Photograph by Giles G. Healey*)

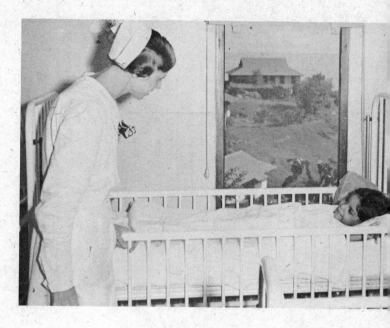

A United Fruit Company Hospital.
(Photographs by Iris Woolcock)

Skipper of a banana ship. *(Courtesy of United Fruit Company)*

The Beverley, early grayhound of a banana fleet. *(Courtesy of United Fruit Company)*

The Camayagua, banana ship of the 1920's.
(Courtesy of United Fruit Company)

The Quirigua, super ship of the 1930's.
(Courtesy of United Fruit Company)

set about skillfully to expand its suburban trade and to aid and sponsor the humble fruit peddlers.

In 1895 Andrew Preston was reporting with "real regret" that Boston Fruit was losing money on its attempted entries into Baltimore, Philadelphia, and New York and that without superior ships the company could even lose its position in Boston. Accordingly Boston Fruit leased another pair of still bigger and faster banana steamships—the *Brookline* and the *Barnstable*. Even Lorenzo Baker admitted that the new steamships were spectacular. In addition to "elegant accommodations for twelve passengers," both ships were "fitted with electric lights and all the modern improvements for the banana trade. . . ." *

The *Brookline* and the *Barnstable* were off on a quarter of a century of lucky voyages, and the green-and-gold tide of banana imports continued to rise. The total of banana imports into the United States during 1890, the year of Boston Fruit's incorporation, was 12,582,000 bunches, an increase of about 3,500,000 bunches over the totals of the previous years. Again New Orleans led with 3,668,000 bunches, all imported from Central America. New York imports passed the 3 million mark, two-thirds of them from Jamaica. Baltimore imports rose to 629,000 as Boston Fruit began shipping Jamaican cargoes to that port. Partly for the same reason Philadelphia imports climbed to 1,518,000. Boston, however, had imported 1,602,000 bunches and of this total Boston Fruit had imported about half.

Storm losses and Central American revolutions in 1891 resulted in a decrease of a million and a half bunches, but 1892 saw the total of banana imports restored to 12½ million bunches. Boston markets remained steady. So did Baltimore markets. Philadelphia imports reached a new high of 1,818,000. New Orleans chalked up a total of 4,483,351 bunches, and

* Quoted from Announcement of December 1, 1893, Hurlbut & Company, ship brokers, New York.

New York passed the 3⅓-million mark with about a million bunches from Jamaica and a million and a half from Cuba. Newer ports—Savannah, Galveston, Tampa, and Mobile—had begun to receive banana shipments. But New Orleans, New York, Philadelphia, Boston, and Baltimore accounted for more than ninety-six percent of all the inter-American banana trade.

At home in Boston, Andrew Preston, produce dealer, was becoming Andrew Preston, financier, corporation man, and shipping authority. But he continued to work and live simply. Since fancy offices bothered him, his own office continued to hold only an old-fashioned roll-top desk, a spindle-legged chair, a turkey-feather duster, a grandfather's clock, and an immense almanac-calendar. There were also a couple of brass spittoons for visitors who chewed. Andrew himself did not chew tobacco, though he did smoke moderately priced cigars and now and then, when mood and companions were right, he would drink rum or a whisky-and-water highball. After many promptings from his family, he began to wear a white open-wing collar and a black shoestring tie. His rich brown mustache grew longer and thicker, and he combed it straight to the sides instead of allowing it to droop.

Through the years some of Andrew Preston's produce-selling principles were becoming better known. He continued to favor low but steady prices and year-round work, and he was sure that in order to stay in the banana game at all Boston Fruit would be obliged to keep expanding its fleet and its markets. He recognized that the banana trade was an enterprise combining farming, transportation, and selling and that each factor was as important to the whole as any leg of a three-legged stool.

Unfortunately, few other banana men agreed with Preston. During 1890 nearly 2000 cargoes of the fruit had been delivered to United States ports, but a great number of those cargoes had been short or of bad grade. Moreover, during the five years between 1885 and 1890, about one out of every seven ships hired to the banana trade had been lost by storm or fire at sea. Repeatedly, too, banana-growing centers had been paralyzed by epidemics of yellow fever and other tropical diseases. In some sections banditry and open revolution had completely halted the trade. In 1890 there were probably no more than 30,000 acres of bearing banana lands in all the Caribbean countries, and about half of this acreage was in Jamaica, most of it in small plots.

At his roll-top desk in Boston, Andrew Preston studied statistics of Caribbean agriculture and finally decided that Cuba was the coming island of the West Indies. Cuban lands were plentiful and cheap, and he knew they could grow bananas. But Lorenzo Baker stood firm for Jamaica. Now that the island was his home he felt a strong loyalty for its fiercely bright sunshine, its dusky crowds, its ox drivers and plowmen and wielders of broad hoes. He admired its mixture of races and respected the agricultural skill of the Negro. He was astonished by the energy of Jamaica's women workers and wrote enthusiastically of the merits of "woman power." He kept reminding his colleagues in Boston that they owed a great debt to the island and were obliged to ship and sell what Jamaica produced.

His colleagues in Boston were doing their best. In 1896 they had leased and put to work two more banana steamships, the *Beverly* and the *Belvidere*, coal burners twenty-five feet longer than the *Brookline* and *Barnstable*, completely modern, with stowage capacity for 30,000 bunches of Jamaica bananas and accommodations for thirty-six passengers.

As his hard-working banana navy steamed into ports with bigger and better cargoes, Andrew Preston was even more industrious in distributing and selling the fruit in Boston and the United States. About one-fourth of all banana tonnage reaching United States ports at that time was either rotten or too ripe for sale. More often than not the transport losses were equaled, if not exceeded, by handling losses. Bananas are a big, bulky fruit which bruises easily. During the 1890's the usual procedure for discharging a cargo was to put two bunches in a heavy basket and have a stevedore carry the basket on his head. This eventually gave way to the practice of shoulder-packing the bunches one at a time.

There was no standardization of the sizes or weights of the bunches. A dollar a bunch was what practically every importer hoped for—and rarely got. There were other irregularities. An inland buyer might buy a carload at a dollar a bunch, only to find that his competitor next door had bought a similar carload the same day for sixty cents a bunch. As a rule the inland orders were telegraphed to a broker or, in the absence of a broker, directly to the importer. The importer or his broker would then select the best fruit for preferred customers. To Andrew Preston, as to any other honest produce seller, this was discouraging, all the more so because the future of the trade lay in developing and supplying the inland markets.

The greater part of inland supplies came by way of the side-wheel river steamers from New Orleans, up the Mississippi to Helena, Memphis, St. Louis, and Cairo, and sometimes via the Ohio to Cincinnati. A side-wheeler could carry as many as 1000 bunches of bananas, and frequently loaded broken shipments of several hundred bunches at rates cheaper than those prevailing in railroad freight. But railroads in the South were becoming more and more interested in bananas. In 1881, the Illinois Central, the Mobile & Ohio, and the Louisville & Nashville were joining in the New Orleans banana trade. The first carload railway shipments of bananas had been sent west of the Missouri River as far as Denver.

March, 1883, saw the banana trade's first awkward experiments with the weatherproofing of railroad cars. Mr. R. A. Patch, a pioneer fruit merchant of Denver, directed the operation.

To withstand the cold weather . . . this particular car was double papered on sides, ends, and floor. The bananas were packed deep in rice straw, a bunk was built for the messenger, a barrel stove installed, provisions secured, and on a rainy dismal day, close to midnight, the car left New Orleans via the Louisville & Nashville Railroad; this routing was necessary because of high water along the tracks of the Illinois Central.

At Henderson, Kentucky, the car was "hoisted," that is, its broad-gauge trucks were removed and standard trucks substituted. Later the car was ferried across the river to Evansville, Indiana, and then forwarded to St. Louis. In this city the shipment was seriously delayed by a strike of the railroad men. . . . It went on to Kansas City, where a Union Pacific train was being held to receive it and, on the seventeenth day of March, ten days after leaving seaboard, the fruit reached Denver. . . . The messenger in charge of the car remained at his post the entire journey. He ate, slept, and lived, as best he could, the whole ten days in the car. . . . The financial returns from the sale of the fruit tended to establish the banana industry on a solid foundation in the Rocky Mountain country. . . . Had the fruit been unprotected and rendered worthless through chilling . . . the industry would have lost many years of its Western growth.

Andrew Preston watched carefully the early Southern and Western ventures in rail shipment of bananas. He was even more interested in the throngs of immigrant banana peddlers and small dealers, most of them Italians, Greeks, and Slavs, who were selling amazing tonnages of the fruit to a rapidly growing public of immigrants. He remembered that much of Boston's banana wealth had come from the sturdy shoulders and fat back packs of the earlier Yankee peddlers.

He delighted in quoting, and may even have written, a short lecture entitled "Lesson of the Banana Man":

Almost anybody can do things with plenty of capital, but it takes a real merchandiser to do business on a scanty amount of cash. The banana peddler loads his cart in the morning with, say, ten dollars' worth of fruit. He returns at night with an empty cart and fifteen dollars in cash. He turns his capital maybe 300 times a year. On a gross yearly business of $4500, he makes some 300 separate profits of 33⅓ percent, and all on an original investment of ten dollars plus the cart and his time. . . .

Preston was also certain that his trade required a more widespread farm front. Lorenzo Baker, the nautical president of Boston Fruit, agreed. During the 1880's, Jamaica's banana farms had been favored with amazingly good luck. Year after year the verdant island had escaped hurricanes. Traders declared that the island's climate had changed. Baker smiled at their optimism. Any adult Jamaican remembered at least a dozen hurricanes that had scattered and flattened banana plants like spilled toothpicks. As a veteran sailing man Lorenzo Baker had a deep respect for tropical tempests and he knew that the storms would strike again.

Therefore, like Andrew Preston, the captain from Cape Cod favored the development of new sources and, consequently, a spreading of risks. He did not share his junior partner's enthusiasm for Cuban lands, but as a fo'c'sl geographer he favored the rich, sparsely settled island of Santo Domingo—many times bigger than Jamaica and much closer to Boston. So Captain Baker, whom the Jamaicans knew as Cap Lorry, made a prospecting journey to Santo Domingo. Simon Dumois, another successful trader in West Indian bananas, accompanied him. The eastern two-thirds of the island, now the Dominican Republic, was then known as Dominica. For generations it had been looted by citizens of Spain, England, and France, further ransacked by pirates, and attacked by the rebel slaves who had taken over Haiti on the west edge of the island.

After weeks of searching this wilderness, Captain Baker bought for Boston Fruit a large plantation, known as the Martinez Estate. It included about 40,000 acres, for which

Boston Fruit paid about $60,000. In view of the times and the hazards, it was no bargain. Spanish-grant land titles were unreliable, and there was no established government or police force. Labor was scarce, and the local population consisted principally of transient squatters who settled on any bit of land they chose, built a *manaca* shack, and stayed on indefinitely. Their chief occupations seemed to be fishing, hunting native deer and guinea hens, and raising flocks of undersized Dominican goats.

Most of the estate Baker had purchased was virgin forest. There were no roads or railroads and bananas, when and if they were grown, would have to be hauled by bull cart over rough trails to the sea.

After a great deal of searching, Captain Baker hired a Swedish engineer, D. A. F. Sanftleben, as his Dominican manager. Sanftleben tried to recruit squatters and other local labor. He offered wages of a dollar a day in United States currency or French gold and promised to supply cattle, carts, and palm shacks free of cost. But the local citizens had never seen money before and had no imaginable use for it, since there was nothing to buy. Baker directed his manager to try paying wages in useful merchandise, such as cured meat, cotton cloth, perfumes, ribbons, and shoes. This attracted a work force of 800 natives who proceeded to clear fields in the wilderness and blaze the first cart roads to the sea. The workers were happy with the barter wages and all was well until smallpox, dysentery, malaria, and other virulent diseases began to swoop down on the colony. No sooner were the epidemics brought under control than the revolutions began. Without formal notice all the male plantation workers would find themselves drafted into one rebel army or another to fight against whatever war lord happened to be in power. That meant exchanging broadaxes and machetes for long-barreled rifles, many of them old-style Springfields or Kraggs discarded by the United States Army.

Nevertheless, the Dominican banana farms began to take shape. Baker and Sanftleben arranged a routine for "renting back" the conscripted plantation workmen, negotiating with the contending generals to have soldiers released for harvesting and handling bananas whenever the ships came in. So the draftees would come down from the hills and put aside their rifles and bowie knives until the fruit was harvested and loaded on the lighters. Then they would take their pay in gold or silver coins, pick up their weapons, and return to the business of guerrilla warfare.

It took six years to clear the fields and plant the bits. Early in 1898 the first export of 13,000 bunches of Dominican fruit went steaming away to market. In celebration, Bill Newsome, the new Dominican manager who later became Andrew Preston's senior vice-president, treated all his work force to a fiesta of goat barbecue and brought out his big new gramophone with the morning-glory horn and the ebony case of twelve cylindrical records. When the feasting and dancing were done, about three days later, the crowd was entertained by a succession of cockfights, with a handout of good rum to celebrate each round of the contests.

As the Dominican fields came into production, Lorenzo Baker planned a ten-mile narrow-gauge railway to link the banana fields with the sea. The plantations remained in bearing for most of a decade. But gradually they faded away, the jungle crept over the fields, and the midget railroad sank into ribbons of rust. The principal reason for the abandonment of the project was that the pioneer from Brooklyn, Minor Cooper Keith, had cultivated better banana lands far from Santo Domingo.

After careful study of the records, Mr. Preston—even Captain Baker had begun to call him Mister instead of Andy— had decided that more bananas had to be planted in widely separated places, so that no principal part of the supply could be wiped out by any one hurricane or flood. A "blowdown" causes heavy and sometimes ruinous losses to the banana farmer. But to the importers these losses are enormously magnified. Costly ships, representing large capital investments and a huge operating overhead, are left without cargo. Railroads and piers stand idle. Stevedores wait with nothing to do. Established markets are lost by forfeiture. Even large banana companies can be ruined by a single hurricane if all their fruit grows in the paths of such storms. But while Andrew Preston continued to think about spreading the risks, Minor Keith was practicing it.

When Boston Fruit began in 1885, the name Minor Cooper Keith had meant practically nothing to Andrew Woodberry Preston and his company. By 1890, every banana grower and every noteworthy banana seller was hearing a great deal about Minor Cooper Keith. The little man from Brooklyn had become the world's largest producer of bananas. Keith companies were growing the fruit in Costa Rica, Nicaragua, Panama, and continental Colombia in quantities which could deluge any market port of the United States. Therefore, it was not at all surprising that late in December, 1894, Minor Cooper Keith, leathery brown from tropical sun, appeared in Boston to sign a paper which authorized the Boston Fruit Company to sell within the United States north of Cape Hatteras all bananas grown and exported by Minor Keith's Colombia Land Company, Ltd., and his Tropical Trading and Transport Company. The commission was to be two and a half percent.

Minor Keith was driving a good bargain. He had acquired as his Eastern sales agent the most successful banana-selling establishment in the United States at a commission rate of only half the average then prevailing. But Boston Fruit had also bargained shrewdly, for it was gaining access to the best source of exportable bananas. That ended the persisting nightmare of Andrew Preston and Lorenzo Baker—the possibility of finding their company put abruptly out of business by hurricane destruction of the Jamaican banana crop upon which Boston Fruit was largely dependent. With a large supply assured, even though the bananas belonged to Keith, Boston Fruit could certainly fill its ships and hold its trade.

During 1895 imports into the United States exceeded 18 million bunches. New Orleans kept its place as the foremost banana port with a third of the nation's total. New York was second and Boston third. Steadily banana production was swinging toward coastal Central America and away from the West Indies, even though death rates in Central American ports continued to be 150 per thousand citizens annually as yellow fever, malaria, and other tropical diseases struck down many of the banana farmers.

While banana bankruptcies continued in many United States ports, thousands of citizen farmers from Mexico to Ecuador were beginning to grow the fruit. Hawaii had begun to raise bananas and ship them to San Francisco. Banana men of New Orleans were alarmed by this unexpected turn of events. The Hawaiian fruit was the Cavendish, a fibrous-cored banana. The Pacific bananas were comparatively expensive— about eighty cents a bunch loaded in Honolulu (approximately three times the farm prices in Jamaica or lower Central America), and baling, sea packing, and freight raised shipside prices at San Francisco to at least sixty dollars a ton. That meant resale at the standard local price of twenty-five cents a dozen. Nevertheless, San Francisco had slipped into the running as a pioneer banana port.

The "banana crowd" of New York had begun to meet at lunch, and frequently for afternoon highballs and beer, at the Hoffman House, facing Madison Square. In the immigrant-crowded city, the banana trade continued to grow and prosper. In Philadelphia, one importer, John D. Hart, was handling a million and a half bunches yearly—all from Jamaica and Cuba—but the partnership of Hippolyte Dumois in New York, which imported bananas grown by Hippolyte's brother Simon in the wilds of Banes, Cuba, had tied Hart for first place among the independent importers and increased New York's banana total for 1893 to 4,280,000 bunches—considerably more than one bunch for every person in that city. During 1893 the Atlas Steamship Company had brought to New York about 850,000 bunches of bananas from the new Costa Rican plantations of Minor Cooper Keith. The British Honduran Aspinwall Fruit Company, its cargoes carried by Aspinwall Mail steamships, was shipping more than half a million bunches a year into New York, while the British-operated J. E. Kerr Company, with plantations near Montego Bay, Jamaica, had introduced the banana auction system to Manhattan brokers and was unloading as many as 900,000 bunches a year.

At least twelve smaller importers were active in New York, and brokers at shipside had begun to hear banana auctioneers who shouted, " 'Nanas; 'nanas one-one-one; 'Nanas two-two-two; 'Nanas three-three-three—'Nanas go a dollar-fiftee."

Banana companies continued to fail, but new names took their places.

In Baltimore Henry Brothers had vanished into bankruptcy, together with the J. E. Bell and Company and the A. B. Bulack Company. The Monumental Fruit Company failed after only one month of operation. J. M. Ceballos and Company was also finished. Indeed, customhouse records showed that the Buckman Company was the only one of Baltimore's banana firms that had grown steadily during the 1890's, pushing ahead from 988,000 bunches in 1896 to 1,498,000 in 1899. In New York the American Fruit Company, which Boston Fruit had helped organize in 1892, for several years imported shipments averaging 100,000 bunches a year, but in 1899 when Boston Fruit was supplied for brokerage an almost unlimited reserve of Keith-grown bananas, its total jumped to 2,600,000 bunches.

Mobile, Alabama, had suddenly become an important banana port. In 1892, the Mobile Fruit and Trading Company, an independent firm capitalized at $12,000 and headed by Herbert L. McConnell, had chartered one rusty steamship which made two trips a month between Bluefields, Nicaragua, and Mobile. McConnell presently chartered three more ships and increased his imports to half a million bunches a year. Also in Mobile were the Snyder Brothers, who were joint partners with Minor Keith. Within four years they were importing and selling about three-quarters of a million bunches annually. Mobile acquired another noteworthy banana firm in 1894—Orr and Laubenheimer. This was a $150,000 corporation which owned one banana plantation at Bluefields and another at Belize, and chartered tramp steamships to bring in eight cargoes a month.

Many of the colorful old-timers of the early New Orleans trade had died before 1890, and others were resting in quiet parish almshouses. But new and even more vigorous successors had taken up where they had left off. The Southern Pacific Steamship Company in 1891 brought into New Orleans a million bunches, but the J. L. Phipps and Company, selling only Minor Keith's bananas, had become the city's largest dealer with annual imports totaling one and a half million bunches. Because of glutted markets, poor distribution, and enormous losses from spoilage, the number-one local banana firm never made money, and during 1895 it plunged abruptly into bankruptcy.

While Boston Fruit was undergoing corporate repairs in 1890, the Bluefields Banana Company, with an authorized capital of a quarter-million dollars, was established at Galveston, Texas. It was a rough-and-tumble importing firm which hoped to grow bananas in the hot coastal lowlands of Nicaragua, ship them north by tramp steamship, and sell them to brokers in the United States. The president and resident tropical manager was Jacob A. Weinberger of Mobile, Galveston, New Orleans, and the Caribbean. He was an affable Southerner, who gambled wildly for the love of gambling, and mixed an excited English and dog Spanish with violent gestures in a highly original language.

Jake had begun his tropical trading during earlier and leakier schooner days as a combination shipside peddler and coastal trader. During his twenties—before there were any regular ship runs to the Central American or lower Mexican coasts—Jake began schooner portage of broken-lot merchandise and novelty goods to the tiny tropical ports, where he traded ribbons, kerchiefs, horns, shoes, cotton goods, mouth organs, or practically anything buyable along the shores of the Caribbean.

Since few of the jungle-port citizens had any money, Jake exchanged his sidewalk merchandise for good will and whatever produce was locally available. Such produce usually consisted of green bananas, ripe coconuts, and gaily colored parrots and macaws. Some of the parrots had been tutored previously in illiterate Spanish or profane English, but all the birds were beautiful, and pet-shop keepers in the States could sell them. Accordingly, Jake Weinberger became known as the Parrot King. He found delight in that unique sphere of royalty. He liked both parrots and people. As he sold more parrots he made more friends, bought more merchandise for barter, earned greater profits, and almost instantly lost them. Before his contemporaries had thought seriously of calling him Mister Weinberger, Jake had acquired homes in Galveston and New Orleans, begun a family, and made lasting friendships with many shipping men and produce brokers.

In New Orleans, as in Galveston, Jake Weinberger became a sort of Paul Bunyan of the banana game and the subject of unending folk yarns. Typical of these is the one that tells how Jake, on a Saturday noon, made a profitable sale. With the money burning in his pocket, he telegraphed his New York broker to begin buying cotton futures. New York offices were closed on Saturday afternoon, but somebody in New Orleans remembered that the Liverpool curb stayed open till late Saturday evening. So Jake promptly cabled Liverpool, put all his folding money on British cotton futures, and lost it all before the market closed Saturday night.

Such stories as this one are indicative of the spirit of the banana game in the nineties. In New Orleans the old-timers still tell you that it took such men as Jake Weinberger to get the banada trade born and off to a good start.

In sultry, mosquito-harried Bluefields, Jake Weinberger took over in the manner of a white-skinned Emperor Jones. He liked the Nicaraguans, treated them hospitably and generously, gave the children candy and dolls and the men stiff drinks. It was not strange that the Nicaraguans liked "Hacob," worked for him, grew and harvested bananas for him, and helped him turn hot and swampy wastelands into productive fields.

The Bluefields Banana Company lived, in one way or another, until 1896. During its first two years it carried the fruit only to Galveston, then plunged into the banana maelstrom of New Orleans with imports that soon climbed to three-quarters of a million bunches yearly. Early in 1896 the team of Weinberger and Belanger joined the New Orleans-Belize Royal Mail Steamship Line with Oteri and Company and J. B. Camors in a merger (the first among many in which Weinberger was to be involved) called the New Orleans Banana Importing Company. The company immediately failed, the *Times-Picayune* stated, "because of friction among members."

Friction was more or less common along the New Orleans banana front, and it led to bankruptcies, hurried reorganizations, and more bankruptcies. For example, in 1896 W. H. Brown and B. J. Harris, both owners of banana plantations in the Bluefields countryside, formed a partnership called the Caribbean Banana Company. It lasted from February to December before tumbling into bankruptcy. Four years earlier John Wilson and Luigi del Orte formed the John Wilson Company and for five years imported bananas from Colombia. When this partnership exploded in 1897, its liabilities amounted to twenty-three times its original capitalization.

Meanwhile the firms of Orr and Laubenheimer, Jacob Weinberger (who, corporately speaking, was then the Weinberger Steamship Company), and the remnants of the Caribbean Banana Company were merged to form the Bluefields Steamship Company. Minor Keith had taken over the Snyder Banana Company with its 6000 acres of banana plantations in Bocas del Toro (Panama); while John G. Wood, who described himself as the last of the "honest banana independents," withdrew from the trade and opened a saloon.

CHAPTER FIVE

STRENGTH IN UNION

IN ORDER to raise or buy its produce, build or lease and operate tropical railroads and ships, and distribute its wares in the United States, the banana trade required a great deal more capital. But because of its past record the trade was not accepted as a satisfactory credit risk and its capital status remained depressingly low.

Wild risks of capital and workmen's lives and anarchy in competition were ruining the trade's future as well as its present. If the industry was to survive at all a new orientation was imperative.

Attempts to set up fair-practice associations in such banana ports as Charleston and Baltimore had been unsuccessful. A working majority of New Orleans banana merchants—including Jake Weinberger and his brother Charley; Minor Keith and the Snyder boys; Orr and Laubenheimer; and Camors-McConnell—had joined in what they called the Southern Banana Exchange, formed, so it was said, "to do away with cutthroat practices in the New Orleans banana trade."

98

The Exchange died after two months, but the cutthroat practices continued.

There were other considerations which persuaded the bankers that the banana business was not a good investment. Inland markets were being neglected. The five port cities that were receiving at least ninety-five percent of all bananas shipped to the United States and consuming more than eighty percent of them, represented only sixteen percent of the buying public of the United States. Yet the trade continued to pour torrents of bananas into congested port markets.

In Boston, Mr. Andrew Preston was making bold plans. He proposed to establish a banana-marketing company, capitalized at $10,000 and owned outright by Boston Fruit. The new organization was to be relieved of all obligation to earn a profit; the purpose of the new company would be to dispatch bananas from shipside to inland United States markets. Mr. Preston named it the Fruit Dispatch Company.

The tropical situation was almost as discouraging as the domestic one. The possible growing range for bananas followed the warm rainy lowland areas along some 5000 miles of Pan-American coastline from Vera Cruz, Mexico, south to the Amazon River. Jamaica was the happy exception in being a heavily populated and highly livable island where great quantities of bananas were being grown regularly and efficiently. But continued reliance on the one tiny, hurricane-threatened island was suicidal for the banana trade as a whole.

The banana trade begins with farming and, with few exceptions, life on the little banana farms, the acre or half-acre clearings that ordinarily fronted the river banks or the sea, was rather dismal. Life and work on the bigger banana farms was little better, for there, too, were sodden humidity, heat nightmares, rains and fevers, polluted waters, and, worst of all, unbearable loneliness. It was a life for renegades or hopeless men.

Social historians have learned much of farm life in the
United States by studying successive issues of that distinguished folk document, the annual catalogue of Sears, Roebuck & Company. But the Sears Roebuck catalogue rarely got
to the banana frontiers of the eighties and nineties. As an
alternative one can refer to the formal inventories of those
jungle frontier farms. Here, for example, are the goods and
chattel of one of the first banana plantations, established in
1890 and owned by Charles De Lerno and Santo Oteri of
New Orleans:

In the town of Ceiba, Rep. of Honduras, together with the buildings, structures, and other improvements thereon and about 800
acres of land, the whole being valued at $41,000 cash in hand
. . . ; 1 house and lot with sheds; 1 roll-top desk; 1 high desk
chair; 1 clock; 1 hatrack; 1 tin mail box; 3 cuspidors; 1 water filter
and stand; 3 oil lamps; 2 galvanized buckets; 1 hoe; 1 hammer; 1
dining-room table; 6 dining-room chairs; 2 iron pots; 2 iron
skillets; 2 new mattresses; 2 old mattresses; 2 new pillows; 5 old
pillows; 4 rocking chairs; 9 straight chairs; 3 wash stands; 3 wash-
stand sets; 3 old bed springs; 3 mosquito mantles; 17 sheets; 24
face towels; 12 bath towels; 8 lanterns; 1 rowboat complete; 36
coconut baskets; 75 banana mats (mule); 12 pairs rowlocks with
sockets; 2 large anchors; 2 barrels sulphur; 3 charcoal furnaces;
2 sacks charcoal.

Banana laborers in those days cleared the fields with axes
and machetes, or with fire. They planted bits of the bulbous
banana roots in shallow holes, and as the lusty shoots climbed
toward the sun they chopped back the encroaching grass and
weeds with machetes. The banana plants grew rapidly, and
the really big job was that of reaping the heavy green fruit
and delivering it at shipside.

The incidental work of the farmers included a primitive
sort of housekeeping, made the more difficult by the lack of
fresh meats, poultry, eggs, green vegetables, or fruits, and by
the sodden air which causes clothing and shoes to mold and

mildew. Those who could afford to subsisted on imported canned goods. Drinking water, another perennial problem, required charcoal filters and sulphur treatment. There was no real defense against the heat or the fevers—the malarias that plagued all the low countries and sometimes swept far inland; the murderous yellow fever, or "black vomit"; and, recurrently, the ruinous dysenteries and many other mysterious diseases and infections.

Disease was the most powerful enemy of the first banana frontiers. But there were many other enemies. Outlawry and violent crime resulted from the lack of law enforcement agencies and the unchecked immigration of hardened criminals from the United States and Europe. There were no public schools and no hospitals. Only the ships, worn and aging tramps that called at or near the local port once or twice a month, linked the banana farms with the world outside. In these early years, the great moment for the banana outposts came when the ship pulled into port. The residents would run to meet it, water buckets in hand, in eager hope of receiving a sliver of real, honest-to-goodness ice, the remains of what had been a thousand-pound block stowed deep in the ship's hold at New Orleans. Sometimes there would be ten, or twenty, or even fifty pounds of ice left. But more frequently there would be none at all, not even a cool drop of water.

About this time the newspapers had discovered something they called Big Business. No banana companies had yet been rated as Big Business, but Andrew Preston was beginning to believe that if the international banana trade was ever to be secure it would have to become Big Business by way of a confederation of far-flung properties that could somehow be united on the broad principle that standing together is preferable to failing separately.

The American commonwealth itself had been founded on

that hypothesis, and Andrew Preston considered the United States itself the foremost business development of the century. Many other Americans believed that. The nineteenth century had been the greatest business century, the most imperialistic and profit-conscious era in history. And for most of the Americas it had been a century of at least nominal liberation.

The badly governed agrarian Spanish colonies of South America and Central America had slipped through the meshes of Spanish sovereignty. Brazil had snapped the ties binding her to Portugal. The brief Spanish-American War had yielded Cuba, the Philippines, and other ocean-bounded real estate to the sphere of the United States of America. The Century of Empire was dying as it had lived—by empire.

The closing year of the nineteenth century found the United States well into an era of big business and bigger combinations of businesses, many of which were playing a rough-and-tumble game and making the rules as they went along. There were a number of statesmen in the federal government who recognized that ten percent profit was good, twenty percent twice as good, and one hundred percent ten times as good.

There was still no banana monopoly or any remote beginnings of one. Boston Fruit, the most respected of the banana firms, was temporarily prosperous, but it was neither huge nor impressively wealthy. Cautious bankers continued to regard Minor Keith as a bizarre young plunger. There was still no "really important money" in the trade, and though the Spanish War had awakened some of the United States public to the fact that people actually lived in the Caribbean countries, mention of the banana trade conjured up visions of rusty ships that unloaded cargoes to be peddled on side streets by swarthy, mustached Italians, sometimes with monkeys on brass chains. It was not a moral disapproval of the imperialistic nature of the banana trade that kept investors away. Public sentiment was substantially in favor of what various Ameri-

can leaders were calling, without any implication of re-
proach, commercial imperialism. "Respectable business"
merely doubted that the banana trade was respectable business; that is, a sound investment.

As of January 1, 1899, at least forty-four banana importers
were still in business, and in spite of the Spanish-American
War, which had blockaded Cuban shipping and taken at
least twelve steamships off the Caribbean runs, in spite of
yellow-fever epidemics and West Indian hurricanes, banana
imports had totaled about 17,000,000 bunches. During the
year the three Minor Keith companies, Snyder Brothers,
Tropical Trading and Transport, and Colombia Land Company, had grown about forty percent of all bananas sold
in the United States.

From Boston, with the help of its new sales affiliate, Fruit
Dispatch, Boston Fruit had sold about 6 million of the total
17 million bunches, though it had grown or purchased only
about 2,200,000 bunches. At least temporarily, Boston Fruit
was flourishing. Its direct imports of bananas had doubled
between 1890 and 1899. Superior produce merchandising supported by superior shipping was making handsome profits. In
the eight years following the reorganization of 1890, dividends had averaged about twenty percent annually, and by
the end of 1898 the total assets of Boston Fruit were being
estimated at between 3 and 4 million dollars.

But the success story was not nearly so smooth as it sounded.
The venture had relied heavily on the excellence of Jamaican
fruit, and Jamaican weather, long benevolent, was beginning
to change. During 1898 hurricane after hurricane had swept
over the island and destroyed at least five times as many
bananas as the capable Captain Lorenzo Baker had been
able to export. Though both Preston and Baker had hoped
to grow about half the bananas they sold, as of 1899 Boston
Fruit had only about 8000 acres of banana plantings, which,
even when not molested by hurricanes or floods, could supply

only about one-tenth as much fruit as the firm was selling. Port prices of bananas grown by independent farmers of Jamaica were rising steadily, and already the best fruit was coming from Central America and Colombia, not from any island. Though Boston had become a year-round banana port, and though Andrew Preston was to the Hub's fruit trade what the Lowells and the Cabots were to Beacon Hill, in order to stay that way Boston Fruit had been obliged to sell about twice as many bananas in the bitterly competitive markets of New York, Philadelphia, and Baltimore, as in the old home town. And more than two-thirds of all sales were on a very small commission.

All in all, Andrew Preston favored beginning the new century with a refurbished banana firm big enough to produce the fruit in several different countries, or at least in areas larger than the destructive swath of any storm, and to ship and distribute it to all desirable markets in the United States. He realized that such a remodeling would require a great deal of new capital, but he was confident that freight and passenger traffic to and from newly "liberated" Cuba was on the increase and that banana ships could be profitably loaded with southbound freight.

As Andrew Preston continued to weigh and measure ideas that the bankers politely termed "eventual possibilities," fate, with the abruptness of a September hurricane, ruled that Boston Fruit should grow bigger quickly—fate incarnate in the person of Minor Cooper Keith.

The year 1898 had been particularly unlucky for Keith. To start the procession, a New York investment banking firm that had extended short-term loans to Keith's Tropical Trading and Transport Company had tumbled into bankruptcy, thereby leaving Minor Keith the unpleasant choice of paying off about 1½ million dollars in ninety-day notes or closing the company. With superb nonchalance he had showed his cards to the leading families and the general public of Costa

Rica. Knowing that in the tropics the vines see and the trees and walls hear, Minor Keith had permitted the story of his plight to infiltrate by rumor.

Costa Rica liked Minor Keith, who seemed even more heroic to Costa Ricans now than when he had married a president's daughter thirteen years earlier. Through hell and jungles and impassable mountains Keith had built Costa Rica's first railroad and with it had launched for Costa Rica a new banana industry and a new economy. In this hour of need the president of Costa Rica offered the official credit of the country, and hundreds of Costa Ricans, rich and poor, came forward with money to be accepted as loans or gifts as Señor Keith's convenience should direct. Costa Ricans are like that. And so was Señor Keith, who accepted the loans and eventually repaid in full.

With the generous help of Costa Rica, Minor Keith weathered the first crisis of 1898. But bad luck continued. Pestilences harassed the Keith banana plantations. Yellow fever flared again at Limon. Floods ripped away costly bridges and railway grades. A train was spilled over a flood-weakened trestle and destroyed. Storms blew down hundreds of acres of banana plantings. Fire destroyed two of the Keith commissaries and at least $90,000 worth of uninsured merchandise. Then, during October, Hoadley and Company, of New Orleans, another principal distributor of Keith bananas, went bankrupt with about a million dollars of Keith banana money in the tills. Unfortunately, Minor Keith was a partner in Hoadley.

When Señor Keith boarded one of his own banana ships for New York and waved good-by to all the Costa Ricans who had come to see him off, the *gran don* appeared strangely unsteady on his feet. After the undersized tub of a ship had cleared Limon's coral shoals, he remembered belatedly that he had forgotten to throw dimes and quarters to the children ashore. But he remembered to wave from the rail. When the ship nosed to sea he called jauntily to Captain Josh Edmiston, the skipper: "Make me for free, Josh! I still own the line. So fork out the best you got. When I come back—maybe I'll be carrying a Bible and a black umbrella. *Sabe?*"

Captain Edmiston understood. "Shore, boss! You mean you might come back a preacher ridin' for half fare. . . ."

Andrew Preston and his men were not particularly surprised by another visit from Keith. They welcomed his call. Boston Fruit had survived in no small part because of the Keith properties, which were actually supplying about five times as many bananas as all other banana farms owned by United States citizens. Because of his bravado and unfailing personal charm, Minor Keith was unquestionably one of the best liked Americans south of the Rio Grande. As organizer and head man of three banana companies that owned, leased, or held concessions for more than 200,000 acres of tropical lands and employed more than 12,000 tropical workers, and as builder-supervisor of Central America's best railroad, Minor Keith was, at fifty, a man of power and a citizen with a future as well as a past.

But in terms of hard cash and folding money the *gran señor* was admittedly in a bad way. Andrew Preston listened thoughtfully, and while listening he began to see a working pattern for a really big banana company. So the two diligent banana men, both in middle age, began their negotiations. The *Boston Transcript* stated in four small-type lines that Mr. M. C. Keith of Central America was spending a fortnight in Boston on business. But Henry S. Trott, the New York financial writer, predicted in a *Herald* financial dispatch that a merger of surviving banana companies was imminent.

Undeniably Trott had a nose for news. The Messrs. Keith and Preston really were talking business. Presently others joined the talk. Captain Lorenzo Dow Baker, now fifty-nine and one of the best liked citizens of Jamaica, braved the raw March weather of Boston. A distinguished Hub financier, T. Jefferson Coolidge, dropped over from the Old Colony Trust, and a young Boston lawyer, Bradley Webster Palmer, was among those present. Other bankers and banana men joined the group and the ultimate outcome of their conversations was revealed on March 20, 1899, with the formal incorporation of what was called the United Fruit Company, a New Jersey corporation with an authorized capital stock (still unsubscribed) of 20 million dollars.

In the best New England tradition, the bold venture began with a maze of preliminary swaps and inventories, with good traders matching better ones. Minor Keith was in the position of having to trade distant real estate in lieu of cash, and having to acquire a great deal of cash quickly. But first there appeared painstaking inventories of Boston Fruit, showing net assets in properties and good will of $5,105,000; that amount to be paid for with United Fruit Company stock at par, an initial block of 51,050 shares. The detailed "write-off" read:

1. Boston Fruit, Original, 5000 shares @ $635.50. Total $3,177,500 payable with 31,775 shares of United Fruit Stock at par.
2. In addition to the 5000 shares of Boston Fruit, Original, exchanged for 31,775 shares of United Fruit, Boston Fruit received for United Fruit stock:

Banes Fruit Company	4550 shares at $300	$1,365,000
Dominican Fruit Company	1000 shares at $250	250,000
American Fruit Company	260 shares at $250	65,000
Quaker City Fruit Company	250 shares at $250	60,000
Buckman Fruit Company	250 shares at $250	62,500
Sama Fruit Company	600 shares at $208.83	125,000

Thus from the beginning Boston Fruit controlled the "confederation" called United Fruit, whose officers were preponderantly Boston Fruit men:

President and Director—Andrew W. Preston, Brookline, Mass.

First Vice-president and Director—Minor C. Keith, Brooklyn, N. Y.

Second Vice-president and Director—Lamont G. Burnham, Boston, Mass.

Director—T. Jefferson Coolidge, Jr., Manchester, Mass.

Director—Kenneth K. McLeren, Jersey City, N. J.

Secretary—Bradley W. Palmer, Boston, Mass.

Treasurer—Charles A. Hubbard, Boston, Mass.

Four of the original partners of the first Boston Fruit were directors. Captain Bill Anderson remained head of the fleet. Bill Newsome, the big Boston Irishman, was managing in Cuba what was known as "Preston's Cuban folly." Bradley Palmer, who had been described as "that young whippersnapper that follers Mr. Preston," was solicitor and lawyer-secretary. Captain Lorenzo Baker remained tropical manager.

Meanwhile much attention was given to the properties of Minor Cooper Keith, whose trump card was the Tropical Trading and Transport Company, launched in Costa Rica and chartered in London as "a growing concern" with an authorized capital of 800,000 pounds sterling. Early in April, 1899, Minor Keith traded the entire outstanding stock of the Tropical Trading and Transport Company (389,000 common shares, at one pound sterling per share) along with 500,000 shares of the Snyder Banana Company and 3400 shares of his Colombia Land Company, Ltd., for a total of $3,964,000 in United Fruit Company stock at par.

With refurbished credit and a valise full of stock certificates that few bankers could afford to spurn, Minor Keith felt a great deal better. He was able to begin paying all his debts, and after twenty-eight rip-roaring years in the tropics, he was at last financially independent. So the colorful citizen of the Americas presently returned to Costa Rica in distinguished company, with pockets bulging with dimes and quarters for the Costa Rican children. He also brought trunks full of gifts for the adults and a renewed determination to push along with tropical railroading.

The Boston press reported that the "leading financiers" of the city enthusiastically acclaimed the founding of the "greatest banana firm." Andrew Preston noticed that the leading financiers were able to hold their enthusiasm in check. Of the 200,000 shares of United Fruit stock authorized, only 16,000, or $1,600,000 worth, had been sold by the date of incorporation and a bare $1,000,000 more was sold after great effort during the weeks immediately following. Captain Lorenzo Baker remarked sharply that the new venture in high finance was like selling talking parrots at a thousand dollars apiece and taking the pay in talking parrots also worth a thousand dollars apiece.

Andrew Preston, by nature a stay-at-home, made ready for purposeful travel. With a mere thirteen percent of the authorized stock actually sold for money and with plenty of stock to trade for cash, he packed his bag and set out for New Orleans to further the cause of banana confederation. During the busy month of April he bought the total capital stock of the Machecca Brothers' Belize Royal Mail and Central American Steamship Company for $400,000 in the common stock of United Fruit; and for the same consideration he enlisted in United Fruit the "property and good will" of Santo Oteri and Son.

By the end of its second month United Fruit had become a working association of twelve banana firms with established properties in Boston, New York, Philadelphia, Baltimore, New Orleans, Cuba, Jamaica, the Dominican Republic, Costa Rica, Panama, Colombia, and Nicaragua.

From New Orleans the new president of the newest and biggest banana company sailed for Costa Rica to take a look at the tropical assets. Bradley Palmer, several other veteran banana traders, and the boss's daughter Bessie went along.

Boston Fruit alone then had a mere 6000 acres of harvestable bananas and owned, all told, about 33,000 acres (about 51 square miles) of tropical lands, most of which remained profitless wilderness. Boston Fruit had earned and held leadership in successful shipping and selling of bananas. But Minor Keith had contributed the decisive tropical properties. Within nine months the first annual report of United Fruit announced a first dividend of $2.50 per share, the first of an unfailing succession of dividends, and told how the youngest of banana firms then owned or leased about a quarter-million acres of tropical lands in Colombia, Santo Domingo, Cuba, Jamaica, Honduras, Costa Rica, and Nicaragua. Of this, 66,000 acres, or more than 100 square miles, were under cultivation—about 44,000 acres in bananas, 8000 acres (near Banes, Cuba) in sugar cane, about 4500 acres of native coconut groves (in Jamaica), and most of the rest in livestock pastures. The new working association was employing nearly 15,000 citizens of the tropics.

The fleet of the new company included eleven steamships, ranging in size from 600 to 1000 tons; and these were supplemented by twelve to thirty rented or chartered ships. The company also owned 112 miles of railroad, most of it linking coastal banana properties with the sea. The railroads boasted almost 300 boxcars and flatcars and seventeen locomotives.

In Honduras, Costa Rica, Colombia, and Cuba, rural citizens were walking miles to get a first look at the little puffing engines. The oldest of tropical locomotives was the ancient link-and-pin veteran *Panchito*—more formally, No. 1-1888-966. *Panchito* was brought to Cuba in 1899 by the Dumois brothers and set on the six miles of narrow-gauge which led from Banes village to the first clearings that were to become fields of sugar cane. They named it *Panchito* because, so the story went, Pancho Paincero, the strong man of Banes, came to work early one morning and, finding the locomotive derailed, picked it up bodily and set it back on the track. On his eightieth birthday, Don Pancho bet that he could pick up

Panchito again. Out of professional pride *Panchito's* engineer
refused to take him up on the offer.

Andrew Preston looked at his tropical properties with great
satisfaction. He knew, however, that unless the sales establishments in the United States were greatly improved the tropical
properties would be valueless. Back in Boston the stocky
produce seller returned to tending his small but already
promising subsidiary, the Fruit Dispatch Company, of which
he was also president. Within four months United Fruit had
offices in New Orleans, New York, Philadelphia, Baltimore,
and Mobile as well as in Boston, and by the end of its first
year United Fruit at the ports and Fruit Dispatch beyond the
ports had succeeded in importing and selling about 11 million
bunches, for that particular year slightly more than half of
the entire banana supply of the United States.

But the records were erratic and not particularly revealing.
The Boston trade climbed above the 2 million mark while the
New York trade tumbled from 1,800,000 in 1898 to a third
of a million in 1899. Due in some measure to the war, other
port tallies were even more unstable, but they remained
unstable even after the war was substantially forgotten and
Fruit Dispatch had taken over all selling.

During its first year, United Fruit was Boston's only banana
importer, and its gross profit amounted to $500,000, or
twenty-five cents a bunch on the 2 million bunches sold. In
New York, the new organization had six powerful competitors. In Philadelphia it met spirited competition from the West
Indies Trading Company and Monumental Trading Company
but nevertheless sold almost two-thirds of the city's banana
supply for a slender profit of $51,494. In Baltimore, too, the
new banana union had a modest success with a recorded profit
of about $64,000. In New Orleans, United Fruit worked hard-
est—only to lose about $100,000. Mr. Preston described the
situation as "speckled." The new company was able to earn
a gross profit of about ten cents a bunch "with lots of good

luck," which obviously could be discontinued without advance notice. By 1900 nearly a hundred banana firms had already failed and there was no real assurance that any one would succeed. United Fruit's president was heard to remark, "United we stand—maybe."

In company with Bradley Palmer, his young lawyer-secretary, Andrew Preston began another pilgrimage to the southern seaboard. Mobile—a good year-round banana port which was receiving half again as many bananas as all Boston —was the first stop. There Preston succeeded in taking Camors-McConnell and Company, importers of bananas from Bocas del Toro, into United Fruit, trading stock at par for 240 of the 280 shares of the Camors-McConnell stock.

That done, Mr. Preston and his secretary went on to New Orleans, banana capital of the world. There he proceeded to buy for United Fruit, with its still plentiful stock, half the $20,000 capital stock of the surviving banana firm of Orr and Laubenheimer. Next in line was the reorganized Bluefields Steamship Company, importer of Nicaraguan bananas, which agreed to trade half of its 1000 shares to United Fruit for $500 of the latter's stock per share. Thus another quarter-million dollars' worth of the neat new printed matter was taken off Mr. Preston's hands. After this, he and his young secretary called at the modest offices of the Camors-Weinberger Banana Company, where they found Jacob A. Weinberger, the former parrot king and shipside tropical trader, directing the discharge and counting-off of a shipload of rather ripe bananas. Jake was in a typically gracious mood, and when Andrew Preston came forward Jake shook his strong, plump hand and began leading him toward the Opal Bar. "Bring your little boy along, too!" he roared. "Wouldn't hurt to let him set and listen and maybe take a sody pop while you and me have a short one!"

They sat in the deep cool shadows of the saloon, and before they rose United Fruit had won its sixteenth member. Mr.

Preston's offer included purchase with $40,000 in United stock at par of 200 shares, or one-half the stock of Camors-Weinberger. They shook hands on it. Before office hours next day one of Jake's friends urged him to pull out his acceptance and raise the ante. Others in New Orleans were giving the Boston whale the harpooning of its life. But Jake said no. He had given his promise and shaken hands on it. And Jacob Weinberger was a man of his word.

The mergers continued. In Baltimore, Juan M. Ceballos' reorganized Monumental Trading Company, with a capital of $25,000, was importing Jamaican bananas. Señor Ceballos divided his assets into 250 shares, traded 126 to United Fruit at par, and kept 124 for himself. In October of its first year, United Fruit quietly organized another New Jersey corporate offspring, called it the American Importing and Steamship Company, with a capital stock of $25,000, and planned to run Jamaican bananas into Philadelphia. After three years of regular losses this subsidiary faded away.

For a cash payment of $46,133.09 United Fruit next bought 1260 of the 2500 shares of the Atlantic Fruit Company, then engaged in selling Jamaican bananas in New York, Philadelphia, and Baltimore. Atlantic's president, Joseph di Georgia, remained in charge. Shortly after this deal, Mr. Preston went again to New Orleans to rap at the dark-green doorway of the Vaccaro Brothers, a Louisiana corporation capitalized at $200,000 to transport and sell Honduran bananas in New Orleans. United Fruit paid $170,000 in stock for half of Vaccaro's assets but left the three Vaccaro brothers to proceed in their own unique fashion, without United Fruit direction or directors. The Vaccaros did, and in 1906 the brothers Felix, José, and Lucas, all veterans of New Orleans' French market, launched a new and bigger Vaccaro Brothers which eventually became Standard Fruit, the second largest banana company of the Americas.

Andrew Preston gave his word that in no instance would United Fruit representatives serving on the boards of any associated banana firm vote against the interests of the previous ownership. He reminded the trade that United Fruit was a federation working for survival in one of the most hazardous international trade ventures. He repeated that United Fruit was not and had no intention of becoming a trust.

In line with this policy, after United Fruit had acquired majority stock in nine banana firms, Andrew Preston announced what he termed a "second period in the process of confederation." United Fruit now refused to hold or accept a majority stock in any associated banana firm or to place more than one director on the board of any associated firm. Shortly thereafter Andrew Preston announced a "third period," in which United Fruit began withdrawing entirely from its working associates. "They can play that one on their pianos!" said Mr. Preston.

But some banana men were in no mood for such concessions. Frederick N. Steely, of Chicago, proceeded to wage and lose a 15-million-dollar suit against United Fruit for violation of the Sherman Antitrust Act. By 1910 the largest banana company had parted with all stock in its four remaining associated companies.

Competition was far from dead. Even in Boston, known in the trade as "Andy Preston's town," strong opposition was appearing; first the W. W. and C. R. Noyes Company; then the Atlantic Fruit Company and the Dumoise-Nipe Company; next the American Importing and Transportation Company and the Caribbean Fruit Company. In spite of the sturdiest efforts of Andrew Preston and his selling force, home-town profits appeared to be frozen at around half a million dollars a year.

In New York, where the banana game was even fiercer, United Fruit began gaining. Average profits were lower than those in Boston, save for the jack-pot season of 1902. But volumes climbed higher. Even so, the competing Atlantic Fruit Company soon crowded to first place in New York. In Philadelphia, the new United Fruit managed to sell about two-thirds of the yearly 2½ to 3½ million bunches at rather unpredictable profits—$51,494 in 1900; $224,975 in 1901; $306,105.42 in 1902; $181,364 in 1903; $62,204 in 1904; and $52,093 in 1905.

In Baltimore the newest and biggest banana firm sweated out a first year's profit of $64,208.23, barely broke even the second year, and then began a succession of annual balances in the red—$156,685 in 1902; $36,760 in 1903; $110,179 in 1904, and $184,692 in 1905. There was no ready market in Baltimore. In near-by Charleston the new banana firm lost $37,540 during its first year of selling in 1902, then worked much harder in 1903, sold nearly three-fourths of the port's entire supply of bananas—and lost $90,135. After a ruinous Jamaica hurricane, Charleston was out of the banana trade for three years. In 1906 United Fruit came back to Charleston without competition but nevertheless lost $33,324. Again in 1907, in 1908, and in 1909 it held all the Charleston trade and lost, respectively, $21,629, $22,377, and $14,026.

In the banana-glutted port of Mobile, where ten other banana firms were fighting it out, United Fruit worked hard but lost money. In New Orleans prospects were brighter. After a first losing year, United Fruit began delivering half or more of the Delta City's formidable banana total while establishing in New Orleans a Southern division which included about two-thirds of the United States—east to Ohio, Pennsylvania, and Florida; north to the Great Lakes; and west to the Pacific. The venture was big, and after some time it became profitable. During 1907, when New Orleans' banana imports were more than 10 million bunches, United Fruit supplied about sixty percent of the total at a profit of 2¼ million dollars.

Keith bananas and Preston merchandising were beginning

to take. But the trade was not one to be described or measured in terms of port statistics or corporate shares or localized profits and losses. It was best appraised in terms of men— especially a stocky, mustached, middle-aged produce salesman in Boston and a rather slight, white-haired, and white-bearded old man in Port Antonio, Jamaica.

Back home in Port Antonio, Captain Lorenzo Dow Baker, at sixty-five, was resting as he watched the passing ships. But he continued to direct a busy ship-and-cargo agency and to make comfortable his numerous Cape Cod relatives. Captain Baker had become one of the biggest landowners of Cape Cod as well as Jamaica. Principally for sentimental reasons, he had bought thousands of acres of Cape Cod coast front and cranberry marshes—"enough blame cranberries," he estimated, "to give a bowlful of Thanksgiving sauce to everybody in the whole dadblamed world." He had built an inn at his old home port of Wellfleet; bought an excursion boat to serve it; put his son, Lorenzo Dow, Junior, through Bowdoin, and other-wise needled into green envy a number of Cape Cod neighbors who had so bitingly ridiculed Lorenzo's first stubborn ventures in the banana trade.

CHAPTER SIX

JUNGLE GROWTH

UNITED FRUIT'S EARLIEST WORK in tropical agriculture followed the trails already blazed by Minor Keith in the rich Zent Valley of Costa Rica. During 1900, its first full year, United Fruit's direct investments in tropical farming amounted to 2 million dollars. Eight thousand acres of jungle had been cleared and planted with bananas. This was more than Boston Fruit had ever owned. For the banana trade 1900 was an important year. The jungle-fighting force reached the unprecedented figure of 15,000 men. Forests were slashed. Jungles and swamps were drained. New plantations were surveyed. Tens of thousands of banana rhizomes were buried in shallow holes, and soon new fields and farms were born.

Yellow fever, malaria, and dysenterys remained. But this time workmen died singly or by twos or threes—not by the dozens or scores as they had died when building the railroad for Costa Rica and Minor Keith. The new banana company rebuilt a hospital originally constructed by Keith on the heights near Bocas del Toro in Panama, and at Limon, Costa

Rica, set up a sick camp under the profane but able steward-
ship of Jack Marti, former tender of Limon's Fourth of July
bar. Jack served as nurse, doctor, tyrant, and confessor to
hundreds of fever-stricken patients.

But United Fruit's first banana plantings succeeded primarily because of the workers—the handful of *hombres* who
knew good banana lands when they saw them; the tough,
sinewy, hard-drinking engineers who surveyed farms and laid
out drainage systems; the railroad location men from the
States; and, no less important, the black Jamaican farm
workers, who were able to withstand the fevers and who
knew more about banana raising than any other people in
the hemisphere.

On March 20, 1900, Andrew Preston's cautious report to
his 361 stockholders put the "reasonable" value of all United
Fruit's tropical investments at 17 million dollars. The new
federation of banana firms owned 212,394 acres in Costa Rica,
Cuba, Honduras, Jamaica, San Domingo, and Colombia, of
which 66,000 acres were under cultivation—about half of this
in bananas, most of the remainder in sugar-cane fields and
coconut groves. United Fruit also owned 11,945 head of cattle,
1,977 horses and mules, 112 miles of light railways with 17
locomotives and 289 freight cars, a sugar mill in Cuba, tow-
boats, launches, wharves, and docks, and 10 small steamships.

The pioneer banana farmers had established a method of
banana planting. Gangs of woodsmen, armed with broadaxes,
first cleared away the dense underbrush and vines and felled
the largest trees. They dug drainage ditches to relieve the
land of standing water before staking off the sections and
planting the bits. The logs and underbrush were left to rot
and enrich the already fertile earth. Above the moldering
debris the green banana leaves and stems climbed to man's
height within three months, to rich harvest within a year.

The sweating *Yanquis* had begun to speak the language of
banana farms. They had discarded the term "banana tree" and

substituted "stool" to designate the self-perpetuating root clumps. They were setting out the *hijos* or bits—banana-root bulbs—in the rich, well-drained earth, about 400 of them to the acre, and the banana plant, fed by the rich valley earth and growing in a fog of humidity and warmth, rapidly converted soil food into plant tissue.

To perpetuate the harvest, the banana-wise Jamaicans waited until the major plant stem approached the blossom period and cultivated carefully the *plantilla* which grows from the parent root. Then, in proper time, they let still another replacement or sucker grow, so that soon the parent stool was producing harvestable fruit twice yearly instead of only once, as it would have done without cultivation.

Cut off a half-grown plant and overnight an inch or more of tender new growth will appear. Jamaicans swear that one can hear the banana plant grow. If you doubt it, they say, walk into a banana grove on a humid night after an evening shower. Stand beneath the dripping leaves and listen. You will hear a subdued cracking coming from the surrounding stools of bananas. "*Sí, señor*, it is the pain the plant feels when it must grow so fast."

Jamaican fruit reapers work with skill and dexterity to harvest the fruit at precisely the right day and hour. When a green bunch is reaped too thin, or immaturely, the fruit will not ripen with its natural flavor; if the bunch is cut a day or two late it will ripen prematurely, damage adjoining fruit in shipping, and prove a costly loss to the shipper.

The reapers are armed with flat, broad knives fitted to the ends of long poles. With this instrument the cutter hacks into the porous stem of the bearing plant and makes a notch a few feet below the heavy bunch of fruit. This causes the tree to bend down gradually so that the fruit bunch balances easily on the shoulder of a second man who waits to receive it. As the falling bunch is caught, the cutter takes a sharp machete from his scabbard and hacks off the plant stem. With another

deft stroke he cuts off the long hoselike blossom stem which
hangs from the under tip of the fruit bunch. Then he cuts
down the fruit-bearing stalk at its thick and porous base, so
that the *plantilla* or next largest shoot may grow and within
six months bear another bunch of bananas.

The "shoulder man" carries the bunch to a waiting mule
and slips his burden into one of the three basketlike holsters
on either side of the animal. When the pack is loaded, the
mule driver leads the mule along a field path beneath thick
canopies of dark green and brown-fringed banana fronds to
the tramway.

At Number 131 State Street, in far-off Boston, this new
tropical knowledge was being integrated into a system of
banana production which Andrew Preston termed a "centralized planting program." Some of the firm members favored
Boston Fruit's retaining its earlier island plantations as future
sources of bananas. Minor Keith, eloquent in debate and
devastating in logic, eagerly tore their arguments to shreds.
He pointed out in vivid and profane metaphor that, for reasons
best known to God, Caribbean crops were unpredictable: a
bumper crop was often followed by a poor one; a drought by
a flood or a hurricane. Jamaica had been spared major hurricanes for ten bountiful years, but now the lucky streak was
broken.

Late in 1899 hurricanes had hit Jamaica again. Early in
1900 a freak storm had destroyed about nine-tenths of the
island's banana farms. The company's Dominican plantations
were also storm-beaten, and Cuba, Minor Keith insisted, was
too cold for profitable banana growing.

Andrew Preston, who listened more than he spoke, had
already quietly decided to plant the Cuban banana lands
with sugar cane. Meanwhile, Minor Keith, who had actually
planted more acres of bananas than anyone else in the trade,
convinced Preston that the time had come to think about an

additional spreading of storm risks and a far greater volume of sales. During its first year United Fruit had shipped and sold about 11 million bunches of bananas at a net profit of slightly more than eight cents a bunch, or about four dollars a ton. Andrew Preston was confident of a potential demand far in excess of 11 million bunches, and that, he felt, justified large new banana divisions.

United Fruit began to expand its Costa Rican holdings. Keith's Northern Railroad had pushed on to San José. Preston thought that it could be made the most important of all banana railroads. So Costa Rica's coastal valley lands were chosen as the location for a first mainland banana center. Lush yields were promptly forthcoming from the pioneer Costa Rican division—presently more than 5 million bunches a year. Puerto Limon became the largest Central American Caribbean port, and bananas, second only to coffee, the foremost crop of Costa Rica.

Panama was next in the expansion program. In 1903, United Fruit opened a major division at Almirante, fronting the Caribbean, not far from Minor Keith's earlier plantings at Bocas del Toro. The beginning was good. The soil was rich, and the countryside deep, wet, and sheltered. A first 20,000 acres were planted. Nearly 300 miles of narrow-gauge railway radiated from Almirante, the new banana capital. Jamaicans worked the farms, and banana yields climbed to 3 million stems a year.

Colombia, where Minor Keith had acquired a 12,500-acre tract near Santa Marta in 1875, had long been famous for its bananas. But prior to the coming of the *Yanquis*, the fruit had never been exported, even though Santa Marta harbor, in a protected bay, is one of the best ports in South America. The valley lands back of the port are hot and comparatively dry. A quarter-century earlier Minor Keith had planned surface irrigation from swift, clear streams that are fed from

the snows of the Sierra Nevadas, farther inland, but the plans
had never been realized.

Along nearly thirty miles of a valley paralleling the Rio
Frio, United Fruit planted banana farms. Approximately half
of the total acreage was in the hands of citizen farmers.
Eventually United Fruit banana plantings covered more than
20,000 acres of the rich, well-irrigated Colombian lands;
ninety miles of railway were completed; and, in 1924, nearly
8 million bunches of bananas were exported.

Jamaica remained the most important source of bananas, as
Lorenzo Baker, still proprietor of the L. D. Baker Company
of Port Antonio, had predicted thirty years earlier. In 1914,
Jamaica led the world in banana production, and it held first
place for twenty-five years. Most Jamaican bananas were being grown by independent farmers on tiny plots, some of them
high on the hillsides. Banana fields were also pushing into the
lowlands formerly planted with sugar cane. United Fruit had
planted 8000 acres of Jamaican lands with bananas, about
9000 acres of coconut groves, and 4000 acres of sugar cane.
But those were comparatively small holdings.

In eastern Cuba, United Fruit concentrated on sugar production. During 1907, the Nipe Bay Company, originally
sponsored by Boston Fruit, harvested a first crop of 15,000
tons. Much later, sections of adjoining wilderness lands were
purchased and surveyed, until the potential "sugar division"
covered more than a quarter-million acres. Year after year
forests were cleared until 90,000 acres, about 140 square miles
of land, were planted with sugar cane. Two grinding mills,
each with a daily capacity of 7000 tons of cane, were built
to process the crops. Harbors were dredged, piers raised, and
hundreds of miles of railroads built to link the cane fields with
the sugar mills and sugar ports.

United Fruit undertook another pioneering venture in 1907
with a new banana division in the Caribbean lowlands of
Guatemala. Puerto Barrios, Central America's best natural

seaport, was its original headquarters, and the rich broad valley of the Motagua, longest river in Central America, was its farming locale. The Guatemala experiment proved to be an oversize show window for a new era of tropical agriculture and a working model for still bigger divisions to come.

One comes into the division—known to United Fruit Company men as "New East Guatemala"—from Puerto Barrios, where banana stevedores, black men and brown men, work in antlike files, loading the banana ships from railroad cars piled high with the heavy green bunches. Beyond the piers and the lines of stevedores, each carrying one bunch of green bananas, the port town sprawls, heat-blistered and sleepy. Clustered around the army barracks are the inevitable soldiery—smallish Indians in blue, overall-style uniforms, carrying or dragging large-caliber rifles. They are genial and carefree soldiers, who receive in army pay about ten cents a day and return, after a year or two of armed service, to their respective inland villages with treasuries of tall tales and a fund of metropolitan information. Their officers, well uniformed in khaki, with Sam Browne belts, swagger sticks, or leather riding crops, are likely to be graduates of Guatemala's Polytechnical College. Across from the barracks is a clapboard hotel, from the plaza of which the tourists watch the magnificent tropical sunsets.

The daily train for the interior leaves shortly after daybreak. The trains are vaguely European in appearance. The first-class coaches offer a rather dull assortment of prosperous businessmen and tourists, but passengers in the second-class coaches are a friendly group who travel in a gay, picnicking spirit. They chatter, laugh, and chain-smoke as they dip into giant lunch baskets full to overflowing with fattening pastries and ripe fruits. When the train stops at any village along the way, the second-class passengers poke their heads through the open windows and peer about eagerly for local acquaintances. At the first whistle blast, they reach out to shake hands, wave Sunday-best handkerchiefs, and make hasty, impromptu purchases of additional foodstuffs from vendors who trot along the platform.

At Morales village the banana plants appear, filling the fields with a brilliant green, their huge pink blossoms and high fruit stems moving in the wind. High overhead, black buzzards ride the air currents. They wheel and dip as the sun flashes against their oily black wings.

The railroad forks at the company town of Bananera. One branch winds on toward the western lowlands, while the main line pushes through to the company town of Virginia and uphill to Guatemala City. At Virginia, now completely abandoned, the buildings were intense yellow with bright red metal roofs. There were homes for the *jefes—Norteamericanos;* the division manager, assistant manager, superintendent of agriculture, chief engineer, transportation manager, division inspectors, telephone manager, chief clerk, auditor, and other comparatively permanent executives. There were also a wooden hotel and a building which served as a combination school and church. Lawns and open grounds were well tended, their corners bright with flowers.

Beyond the now forgotten banana town of Virginia is Quirigua, site of one of the more renowned Mayan ruins. Quirigua lives on. Native peddlers stroll about its depot, vending fruits and home cooking. Files of green-headed ducks waddle along beside chickens and lean, dejected mongrel dogs. On a green-carpeted hill beyond the station stood the justly renowned Quirigua hospital, once stalwart and brilliant white against the sun, but now, at least in considerable part a casualty to earthquakes.

Farther on and closer to the banana plantations are the tiny farms of the natives. Most of these people are banana workers, past or present. Their homes, set in cultivated patches of jungle edge and mountainside, are palm shacks roofed with manaca thatch, which does not keep the rain out though it does discourage its coming through. Some of the shacks have yards fenced with bamboo sticks and doorways cluttered with chickens. Most of the Negro farmers speak English. They have taken to the land, and they hold it with a primitive but effective economy. Now and then they sell a hen or two, a box of newly hatched chicks, or a basketful of green coconuts lifted from untended groves near by. Once in a blue moon they make a major sale of a pony, a burro, or an aging cow. Beyond these communities are the native Spanish-Indian towns with clusters of adobe homes, army barracks, spired churches, and shaded plazas.

Within their own well-surveyed boundaries the company banana farms operate according to an agricultural master plan. The overseer, or *mandador*, is in charge. He lives in a one-story bungalow with a screened piazza, a living room, dining room, two bedrooms and a bath, a kitchen, a servant's room, and an office. For each overseer's home the company supplies a cook and sometimes a yard boy or other servants. Furniture, silver, and linen are also furnished by the company. It is almost inevitable that flowering hedges, beds of roses, and hibiscus will ornament the open lawns.

During its early prime (about 1920) the Guatemala division included about twenty-five bearing farms, ranging in size from 400 to 1500 acres. Each farm was subdivided into sections of ten to thirty acres and interlined with midget railways along which mules or noisy gasoline cars pulled heavy cartloads of bananas.

The stalk-littered fields were spiderwebbed with mule paths that wound among fallen logs, beneath silent arches of banana plants, and across little log bridges that spanned the deeper drainage ditches or the lagoons full of brackish waters, reeds, and, sometimes, dozing alligators. In general that picture remains typical.

Only the banana plants seem large. Men seem puny and incidental by comparison. But browned men, most of them equipped with the broad-bladed machetes, work almost incessantly to perpetuate the harvests. For a banana farm is never really finished until it is abandoned. The producing acreage requires constant replanting by the process of digging suckers away from the roots and resetting them. This work is called "supplying." As this work proceeds, other operations are necessary: the green fruit must be harvested, the land drained, the soil spaded, dead leaves trimmed. There is an unending series of additional tasks, some of them amounting to major engineering projects.

The overseer, who is usually assisted by a timekeeper or assistant overseer, is directly accountable for the entire farm and its labor force of 125 to 200 workers per thousand acres of cultivation.

Ordinarily banana farmers work in the forenoon, from dawn until nearly midday. While the laborers take the afternoons for siestas, the overseer and his timekeeper must fill out interminable reports and records—weather reports, fruit estimates, pay rolls, harvest tabulations, reports of acreage and livestock, work contracts, requisition slips, sick lists and hospital records, over-all farm budgets, and an individual account for every worker on the farm.

The original Guatemala division demonstrated the practicability of a co-ordinated leadership. A division manager is nominal head and senior diplomat of such an organization. The superintendent of agriculture supervises the operation of all farms, orders fruit harvests, and tries to fill the division's quota of exports. In charge of each district, usually 5000 to 10,000 acres of producing farms, is a district superintendent of agriculture who, with the assistance of a chief clerk and other clerical workers, keeps complete records of each farm, from first survey to final abandonment.

The central fruit department maintains general supervision of the grade, quality, and quantity of bananas exported; keeps records of all harvests, ship loadings, and production estimates for each one of the farms; and serves additionally as general trouble shooter and watchdog.

The engineering department is also part of division headquarters. The chief engineer, with his staff of assistants and clerks, directs land surveys, the planning of new farms, the building of levees, tramlines, drainages and irrigation systems, bridge and road construction, water-supply installations and other construction projects.

A central machine shop overhauls, finishes, repairs, and frequently manufactures an endless line of equipment—from locomotives, bridge spans, flatcars, and rum vats to toilets and cotter pins. To supply some of the repair materials and merchandise required to keep tropical plantations in harvest is the work of the company-operated materials and supplies department—the "M and S"—which buys, stores, and distributes tens of thousands of needed articles—motor parts, paint, tile, nails, screws, nuts and bolts, farm tools, riggings, ropes, cables, coffins, stoves, and furniture. A full list would run to hundreds of closely printed pages.

There is also the merchandise department, a tropical version of a department store, with numerous local branches, each selling most or all of the everyday requirements of banana workers and their families—groceries, shoes, clothing, hats, china and glassware, bolt goods, staple drugs, tobaccos and liquors, and much other merchandise. In the deep tropics, as anywhere else, workaday people will not keep on working unless they can buy goods with their earnings. And since most banana farms are more or less isolated, methodical storekeeping is an essential part of banana operations.

The Guatemala division proved to be one of the first truly cosmopolitan farming centers of the Americas. It began with United States management, Yankee railroading, and the English pattern of tropical plantations. Workers and craftsmen were taken from many nations—eighty to ninety percent of them local workers who were joined by technicians and clerical workers from the United States, Canada, Mexico, England, Scotland, Spain, and Jamaica—in all a working establishment of about 10,000 Indians, Negroes, and white men.

About one-fourth of all goods consumed were from sources beyond the Americas—matting, rugs, and novelties from China; rice from Siam, Burma, and Indo-China; chinaware from England and Wales; jams, candies, saddlery, woolens, and whiskies from England; butter from Denmark; paper wrappers, roller bearings, and matches from Sweden; watches, candies, and novelties from Switzerland. From Italy the banana-farm centers bought wines and straw hats; from France, perfumes, soaps, and dress goods; from Norway, sardines; from Spain, olive oil and wines. Cutlery, steel rails, barbed wire, sheet steel, iron roofing, knives, machetes, lanterns, car wheels, and medical supplies came from Germany; window glass, table glassware, cutlery, earthenware, hosiery, and ironwares from Belgium; whisky and linens from Ireland; fuel oil, beer, and hard fibers from Mexico; cigars and rum from Cuba; cement, codfish, potatoes, oats, flour, and canned salmon from Canada.

The Guatemala division accounting department consisted of rooms full of accountants, chief clerks, assistant chief clerks, cashiers, and paymasters. In offices, clubhouses, warehouses, *bodegas*, and farm piazzas, adding machines totaled shipments of the fruit which had become a world commodity.

In Guatemala, as in other banana farm centers, the telling of stories has become a favorite form of recreation, and a great number of them concern the banana mules. In the low, wet countries mules can pack out bananas when tractors or trucks would sink into the mud and horses or oxen would die of exhaustion.

If you are so foolish as to ride a banana mule, you first lift aboard the ponderous McClellan saddle with its hooded box stirrups. The mule waits sleepily. You slip into the saddle, expecting only lazy obedience. But suddenly the mule rises on its hind legs and makes three or four nimble but stiff-legged leaps. You fly through the air head foremost and, if you are lucky, nose-dive into soft mud. Otherwise, you may be hurt. You rise and remount, expecting to be thrown again. But this time the mule trots meekly along the trail. Your foot protrudes in the stirrup. Deftly the mule turns his head and bites your toes. Chances are that the mule will not bite you again. Instead he will fall down on top of you, or carry you into a swollen stream and leave you there to drown. Kindness will do no good. The kinder you are, the more fervently and maliciously does the creature scorn you.

Thinking to avenge yourself, you feed the animal tin after tin of dehydrated beets, onions, and carrots, pour the mule a tubful of water, and stand by to watch the creature swell up. The mule does swell, but it does not burst. Next day you may again ride it down the road. At the worst mudhole the mule hesitates between the dry spots to the left and the dry spots to the right, then wades deliberately through the deepest mud of the middle, leaving you plastered to the armpits. Or it may, without any encouragement from you, begin to gallop stiffly and eventually stumble into an evil-smelling lagoon. Then the mule will scramble out, fall over a log, and leave you counting your fractures.

"Old Guatemala," like other banana divisions, has a fund of untrustworthy proverbs. One of these says that a man can never understand the banana game until he understands banana mules. No human being can possibly understand banana mules.

There are other items about which one meditates during the hush of the tropical noons, or at night while listening to the Caribbean pounding at its phosphorescent beaches. There is, for example, a tropical folk tale heard, with variations, from Honduran Caribs, Guatemalan Indians, and Nicaraguan

Chinamen. It is the story of the primeval Central American monster, the sesimite, a man-beast of giant size which for untold centuries has ambled through the folk literatures, if not the actual mountains and forests, of those Americas.

While running an investigation line in the area of Toloa Lagoon, Honduras, a banana engineer, whom we may here call Charlie, saw one of his stake drivers making a headlong dash for camp. Somewhat surprised, Charlie swung his transit about and stared through it into the distorted face of a huge and hairy beast. The monster was several hundred feet away but the lens of the transit made the creature appear within arm's grasp. Charlie, too, whirled and ran.

That night Charlie resummoned his courage, took a powerful flashlight and a shotgun loaded with buckshot, and went back to the lagoon boundary where he had seen the sesimite. After several hours of walking and waiting, "a gigantic shape with fire-lighted eyes" arose from the pathway before him. Charlie tried to run, but his legs seemed paralyzed. The creature lumbered toward him. Frantically Charlie raised his shotgun, took aim at the advancing body, and jerked the trigger. "The creature gave a hideous, unearthly yell" and dived into the swamp, apparently not seriously injured by the charge of buckshot. Charlie returned to camp, walking backward most of the way.

The story goes that poor Charlie was a wreck for weeks, unable to muster courage to return to the lagoon and recover his transit, and unable to find anyone who would be his proxy. After a time he did venture out again, and this time he killed the sesimite, which, Charlie's workmen say, was a sort of ape about six feet tall with a long flowing tail like a horse's. *Oso caballo*, the natives called it, the same sort of back-country ogre about which the Honduran historian, Caville, had written some two and a half centuries before Charlie was born.

There may or may not be sesimites in the banana lands.

But there are several forbidding types of known animal life—jaguars, wildcats, gorilla monkeys, and, even more repulsive, the tapir, or mountain cow, a weird beast with a flexible snout, small eyes, piglike ears, and short thick legs supporting a large, barrel-shaped body. A banana man, describing the beast, says:

The tapir travels alone and does most of its feeding and moving about at night. It is usually encountered in deep forests, near lakes or streams. The buck has a shrill whistle similar to that of a buck deer. When startled the tapir starts off like a shot, plowing wildly through the bush. When attacked by a jaguar the tapir runs for water, does not bother to swim, but walks on the bottom, forcing the enemy to let go his hold or drown. . . .

But the native animal life of the banana lands is very limited in variety. The bird life is not nearly so exotic as fiction writers are inclined to represent it. Most numerous of the tropical birds are the common black buzzards—repulsive but, practically speaking, indispensable, because they are nature's own sanitary police, ever at hand to gorge on dead flesh, which would otherwise serve to spread disease.

Seen at close range, buzzards are indescribably ugly. Yet some of the bird life of banana lands is breathtakingly beautiful as, for example, the bronze and gold macaws, and red-and-green parakeets (these squeak like rusty wheelbarrows) and the shiny black tropical jay, called *oropendola*, a noisy and quarrelsome bird.

Beyond the railroads and the farms, on the brambled edges of marshes or streams, one sometimes sees the egret, a magnificent soapy-white relative of the heron. In the lowlands the swamps and sluggish streams usually carry mats of rotting vegetation. Frequently one sees aboard these mats the *jacones*, bespeckled, stubby birds that skip happily on the surface of the floating debris in search of water bugs. Most interesting and solacing to the homesick Yankee are the migrant songbirds that winter in the tropics. These include common orioles, catbirds, brown thrashers, cardinals, summer tanagers, and blackbirds. Plovers and sandpipers also come to winter in the banana lands, and on the lakes and coast fronts one frequently sees wintering mallards and teals.

By comparison with the United States the native bird life of the banana country is limited. But the Caribbean lands have an amazing variety of plant life. In Costa Rica, for example, the recorded census of higher plant forms stands at about ten thousand species, with perhaps thousands more awaiting formal listing. Costa Rica is about the size of West Virginia, which has approximately two thousand indigenous plants. Central America as a whole has at least 15,000 higher plant species, which may very well include hundreds of garden, flower, and field crops of the future, along with many valuable trees, cacti, and dye and drug plants.

In the American tropics the banana is a comparatively recent immigrant. It arrived long after Columbus. But a great deal of the life and lore of banana lands is truly ancient—pre-Columbian and pre-Christian. And the banana men of today and yesterday are but another wave of temporarily successful jungle fighters. Particularly along the thousand-mile crescent between the Gulf of Honduras and the Bay of Santa Marta, each successive stronghold of banana growing has occupied the residence site of earlier Americans.

The ancient empire of the great Maya Indians included such past or present banana colonies as Quirigua, in the land now called Guatemala, and the fertile Ulua Valley in Honduras, the greatest of banana centers, which was one of the southern outposts of the Mayan civilization. The Ulua, in fact, is the Nile of the New World, a deep river which carries fertile silt by the millions of tons and so replenishes its broad, rich valley lands. Along the Ulua one sees magnificent white herons and floating islands of water plants. There is a heavy perfume of flowering jungles, and along the river's edge are banana plants which have escaped from cultivation, fruit stems of giant size with stalks of twisted leaves partly filled with pith, so flimsy that they can be cut by a knife blow or flattened by even a moderate wind.

In the drier areas of the Ulua and Motogau basins, banana farmers have picked up many figurines carved in stone—carvings intricate in design and perhaps of religious significance. In banana fields along the Ulua they have found remnants of multicolored pottery, some dating to the fifth or sixth centuries of the Christian era. Other Honduran banana fields have yielded beautifully carved marble bowls and metal fragments which prove that the Mayas were familiar with gold and other metals and carried on trade with various Indians of ancient Mexico and Panama.

The opening of United Fruit's Trujillo division resulted in the discovery of several ancient village sites, presumably built by relatives of the Chorotegas, a Central American Indian nation that was powerful, rich, and enlightened during the era between A.D. 1000 and 1300. Most of the little that scholars know about the Chorotegas was provided by the private explorations and endeavors of Minor C. Keith in the area of Mercedes, Costa Rica, during the 1880's. There he collected Chorotegas pottery, sculpture, and gold work which has since become the property of the American Museum of Natural History.

The Caribs were the last Indian peoples to appear and multiply along the coast of Caribbean Central America, and they have proved to be of exceptional importance to the American banana trade. For the Caribs were, and in some measure remain, the distinguished nautical Indians of this hemisphere. Courageously they migrated in sail-bearing *cayucos* from their earlier homes along the Amazon and Orinoco to various islands of the West Indies. Toward the close of the eighteenth century, the British-claimed island of St. Vincent had become so powerful a Carib stronghold that in 1795, when His Majesty's Government became alarmed at the fraternity between the "Black Indians" and the West Indies French, a British naval force shanghaied several thousand Caribs of St. Vincent, loaded them aboard ships, and dumped them bodily in Roatan, immediately off Trujillo in Honduras. In that way the Caribs became the first citizens of the banana frontiers and the early navigators of the banana coasts.

CHAPTER SEVEN

TO THE SEA IN SHIPS

SHIPS are the practical measuring cups of the banana trade. Virtually all successful banana farms are planned, planted, worked, and harvested with specific reference to the cubic feet of cargo space available. Ships find sustaining markets for the bulky and perishable produce and, in addition, satisfy banana agriculture's voracious, never-ending need for heavy goods.

In 1899, when United Fruit was founded, Andrew Preston argued that there had never been enough banana ships of the right kind. Twenty-five years later Mr. Preston said it again. Like almost all other banana companies, United Fruit began with an acute shortage of ships. It met this challenge by building the "Great White Fleet," which eventually grew into the largest refrigerated merchant fleet owned and operated by United States capital.

When the Spanish-American War began, our Navy was desperately in need of light, fast dispatch ships to carry fleet supplies—long-range ships fast enough to keep pace with the fighting ships. Accordingly, the Navy Department contracted with William Cramp & Sons of Philadelphia to build the four "admirals"—the *Farragut, Dewey, Schley*, and *Sampson*—each with a gross weight of 2100 tons. The specifications called for twin-screw ships 280 feet long over-all—slender yacht-shaped vessels that above all else were fast.

But the Spanish War ended before the four "admirals" could be launched. So the Navy sold them to the American Mail Steamship Company, which completed them, painted them a brilliant white, and early in 1899 put them to sea. American Mail then offered the ships to Boston Fruit on ten-year charter. Andrew Preston accepted. The "admirals" were radical departures in shipbuilding, and no one could be sure of their behavior in tropical seas.

Having offered modest apologies for his landlubber's simplicity, Mr. Preston summarized: "Time is money in banana trade. These are fast boats. Jamaica can grow enough bananas to fill them. . . . They're big, pretty ships and each one of them carries fifty-three passengers and 35,000 bunches of bananas. I'm thinking of the bananas. . . ."

The United Fruit Company was born before the ship-lease negotiations were completed. But Andrew Preston assigned two to the Jamaica-Boston and two to the Jamaica-Philadelphia run. Each ship was scheduled to make at least twenty-five trips yearly and thus assure a weekly service at the respective home port. The *Farragut* promptly established the record time between Boston and Port Bowden, Jamaica—five days and one hour. After fifteen years in the banana trade, the *Farragut* was sold to the Alaska Steamship Company.

The "admirals" kept to their schedules even though storms and many other mishaps overtook them. In the course of a more or less typical voyage, the *Sampson* sighted the U. S. Transport *McPherson* in distress, towed her into Hampton Roads, proceeded on her course, and was run aground by the pilot at the foot of Titchfield Hill, Jamaica. When she worked herself free she was leaking badly, so several Jamaica boys dived overboard and calked the gaping plates with coconut bags. She limped into port for repair and was off on another banana voyage in a few days.

Boston Fruit had owned only one ship. But United Fruit had bought or leased ten additional ships, which Captain Lorenzo Baker, speaking from his Utopian retreat at Port Antonio, had labeled the "Rusty Stinkers." The flotsam banana fleet included the 1500-ton *Anselm*, an iron-screw steamship; the 1065-ton *Breakwater*; the 843-ton *Foxhall*; the 948-ton *S. Oteri*, formerly owned by the New Orleans banana firm of the same name; Minor Keith's *Olympia* with a gross tonnage of 1657; and the antique *Sunbeam* and another wooden-screw veteran, the *S. Pizzati*, each of about 500 tons; the *Stillwater*, a 1000-ton steel-screw ship; and the *Scythian*, a steel-screw steamer that had been damaged by fire off Cape Cod and bought by the Preston boys at a marshal's sale.

This banana fleet was not prepossessing in appearance. Its ships were old. None of them had been designed for the banana trade, and most of them were discouragingly slow. Andrew Preston and his men selected three—the *Breakwater*, the *Stillwater*, and the *Scythian*—to be reconditioned at a cost of about $60,000 apiece, and hoped for better ships.

United Fruit did, however, provide the hodgepodge fleet with a house flag—a central diamond of white bounded by two equilateral triangles of deep blue and two isosceles triangles of crimson. Early in April, 1899, a few weeks after United Fruit was incorporated, Preston and several of his directors, the Messrs. Keith, Burnham, Sevilla, and Dumois, had journeyed from New Orleans to Limon aboard the *Anselm*. Preston's daughter Bessie, then seventeen, accompanied them. During their voyage the directors felt that the new company should have a new flag, and the task of designing it was given to Bessie Preston. After many hours below deck Bessie emerged with a design for the flag that has flown on the Caribbean ever since.

Andrew Preston observed that a pretty flag would look even better when flown from good ships. In 1901, as a first determined approach to this goal, United Fruit chartered the *Buckman* and the *Watson*, each of which accommodated twenty-four passengers and approximately 40,000 bunches of Jamaica bananas. These ships were the first to carry the new insignia of the Great White Fleet.

But 1903 proved to be the year of transition for the banana navy. During that year, United Fruit decided to install refrigeration in its ships. This involved building and owning new ships, since no refrigerated craft were for hire or lease. The undertaking was epochal. Any banana man knew that with refrigerated ships the market range of the fruit could be greatly extended, losses from premature ripening minimized, and quality standards raised.

So far as the Americas were concerned, refrigerated shipping was still a theorist's dream, but in some measure British tropical shippers had already accomplished it. Britain's merchant marine was immense, and its stakes in tropical commerce were proportionately large. During 1901 Elder, Dempster and Company, under the guidance of Sir Alfred Jones, had launched three refrigerated ships, the *Port Morant*, *Port Henderson*, and *Port Maria*, on its Jamaica-Bristol run. The following years Elder & Fyffes, Ltd., of London, bought three 3300-ton ships and fitted them with refrigeration equipment.

With six refrigerated ships carrying bananas from Jamaica to English ports, the British were getting into the banana money. But the British type of refrigeration was too bulky for economy. The necessary apparatus took up about a fifth of the cargo space with tubes, fan ducts, and miscellaneous gadgets, all of which made for costly shipping. The fabulously rich London market could bear the extra costs. But the principal United States markets insisted on cheap bananas.

Andrew Preston made plans for a model ship, before contracting for the construction of three new and completely refrigerated ships in a large British shipyard. Changing such a resolution to fact required the merged services of Yankee shipmen, American, English, and Canadian engineers, Irish shipbuilders, English contractors, and American crews.

Preston, Minor Keith, and Captain Bill Anderson traveled to Montreal to discuss with one Llewellyn Williams, a pioneer refrigeration engineer, ways and means for adapting the still primitive refrigerating machinery to ships. Somewhat later Williams reported:

I wished to refrigerate a 'tween-deck space of, say, 25,000 cubic feet as being an adequate experiment, but Mr. Preston decided a whole vessel should be fitted or nothing. . . . Mr. Preston suggested that I visit the various steamers of the fleet and select the one which appeared best suited by its construction for this experiment. He recommended the *Venus*, then owned by the Weinbergers of New Orleans and chartered by the United Fruit Company, and trading between New Orleans and Central American ports. . . . I made this inspection trip and found Mr. Preston's judgment in regard to the *Venus* entirely correct.*

So they began by refrigerating the *Venus*. In New Orleans, greatest of banana ports and the center of banana gossip, Mr. Lee Christmas, vacationing from a revolutionary enterprise in Honduras, got many a lusty laugh at bars and bawdyhouses with the rhetorical question: "Ain't it just like them gahdamned Yankees to commence by refrigeratin' *Venus?*" When the laughter had abated, Mr. Christmas would continue with added proof of his sheer genius for inelegance: "So they take the *Venus* and pad her stern with cow hairs, and put fans and ice bins in her belly! That's Boston, brother! That's Boston!"

* This and subsequent quotations are from the original document of Llewellyn Williams as published in *Unifruitco*, Vol. 5, 1928, pp. 528-532.

The *Venus* was a twenty-six-year-old iron steamship with a total load capacity of 120,000 cubic feet. In 1903 she was a big banana ship. The Williams or Linde "system," was a patented refrigeration process which the Canadian government had already put to severe tests. It was designed to distribute "cool and fresh" air throughout the ship's hull with equipment which required the sacrifice of only five percent of cargo space.

Having placed orders for the necessary air pumps and engines and arranged for bonuses for the first and second engineers, Andrew Preston ordered the *Venus* moved from New Orleans to Cramp Dry Dock in Philadelphia. Here the overhaul was completed in eight weeks, with 190,000 feet of lumber for air ducts and 70,000 pounds of cow hair among the materials used.

Llewellyn Williams noted the progress story:

The vessel underwent considerable hull and machinery changes whilst being refrigerated, and amongst other things was converted to an oil burner, in order that coal bunker space could be used for refrigerating machinery. . . . After the *Venus* had been fitted out and represented in our minds the last word in American refrigerating perfection, she was . . . sailed for Port Limon, Costa Rica, and loaded with a freshly cut cargo of fruit and started for New Orleans with a stowage temperature exactly what banana experts had specified. After a six-day voyage the *Venus* anchored off the New Orleans wharves and waited for three additional days. . . . On the ninth day, the cargo was discharged and the usual classification count made, when, to all our consternation, the ripes were found to be about twelve percent, and, therefore, no better than an average natural ventilated cargo. . . .

That was a bitter, costly disappointment. The baffled refrigeration engineer laid the dilemma to the peculiarly wet tropical air and to the use of brine sprays, which apparently kept the cargo-space air too moist during the fruit-cooling period and too dry the rest of the time. They took the ship back to Limon and again loaded her with bananas. Again the venture failed. The General Office telegram was significantly curt: "*Venus* arrived twenty-five percent ripe." That was as bad as the records of the old sailing ships with their deck cargoes. Engineer Williams hurried to Boston to see Andrew Preston:

I stressed the point that a risk would have to be taken to determine by actual test the lowest air temperature which could be used without detriment to the cargo, and that in so doing there would be every likelihood of damaging if not destroying at least one banana cargo. . . .

Andrew Preston fondled his mustache. "My boy," he said, "I think your piano is all right, but my banana boys don't know how to play it. You better go down and show them how."

Engineer Williams continues:

It would be hard to add anything to this precise statement, and in order to "show them" I requested that he give orders permitting me to carry the cargo at any temperature and under any method of treatment which I considered desirable. He stated that the cargo was worth about seventy thousand dollars, and suggested that, if possible, the two ends of the ship be subjected to different treatment so that the company could obtain the results of the two experiments for the cost of one cargo of bananas. . . .

On this third voyage, the vessel loaded in Port Limon and moist air with the spray system was used at the after end for the first three days, but on the forward end for only one day, and air temperatures as low as 46° were used in cooling down the cargo and the fruit itself was carried to the pass at the mouth of the Mississippi River at a temperature of about 52°, when it was warmed up to 56° and so brought to the New Orleans Wharf ready for discharging.

The cargo turned out less than 2 percent ripes forward and

about 4½ percent aft, again indicating the merit of using the drier air. The result of this voyage was that cargoes were afterward carried with air delivery temperatures as low as 50°, and subsequent voyages of the *Venus* indicated that her fans were too small, but the refrigerating plant was otherwise successful. . . . The fans were speeded up with better results, and the ship functioned regularly in the banana services for . . . five or six years after the third voyage. . . .

To the *Venus*, therefore, belongs the credit for initiating into the United Fruit Company's service the carriage of bananas by refrigeration, so much improved in later years by experience in the Great White Fleet. On returning from New Orleans for another conference with Mr. Preston, at his request I transferred my activities to the staff of the United Fruit Company and with Captain Anderson immediately left for Ireland to do my bit in the construction of the Great White Fleet.

The refrigeration of the *Venus* marked another era in the American banana trade, and without question it surpassed all the other accomplishments of the first five eventful years of United Fruit. As soon as the *Venus'* refrigeration was perfected, Andrew Preston confirmed the contract with Workman Clark for the building of three new and almost identical ships, the *San José*, *Limon*, and *Esparta*, then the biggest and fastest ships ever designed for the banana trade. Each was 330 feet long, 44 feet in beam, and 31 feet in cargo depth, with a cubic capacity of 130,000 feet—cargo space for 45,000 bunches of bananas—and with accommodation for ten passengers. All the ships were fully refrigerated, and each had a rated speed of 13½ knots. All were painted white to minimize radiation from the tropical sun.

These three ships were the nucleus of the White Fleet, which was not yet great. At the time the keels were laid, cautious onlookers predicted that such giant ships could never be filled with bananas. Within a year after the ships were launched the same cautious banana men bemoaned the fact that the ships were not larger. Significantly, even after five busy and relatively prosperous years the leading banana company was nevertheless obliged to borrow a quarter of a million dollars to finance approximately one-fourth of the cost of the three new ships.

The *San José* was first to put to sea—for Port Morant, Jamaica, at a steady twelve knots. From there she proceeded to Limon and loaded a first 40,000-bunch cargo for Boston. Six weeks later, on September 24, 1904, the *Limon* slid down the ways, and a little more than a month later the *Esparta* also went to sea. Three of the best banana ships ever built were in productive service. Skippers Rose of the *Esparta*, Porter of the *Limon*, and List of the *San José* reported successful maiden voyages. That marked the beginning of American banana trade with the refrigerated ship.

The next four to join the fleet were Dutch ships—the *Coppename, Marowijne, Saramacca,* and *Suriname*—compact, efficient ships, each with a gross tonnage of around 3200 and with accommodations for forty passengers. They were good ships in their day, but they were in several respects mystery ships born of a failing and little known venture in internationalism.

The Dutch West India Company, after several unsuccessful commercial ventures in North America in the seventeenth and eighteenth centuries, moved to the American tropics and made its principal stand in the Guianas. The Guiana colonies had never been prosperous. Their peoples, bizarre mixtures of European whites, African Negroes, Chinese, Javanese, native Indians, and wanderers from the Middle East, associated only reluctantly and their settlements did not thrive. Dutch Guiana, or Suriname, had remained a white elephant to the empire as one development scheme after another failed.

In 1905, representatives of the Suriname colonial government came to Boston to enlist the co-operation of the United Fruit Company in the colony's plan for the establishment of banana plantations. Andrew Preston listened to the proposals and sent several of his men to investigate. In August, 1906, United Fruit entered into a contract with the colonial government of Suriname according to the terms of which the colonial government was to finance the cultivation of bananas in suitable areas of the colony and to sell the harvests to United Fruit for export. To provide the ship tonnage necessary, the colony contracted with the Royal Dutch Mail Line of Amsterdam to build four steamships, each with a capacity of 100,000 cubic feet and each fitted with Hall's refrigerating machinery and the United Fruit's air-distributing system. It was further agreed that in event the Dutch Guiana banana venture failed, United Fruit could buy the steamships at their cost price and charter them for the remainder of a ten-year term.

So the four ships were built, two at Belfast and two in Amsterdam, and were launched in 1908. On the inauguration day of President William Howard Taft, Andrew Preston announced the founding of United Fruit's Dutch Guiana Division. But the centuries-old curse that had plagued the Dutch West India Company seemed to continue. One after another the Suriname banana fields began to die of a little-known root fungus called Panama Disease (musae cubense), an insidious parasitical blight that attacks the Gros Michel banana below ground level. The Dutch banana plantations withered away.

Eventually, United Fruit bought the four Dutch ships, painted them white, and added them to the banana fleet. They were good, sturdy ships, but seamen insisted that they were "touched" with the Dutch curse. This nautical superstition was given strength by the greatest disaster in the peacetime history of the banana navy. On Friday, August 13, 1905, the *Marowijne* sailed from Belize, British Honduras, bound for New Orleans. On the same day, a fierce hurricane, originating between Haiti and Jamaica, was reported moving toward the

Yucatan Channel. It passed through this channel on the four-teenth, roared into the Gulf of Mexico, and on the seventeenth smashed with disastrous force upon the port of Galveston.

The last radio message sent by the *Marowijne* was dated 1:30 P.M., Saturday, August 15. When the *Marowijne* failed to appear, United Fruit solicited the help of the United States Navy, which promptly joined in a search of the waters from the Gulf to Yucatan. The search was futile. The Dutch ship had vanished from the seas. Some weeks later, a cork life pre-server identified as belonging to the *Marowijne* was washed ashore on Cozumel Island. The *U.S.S. Jupiter* spotted and picked up several bits of wreckage. In September, the ship was officially reported as missing to the Committee of Lloyds in London.

By 1908 the value of refrigerated banana ships had been decisively proved. In that year United Fruit began con-struction of twelve 5000-ton refrigerated ships, each with accommodations for eighty passengers and space for 40,000 bunches of bananas. The building program was expanded to include five more refrigerated 5000-tonners. Building such a banana fleet involved a maze of associated activities—the building and refurbishing of piers, railway yards, and dock facilities in a dozen tropical ports; the rapid expansion of banana acreages; the laying of hundreds of miles of new rail-roads; additions to the commercial radio-telegraph systems; and a doubling of effort on the part of the banana sellers.

Andrew Preston and Captain Bill Anderson added hours to their already overlong workdays. Their banana ships had become familiar objects on Caribbean horizons, even though United Fruit's Great White Fleet represented only slightly more than one-third of the active banana tonnage. The ba-nana trade was contributing to the building of the Panama Canal. Jamaican laborers, location engineers, tropical rail-roaders, and other work groups recruited and trained by the banana trade had proved indispensable to the earlier and more difficult period of Canal building.

Banana ships had carried most of the earlier cargoes of Canal supplies. Quite obviously, however, the advantages were mutual. Fruit ships had always been assured of northbound cargo from the banana countries. But now the Big Ditch was providing hundreds of thousands of tons of southbound cargoes of steel, cement, timber, glass, machinery, and other construction material as well as food, clothes, drugs, and general merchandise for its thousands of workers. No less important was a new interest in the American tropics, an interest inspired by the great canal. Moreover, the banana trade could now predict that completion of the Panama Canal would further extend Caribbean trade by linking the New World's Mediterranean with the Pacific.

As the Canal grew, so did banana shipping. In 1913, United Fruit built and launched the *Pastores*, *Calamares*, and *Tenadores*, once more the "best and biggest" of banana ships. All three were built in Belfast, and each had a gross tonnage of 6305 and a capacity of 178,000 cubic feet. Each was 100 feet longer than the 5000-tonners which had preceded them. Never before had Caribbean sea lanes seen such ships or such furnishings and interior decorations. Passengers exclaimed, "A banana man's dream of heaven!" and pilots declared, "Creepin' Jesus, you could steer them boats up a tree!"

Having launched the three *magnificos* and increased the Great White Fleet to nineteen passenger-carrying ships, Andrew Preston turned again to the building of prim white banana ships to carry freight (but no *turistas*) south and green bananas north. The banana traders knew by this time that carrying passengers had become an inescapable obligation of Caribbean trade. But they were also aware that passengers and tourists were a perennial headache, that there was little profit in such business, and that a lamentably large proportion of *Norteamericano* tourists were luxury-loving bores who expected infinitely more than they were willing to pay for.

Marine history has proved that passenger haulage is one of the most effective ruses by which shipping companies can siphon subsidies from public treasuries through the strategies of lobbies and pressure groups. But United Fruit ships were built forthrightly to carry bananas. After one plunge into passenger trade Andrew Preston's firm was eager to get back to banana ships.

United Fruit proceeded with the building and outfitting of eight "San" ships—four to be completed in 1915-16, four more in 1919-20. They were to be "medium" refrigerated steamers. The first four, the *San Rito*, *San Andres*, *San Mateo*, and *San Pablo*, had accommodations for only four passengers. Only the *San Mateo*, however, steamed immediately for the banana trade. The other three were taken over by the British Admiralty for use in the First World War. Manned by Royal Navy crews, the *San Rito*, *San Andrew*, and *San Pablo* carried war stores and ammunition across the English Channel, and later to the Mediterranean and Mesopotamia. The *San Rito* was torpedoed and sunk in February, 1918.

A few months later the *San Andres* was torpedoed, beached, and abandoned. George Grant, later the senior shipmaster of the banana fleet, and author of many well-known sea stories, was the twenty-three-year-old captain of the *San Andres*. In the Second World War Grant made a reputation for himself by his lone-wolf tactics in carrying vital food and supplies to our Pacific bases. Refusing to tie himself down to the slow pace of a convoy, he raced across sub-infested and air-patrolled enemy waters, ducking subs and planes and delivering the goods when every hour counted.

Australian-born Hector Harris Robson, now a senior executive of the Great White Fleet, and recently a member of the United States Maritime Commission, was chief engineer of the *San Pablo*, the only one of the British-requisitioned boats to survive the four years of war.

With the signing of the Armistice, the *San Blas*, *San Bruno*, *San Gil*, and *San Benito*, all 3600-ton banana ships, were launched. Soon after this all coal-burning ships of the Great White Fleet were converted to oil. That necessitated costly overhaulings and the placement of fuel storage tanks at strategic points throughout the tropics.

After that came the four black ships of the White Fleet, the *Mayari*, *Maravi*, *Macabi*, and *Manaqui*. These ships, which were slower than the ships of the White Fleet and carried no passengers, were built to carry United Fruit's Cuban-grown sugar. Wallowing low under the weight of sandy-brown sugar and other nonperishable freight, the black ships served as the slow and faithful dray horses of the Caribbean.

But the banana trade required still more ships. Again Andrew Preston's men went abroad to have them built, this time at the yards of Cammell, Laird, of Birkenhead, England. There, in 1924, the three refrigerated "La" ships were launched —the *La Playa*, the *La Mares* (later the *Darien*) and the *La Perla*.

Now that most of the banana fleet had been refrigerated, Preston decided to build three ventilated ships, capable of high speed, which could be used on the shorter runs. That led to the construction, again at the Workman Clark yards in Belfast, of the *Castilla*, the *Tela*, and the *Iriona*, for some years the big three of the banana fleet. They were handsome, costly ships which a decade before would have seemed fanciful extravagances. The Great White Fleet was on its way to an eventual strength of 103 ships with a total tonnage of about 476,000 gross.

The banana navy was also dressing up. Ship's officers appeared in attractive uniforms—trim whites for tropical seas; neat blues for the northern ports.

About the same time, the Great White Fleet was perfecting its routine of nautical engineering to keep pace with the unique and trying demands of tropical shipping.

Shipbuilding for tropical service is a very specialized kind of shipbuilding. The physical strains of tropical service are many times greater than in the temperate zones. The ships must be built to stand the constant strain of high speeds. They must be able to withstand the reefs, bars, and shoals that are a constant menace in tropical waters. They must be able to ride out the violent hurricanes never encountered on transatlantic runs. The complex refrigeration and temperature-control mechanisms must be foolproof—because a single failure can be ruinously expensive. The marine engineering program begun by United Fruit took as its starting point the very highest standards in conventional ship design and added to them the very best specialized engineering for tropical service.

By 1920, "banana navy" was no longer a term of derision. Banana shipping had taken a noteworthy place in the maritime industry of the Americas. But the hurricanes, which Andy Preston remembered from his schooner days, still blew, and storm-wary skippers continued to stand incredibly long watches at the bridges, drinking black coffee, swearing superbly, and pulling into ports with splintered lifeboats, smashed railings, and battered stacks. In Boston, old Captain Bill Anderson, grown heavier and grayer, frowned at the growing caravan of ships, scowled as he recalled his early days as master of a 100-ton schooner, and regarded with quiet suspicion the expanding roster of the Great White Fleet, which in 1920 included thirty-eight steamships. Between 1909 and 1919 the Great White Fleet alone had carried about 15 million tons of general freight and nearly half a million passengers.

Sailors delight in rivalries, and on banana ships there is perennial rivalry between engineers and navigators. One captain and his chief engineer, tired of endlessly debating which one of them the ship could the more easily dispense with, decided to swap places for a day. The chief ascended to the bridge and the skipper went down into the engine room.

After a couple of hours the captain, covered with oil and soot, suddenly appeared on deck.

"Chief!" he called, beckoning wildly with a monkey wrench. "You'll have to come down here at once. I can't seem to make her go."

"Of course you can't," said the chief, calmly removing his pipe from his mouth. "She's aground."

The man who told this story originally was a Great White Fleet engineer who wrote novels in his spare time. He was a big heavy-featured man who usually wore dungarees and talked gruffly of fuel-oil consumption and banana tonnages. His name was William McFee.

Earlier the banana navy had suffered other writing men, including a Baltimore pier monkey, more formally listed as a dock handler, named H. L. Mencken. He was even then a scowling polemicist, whom several of his banana-pier associates remember as a bumptious youngster with a loud voice and an interest in nautical subjects. While the former Baltimore dock hand was assuming his office as literary high priest of the 1920's, William McFee remained the foremost writing man and one of the better engineers of the banana navy.

McFee had been born at sea aboard a three-masted schooner owned and sailed by his New Brunswick-born father. He grew up in a London suburb with an honestly inherited love for the sea. In 1901, when he was twenty, he got an engraved certificate which called him a "qualified" mechanical engineer. He first went to work for a manufacturer of laundry machinery, who denied the accuracy of the certificate's definition. Bill was forced to a hasty decision. He resolved to become a writer and began by contributing skits to a neighborhood newspaper. When his literary income had risen to the encouraging figure of one guinea a month, Bill took a dank cellar room in Cheyne Walk, in London's Chelsea, where he promptly got an overdose, so he recalled, of "babel, blat, and bunk."

So William McFee made a third choice and went to sea as third engineer on the tramp ship *Rotherfield*. He served out five busy years helping to haul copper ore from South Africa to London, cotton from Savannah to Liverpool, case oil from Philadelphia to Japan, general merchandise from London to the Mediterranean. He finished the five years with a rating of chief engineer and a first book called *Letters from an Ocean Tramp*.

Nobody in particular noticed the book or the writer. Then he began a novel, writing and rewriting at sea and in port, during anchor watches in the Mediterranean and in the public library at Glasgow. At Wilmington, North Carolina, Bill McFee finished his book, wrote 80,000 more words, rewrote the entire novel, and waited for a publishing offer. That was in 1912. He had started the book four years before. He found a publisher for it four years later.

A second novel was rejected by all publishers. In downtown New York McFee wrote advertising copy and sales letters for unimaginative businessmen. Despairing of such hack work, he sent all his manuscripts to a literary agent in London and went back to sea as a third engineer for the Great White Fleet. Writing later of this decision, he said, "I recommend this course to all young authors. . . . The sea will evoke from your buried memories an unsuspected wealth of copy. It will soothe your bitterness and assuage your grief. Go to sea!"

As a ship's engineer, Bill McFee "chased bananas" for United Fruit for three years. With the outbreak of the First World War he resigned, returned to London, and shipped as an engineer on transport duty, eventually receiving a commission in the Royal Naval Reserve. He was assigned to the Mediterranean fleet and was in the Aegean when he received a publishing contract and proofs for his long-spurned novel, *Casuals of the Sea*.

McFee was amazed by the energetic praise with which American critics received his books. He called it "Harvard

tradition for lapping the boots of any non-American. . . .
Fawning slop!" Bill swore off reading reviews of his own
books and remained with the banana fleet, working his way
to better berths on better ships. He became chief engineer
on the big *Carrillo*, running from New Orleans to Belize,
Cortez, and Limon, and later went aboard the *Metapan*. He
wrote:

The sea is a good life and I love it. I love the men and their
ships. . . . I stay at sea to keep in contact with reality. . . . That
can be done ashore, but writing men rarely do it. They shut
themselves up in ivory towers or in little sophisticated groups
of their own kind. They get detached from life. . . . I don't care
a blue curse what the public wants. Nor do I worry much
whether I ever make a big name. All I want to do is some hon-
orable work, to do it as well as I possibly can, and there my
responsibilities end.

On shipboard he found time to meditate and write. So he
remained with the banana ships for twelve more years, even
as his writing income far surpassed his engineer's salary. Then
came a dilemma. The boilers needed cleaning. A book had
to be completed. McFee confided his quandary to the port
superintendent in New York. The boss was sympathetic.
"The decision is yours, Bill. Do you most want to be a writer,
or a shipman?"

"I still can't make up my mind," said McFee.

"Then I'll make it up for you," the boss said. "You want
to be a writer."

They shook hands and William McFee quit the fleet that
he had served long and well and went back to the "mysterious
poverty" and the exhilarating adventure of writing books.

CHAPTER EIGHT

ON THE AIR

AT THE LIMON, Costa Rica, headquarters of the United Fruit Company, Mack Musgrave, a Marylander schooled in the newfangled trade called electrical engineering, was supporting the somewhat lofty title of Superintendent of the Electrical Department.

During the summer of 1903 Mack had been delegated by Mr. Preston to proceed to New York or anywhere else that seemed advisable "to investigate the possibilities of radio." It was a vague assignment, but Musgrave accepted it enthusiastically. He began the mission by making a perilous mule-back journey along the jungle trails from Puerto Limon to Bocas del Toro, a distance of about 150 miles. The trip took two weeks of riding and about two months of convalescence, at the termination of which Musgrave reported bluntly that construction of a telegraph and telephone line between the two banana headquarters would be not only wholly impractical but practically impossible. In parts of Costa Rica, Nicaragua, Cuba, and Jamaica, United Fruit had already established telephone and telegraph lines between some of its farms and their respective division headquarters. Now the banana *hombres* were trying to expand the system to connect headquarters in the various countries.

Telephonic and telegraphic systems simply did not work well over such distances. The land lines strung through jungle and swamp were unendingly subject to washouts, floods, hurricanes, boring insects, and the mysterious forces of tropical corrosion. The one established cable station at Colon was inaccessible to any near-by countries, and the only available routing of telegraphic messages from the United States to Central America followed a course which Rube Goldberg might have planned.

Urgent communications from company offices in the United States were first telegraphed to Galveston, Texas; then they were dispatched by cable (usually out of order) via Mexico to San Juan del Sur, Nicaragua; here the messages were transferred to land lines owned and operated by the Nicaraguan government; after much delay, land lines owned and operated by the government of Costa Rica picked up the communications. The latter systems were frequently out of order and, when strife or ill will prevailed between Nicaragua and Costa Rica or the staffs of their respective national telegraph systems, the messages never crossed the boundary at all. But when and if the messages reached Costa Rica's capital, they were dispatched by United Fruit land lines to the Limon headquarters, and then by Carib *cayucos* down the reef-strewn coast to Almirante Bay and Bocas.

Mack Musgrave insisted that this was one hell of a way to operate a banana business, and Andrew Preston agreed with him. The directors of the company were advised that unless United Fruit perfected a reliable system of speedy communication, all the work of the previous years would be undone. The reasons were evident enough. For its very survival the banana trade requires fast and well-managed shipping. In

sought to explain the fantastic slender towers which the foolish *Norteamericanos* had built into the air. Some natives called them super-voodoo. Static noises were known to have caused nervous tropical citizens to run at top speed for miles. Carib medicine men wailed at their altars and slapped charred bones together, in frantic effort to devise counter magics.

Even in the United States, the Preston-Keith experiments with "wireless" were thought to be a piece of insanity, all the more to be scoffed at because the banana men had announced their determination to put radio aboard all their ships at sea. United Fruit quietly purchased the United Wireless Telegraph stations at New Orleans and Burrwood, at the southwest pass of the Mississippi below New Orleans, the latter station for communicating with ships at sea, the former for long-distance broadcasts. In those days five kilowatts was the maximum transmission power in broadcasting. Mack Musgrave set out to raise this to ten.

After a prolonged session of map reading, he recommended Swan Island as the best point for relay to the Caribbean frontiers. This particular island appears on few maps. It is a mere dot of land in the great blue sea, about 900 miles south of New Orleans and some 90 miles northwest of Cortes, Honduras. It is, however, one of the most beautiful islands in all the world—a poet's dream, except during hurricane season.

There were no people on Swan except a ragged, rum-ridden old gentleman who called himself "Captain Adams" and nine or ten colored laborers from Grand Cayman, who fished, hunted game, lived in palm shacks, and spent some part of their time harvesting native coconuts and digging phosphate shale for intermittent export by the Swan Island Commercial Company, a United States corporation which owned all 1300 acres of the mile-by-two-mile island and rather wished it didn't.

Mr. Preston's banana company bought the entire island,

with full knowledge that it had no harbor and that a heavy ship could not navigate within a mile of its sandy beaches.

Mack Musgrave did not see how he could haul tower steel, oil tanks, heavy engines, and generators by rowboat. Nevertheless, he chartered a steamer from New York, employed a construction gang, loaded a heavy lighter aboard, ordered the ship anchored a mile off shore, used the lighter to land cargo on the uncharted beach, and after eight months of work succeeded in building the radio station.

But the station did not function during the static season, which lasts for nine months of the tropical year. Mr. Musgrave therefore experimented, perspired, and waited for better equipment. He did not have to wait long, for shortly afterward Reginald A. Fessenden, who had been broadcasting from Brant Rock, Massachusetts, to Machrihanish, Scotland, with his own invention of 500-cycle rotary synchronous spark sets, reported that signals received at Brant Rock from Swan Island were "strong and of fine tonal quality." Mr. Musgrave proceeded to Brant Rock to investigate. Fessenden eventually agreed to provide his spark transmitters for several United Fruit land stations and agreed further to sell the company 2-kilowatt, 500-cycle rotary synchronous spark transmitters for installation on each of its ships.

So United Fruit was first to put commercial radio on shipboard. The "radical" venture was soon internationally known. Signals from United Fruit banana ships in the Caribbean were picked up by naval craft at Port Said, Egypt, and off Honolulu. In those days these were amazing attainments. But the experiment was costing millions and the banana company was still not rich. Radio was still in its infancy and the National Broadcasting Company, the first of the great networks, did not come into existence until twenty years later. The tube as a detector and amplifier had not been used. In a laboratory on an unimproved stretch of Park Avenue, in New York, Dr. Lee

De Forest was busily experimenting with the "third element" of the radio tube. At Thirty-second Street and Broadway, Mr. De Forest's associate and friend, Thaddeus Cahill, had established "Telharmonium Hall," from which he and De Forest were broadcasting music by "Professor Cahill's Telharmonium machine." That was the first radio broadcast of music.

Mack Musgrave sought advice from De Forest and Cahill and then returned to radio building. He resolved to develop a more powerful transmitting station. So again he went searching for a suitable location and eventually chose a site on Cape San Antonio on the extreme western end of Cuba, fifteen miles from the nearest settlement, more than fifty miles from any railroad, completely lacking in harbor or building facilities, and infested with mosquitoes, sand flies, and stinging scorpions.

Musgrave and his helpers loaded a chartered ship with supplies, building materials, station equipment, and construction crews from Baltimore. He discharged the cargoes in rough sea on small lighters and rowboats. The work crews had to use sledge hammers to break up ledge rock for making cement. They leavened the pulverized rock with beach sand from which they had painstakingly washed the salt. In one way or another during 1909 they built the station—a 250-foot steel tower with umbrella antenna, an operating house, a powerhouse, a storage shed, and a dwelling for the solitary operator. They installed the new Fessenden apparatus and placed a complementary set in the big station at New Orleans.

Cape San Antonio is 600 miles from New Orleans. Indications were that during half the year fairly effective service could be maintained with New Orleans. Transmissions were clearest late at night and early in the morning. This was encouraging. At least it seemed so until the great hurricane struck two weeks after the San Antonio station was completed. The storm blew away part of the station and smashed the rest.

The banana company rebuilt the station, only to have another hurricane level it again.

Nobody knew better than Mr. Andrew Woodberry Preston that the survival and growth of the banana trade depended on the resourcefulness and the inventiveness of its employees in some fifteen nations. The radio venture was no exception. For example, when the next great hurricane struck and erased the Cape San Antonio station, John Cole, old-time radio operator who managed the station, forwarded this report to the main office:

About 3:00 P.M. on September 13th, I took a barometer reading and noted that it was unusually low, about 29.60. . . . I immediately informed the Weather Bureau via New Orleans. . . . Everything was made in readiness to withstand a storm. . . . On the morning of the 14th the barometer was still falling and the wind was increasing and a few minutes after I communicated with Swan Island the wind blew down part of the aerial. Repairs having been made, storm warnings were sent to all ships and repeated. About 9:00 A.M. the entire aerial was blown away and from that time on the wind blew stronger and stronger, and about 11:00 A.M. reached hurricane force. The Cuban Government wind gauge had by this time been blown away, but I judged the velocity of the wind was not less than 100 miles an hour. The barometer was still falling.

Our kitchen was the first to go, then the gas plant, warehouse, and roof of water storage plant were blown down, and some of the iron roofing carried for miles into the woods. Next the tower, which had been guyed with four one-inch steel cables, broke in two about half way up, breaking the guys, which blew straight out with the force of the wind.

The roof of the operating house was next blown off and the windows and doors blown in. Myself, the cook, and engineer were inside at the time, and we then took shelter in the engine house. The operating house, although of steel construction on concrete foundation, was moved about eight feet off of its foundation. The roof and floor of the veranda were wrenched from the house, but the house itself stood, although badly damaged. The engine house, where we went for shelter, stood only about twenty minutes after we got there. This being the last house, we started for the woods. . . .

We got a little protection behind some large stumps. After we were there for about an hour, there was a lull. The wind subsided and we returned to the station. . . . When I found that the barometer was as low as it would go, and the wind again increasing, we decided to go to the lighthouse, three miles away. This is a stone structure and we thought it would stand. . . . It took us about four hours to reach the lighthouse, having crawled most of the way amidst flying sand, timbers, and falling trees. On our arrival at the lighthouse we found that the prisms had been blown in, putting the light out of commission. We found there the wreck of a Honduran schooner. The captain had come in as close as he could get, but before he could get a boat out, the anchor chain parted and the vessed started out to sea. All hands jumped overboard and somehow got ashore. The vessel was blown to sea and disappeared in less than thirty minutes.

We spent the night at the lighthouse and returned to the station on the 15th, finding that all provisions, furniture, and kitchen utensils had been destroyed or buried under the sand. About 10:00 A.M. a native family, carrying five dead bodies, arrived at the station on their way to the lighthouse. We endeavored to clean up a bit and get a place to sleep, but the mosquitoes, gnats, and crabs which invaded the house would not permit.

On the 18th I hired a small sailboat and started for Arroyos, fifty miles distant, but a few miles out sighted a Cuban revenue cutter, which took me on board and landed me at La Fé at night, from which place I proceeded to Havana. . . .

In spite of all its work and spending, United Fruit still had not successfully established uninterrupted radio communication between the United States and Central America. With a stalemate evident, Andrew Preston approved a temporary compromise, a radio and cable system, called "Via Colon Radio." Messages were sent by direct cable from New York to Colon, where they could be delivered to banana ships equipped with the Fessenden radio sets. From the ship towers the messages were transmitted via Port Limon Radio to Bocas del Toro and the banana capitals in Costa Rica and Nicaragua. Steamship schedules were rearranged so that at least one radio-equipped banana ship could stand by in Colon Harbor at least six days a week. This experiment was begun late in 1909. It was costly, but it provided the first really dependable radio-telegraph communication.

The Colon service via banana ships remained until the Panama Canal builders established the first United States Government radio station at Cristobal. Then the banana messages were delivered to the government station for rebroadcast. Nevertheless, "Via Colon Radio" had actually saved the day for United Fruit.

Andrew Preston showed mild boredom at an avalanche of congratulations. He said: "Of course my boys have got something." The banana president reached for his camphored cigar box. "Give us one more year. . . ."

Meanwhile Mack Musgrave devoted himself to recruiting the best operators he could hire and persuaded George Davis, the United States Navy's director of radio organization and research, to become his assistant. Davis directed the reconstruction of the hurricane-wrecked Cape San Antonio station, completed the installation of the Fessenden sets on all the company's ships, and supervised the banana company's experimental radio laboratory at New Orleans.

True to Andrew Preston's prophecy, 1910 was an important year for radio. During that year Musgrave, Davis, and Fessenden introduced the first Fessenden heterodyne at United Fruit's New Orleans and Cape San Antonio stations. They installed improved receiving sets in all the stations, and for the first time commercial broadcasting became internationally trustworthy. These were pioneering steps far ahead of the times. In 1910, though Orville Wright had flown his "poultry-crate" planes, aviation was still in a state of incubation. The automobile industry was also in its earliest period of development. The week in which the first radio messages were sent from New Orleans to Port Limon—in June, 1910—the first transcontinental automobile race began in front of New York's City Hall. The winner entered the gates of Seattle's Alaska-Yukon-Pacific Exposition 22 days and 55 minutes after leaving New York.

That made automotive history. But in the very month that it took an automobile more than 22 days to cross the United States, banana radio was spanning more than a thousand miles in a fraction of a second and repeating the feat every hour and every day of the year.

The Swan Island and New Orleans stations were rebuilt and re-equipped. Another powerful station was erected at Santa Marta, Colombia. The Marconi Wireless Company provided some of the equipment and supplied all the new stations with 50-kilowatt 500-cycle rotary synchronous spark transmitting apparatus. The New Orleans station now spread over twenty acres. Four 320-foot steel masts were constructed and linked with a directional antenna measuring 300 by 600 feet. Two additional 250-foot towers were built at Swan Island, and a similar giant antenna was raised. New power plants and machine shops were required to service the radio stations. Swan Island became the relay point for the stations in Colombia, Costa Rica, Honduras, Jamaica, and Cuba.

Theoretically the newer steel towers were hurricaneproof. But one hurricane which hurled its fury against Swan Island with a recorded speed of 130 miles an hour toppled three of the towers and, in spite of the buildings' reinforcements of steel and concrete, threw all equipment out of order.

Hundreds of miles away, Mr. Andrew Preston penciled a

memorandum on an envelope flap: "Nothing is hurricane-proof."

In New York Musgrave and Davis found a consulting engineer, A. W. Buel, who had designed railway bridges for Minor Keith. Working with Davis, Buel planned a succession of 420-foot steel towers, with 150-foot bridge arms, designed to withstand wind forces of 140 miles per hour. The Buel-Davis tower became standard equipment. Then Musgrave supervised the design and installation of giant storage batteries on the ships to provide power for emergency lighting and of instruments which enabled ship captains to determine bearings from radio beacon stations.

The radio department was formally incorporated in 1913 as the Tropical Radio Telegraph Company, a subsidiary of United Fruit. Soon two new stations were built on the Honduran coast, at Tela and Puerto Castilla, between which points messengers had formerly trotted with their *avisos*.

But Mack Musgrave, who did most to blaze the radio trails of the Caribbean, failed to see his great work completed. Late in 1911 he was granted leave to make an important and secret communications survey in Alaska. Two years later he returned to Seattle to convalesce from overwork and exposure and died there in 1913. George Davis became the head of Tropical Radio.

Between the middle of August and the middle of September merchant shipping in the Caribbean was especially fearful of hurricanes. Davis inaugurated a storm-warning system by means of which ship captains could advise one another of alarming changes of weather. He offered these facilities to the United States Weather Observation Service and appointed all United Fruit ship captains and chief radio operators "special deputy weather observers," whose duties included twice-daily broadcasts of weather reports. These were relayed through Swan Island and New Orleans, supplemented by cabled reports from the Windward and Leeward Islands, and dispatched by land line to the United States Weather Bureau in Washington. The bureau was then able to report the existence of a hurricane, plot its course, estimate its danger, and issue reliable storm warnings for all Gulf Coast shipping. As soon as this storm warning service was available, Tropical Radio began rebroadcasting the official United States Weather Bureau notices to all ships on the Gulf of Mexico and the Caribbean.

The new head of Tropical Radio next began preparations for a system of radio-telephone communication between the United States and Central America. He planned radio-telephone and radio-telegraph ship-to-shore services via tube transmitters and made plans for building at Tegucigalpa, the Honduran capital, the most powerful tube transmitting stations in the hemisphere. Engines, generators, hundreds of tons of construction supplies, and enough steel for a 420-foot tower had to be landed at the Pacific port of Amapala and from there hauled, packed, or dragged by bull teams over eighty miles of jungle and mountainside trails to the remote mountain-guarded capital.

The banana firm began to build a powerful mainland station near Miami, Florida, and another at Managua, Nicaragua. Davis and his staff of Tropical Radio then outfitted all stations with tube transmitting equipment and established for the use of the general public as well as the banana trade the first radio communications system that tied together the principal population centers of the Caribbean area and made them instantly accessible to the United States.

Before the initial network could be put into operation the cost had climbed to more than 4 million dollars. By 1920 United Fruit could afford such an expense. But it may have been significant that bigger and richer business, operating for profit in the same general area, had not elected to undertake it. Though profits were the primary purpose of United Fruit,

Andrew Preston and his company were spending additional millions to satisfy what they considered a critical need of half a hemisphere.

As his chief engineer, George Davis chose William E. Beakes, who had served as Fessenden's helper during the first broadcasts between Brant Rock and Scotland. As his designing engineer, Davis selected Colonel W. P. Rothrock, who had helped build New York's elevated railways. Then he began a systematic selection and training of radio operators. United Fruit accorded every ship operator the rank of purser, with the best accommodations available and a salary ranging from $105 to $140 per month. For radio operators in the tropics the banana company established pay scales of $150 to $250 per month and quarters.

Mr. Preston agreed that his radio boys were playing their piano right nicely, authorized a free medical service via radio, and posted the following order: " 'DH Medico' radiograms will take preference over all other radiograms, excepting S O S calls, throughout the radio service of the United Fruit Company and subsidiary companies. . . ." Another of Andrew Preston's one-sentence general orders announced the beginning of a free medical consultation service by radio from all United Fruit Company hospitals in Central America and all company-operated ships that carried surgeons. This service was provided on request to any ship, regardless of nationality, with sick or injured crew or passengers aboard. Few ships plying the Caribbean carried doctors, and the free medical consultation service was eagerly accepted.

Andrew Preston and his associates sought no public recognition of United Fruit's beneficences. They were using banana earnings to pay for a system of sanitation and hospitalization which was the most ambitious and best integrated of all defenses against tropical diseases. They had accepted radio as an indispensable multi-million-dollar need of banana marketing. In both instances the foremost banana company had worked and spent far beyond the immediate needs of the banana trade. It had gone ahead stubbornly without publicity, fanfare, or press agenting calculated to create an illusion of vast social magnanimity. While other corporations and foundations continued to pound the drums of their philanthropy, the soft-spoken Yankee commission merchant worked on to sell more bananas at lower prices.

CHAPTER NINE

THE MARKET PLACE

IN 1870 Captain Lorenzo Baker of Wellfleet had stated as an axiom that bananas are worth exactly what you can get for them. Port prices in those times were governed by available supply, by bargaining skill, and by a certain amount of blind luck.

When bananas first began appearing at New Orleans and other port markets, the United States diet consisted preponderantly of meat, grain, and potatoes. We were not a fruit-eating or a fruit-growing people. During the 1880's the first California struggles to produce citrus, then called "Sicilies," were a standing joke in produce jobbing. Never, never, said the substantial commission merchants of New York and Philadelphia, would oranges and lemons be grown commercially in California. Possibly there might someday appear in California a few back-yard trees which might bear something vaguely similar to the citrus family, but never for commercial use.

The prophets of fruit have lived hard. During the days of

first banana imports the apple was called the "jobbers' staple." But apple marketing was conspicuously unstable. There was no cold storage then. Freight schedules were highly unpredictable, and during nearly half the year fruits were all too likely to come frozen or frosted from the cars. After the Christmas holidays apples, if any, emerged as one of the choice luxuries of the grocery. As one instance, during February and March, 1880, boxed apples grown in California were wholesaling at twelve dollars a bushel in New York, while scarce supplies of oranges and lemons, imported directly from Sicily, were selling for thirty cents a pound and fifteen to eighteen dollars a box. In most United States seaports bananas were a known fruit, but for good reason they were an erratic, seasonal entry, ever hazardous to sell.

As we have already noticed, the early banana trade was an epic of befuddled audacity. Ships recruited haphazard banana cargoes, paying in money, trinkets, hard liquors, or rash promises, depending on the moods of the tropical seller and the supplies of the fruit at hand. There followed the crazy-quilt patterns of wasteful loading, the massing of deck cargo which was frequently washed into the sea and usually splashed with brine; the prayerful or profane dash for market port—frequently ended with cargo rotting; the completely haphazard undersupplying and oversupplying of port markets; the tactics of inland jobbers, who would receive bananas on consignment, stand by until the produce was dead ripe, then offer a ruinously low bid which the shipper could not refuse.

The pioneer banana trade reeked with disorder; sale by the bunch, giant bunches or pygmies at an identical price; sale by "ship run"—dead ripe, half ripe, or completely green as the ship delivered them; the "stacking" of carload shipments— good bunches immediately behind the car door, the rest trash. As a general proposition the banana trade was as unstable as any.

Dirt cheap in one town, bananas were frequently an ex-

pensive luxury in another. Andrew Preston wanted to do
something about that by establishing a common port price
based on average tropical costs plus transportation and
handling charges. Employees of Fruit Dispatch were directed
to refuse the sale of bananas to fraudulent jobbers. This policy
resulted in the destruction of great quantities of otherwise
salable fruit, but honest fruit dealers welcomed its enforcement.

Fruit Dispatch had begun in Boston and New York. The
first branch office was opened at Pittsburgh early in 1899.
Later in that year other banana-selling branches were opened
in Buffalo, Cleveland, Washington, D. C., Richmond, Chicago, Detroit, Columbus, Cincinnati, Indianapolis, Kansas
City, St. Louis, Minneapolis, New Orleans, and San Francisco.
The initial list of fifteen sales branches included the key railway centers of the United States. If unwanted at one center,
the banana cars were routed to the next, until all the fruit was
sold.

But the bananas required protection from winter freezes
and summer heat. That called for ventilation of railway
freight cars, for boxcar stoves in winter, for car icing in summer, and for attendants or "messengers" to ride through with
the cars and see them safely delivered to the inland buyers.
One of the old-timers among the messengers writes:

When I joined forces with the company in 1902, I was shipped
out on the road right away at a salary of $11.54 a week as a
banana messenger for a cold winter run. . . . I left New York
with a string of five or six cars of bananas for Rouses Point, with
orders to put the fruit in the roundhouse there. The roundhouse
ain't a fruit house, but it gives some protection against the zero
temperatures in that part of the country during the winter
months. Of course we had to warm the banana cars with stoves,
too, and our stove equipment was short. So when I got to Rouses
Point with the five or six cars, I didn't have enough stoves to
heat up the bananas. And I didn't have much time. So I had to

invent a heater right off. So I borrowed a quarter-inch steel plate from the railroad and put it on the floor of the car, after having removed the fruit from the doorway. Going through the scrap heap, I found a lining of an engine smokestack and put it over the brake shoes. That was my stove. After using a few shovels of live coal, I was able to get some heat in the fruit—anyway so it didn't freeze black.

During the previous year the inland banana trade, insofar as there was any, had prospered during the summer, when the green bunches would ripen without any particular nurture or encouragement. In the tropics, however, bananas can be made ready for harvest virtually any day of the year. Stretching the marketing season was therefore a necessity. This made imperative improved methods of handling and storing the fruit. But small shopkeepers or peddlers, accustomed to selling bananas by a single bunch, could not be expected to learn and apply the technique of banana ripening. That task was up to the jobbers or dealers, who could afford to build and equip temperature-controlled ripening rooms and the other costly facilities that were required.

In the United States railroads were refusing to accept the bare green fruit as it was discharged from the ship, for it was almost certain to spoil before reaching its destination. That raised the problem of designing containers suitable for far-inland shipment—containers that would protect the fruit and permit the ripening process to continue unhindered during transit. Fruit Dispatch workers eventually devised a container known as the banana drum, made of jute board and veneered strips of lumber, sized to hold the banana bunch tightly, with paper or straw packing. The drums are light and compact, and for the United States banana trade their introduction proved to be of great importance.

Since his earlier encounters with Captain Lorenzo Baker on the Boston water front, Andrew Preston had argued for a system of inspection, grading, and weighing of all bananas at shipside. But the trade had preferred to ignore him. Dishonest importers obviously wanted no part in such a plan, and the minority of honest importers had not succeeded in perfecting a method of uniform grading, though a few had tried.

Nevertheless, Andrew Preston was stubborn. Fruit Dispatch introduced a routine of banana classification by size of the bunches, depending on the number of "hands" or clusters of bananas on each bunch—"nines" for all bunches with nine or more fully developed hands (occasionally a bunch has as many as fourteen hands); "eights," "sevens," "sixes," and "fives" for the smaller marketable bunches. Next came estimates of the appearance, quality, and general condition of the fruit—good, fair, or poor. By such a grading process at the port of entry, the buyer could be certain that a carload of bananas was no longer thrown hastily together and that individual bunches would not be arranged deceptively within the car.

In 1910, after eleven years of persuasion, Andy Preston completed arrangements with the New Orleans Board of Trade, a disinterested and respected business club, for the employment and direction of skilled fruit inspectors, each one duly bonded, to stand at each car door and inspect and approve every bunch of bananas placed in every car, making certain that the stevedores carried their burdens carefully, and rejecting every stem of ripe, shattered, or otherwise inferior fruit. The rigid inspection was supplemented by an equally impartial weighing of all fruit by bonded weighers, working under city and state license. The gross weight of each freight car was checked before and immediately after loading.

Although these were purely voluntary regulations, they were the first ever effected in interstate banana trade. As soon as the official inspection and weighing under New Orleans Board of Trade direction had been proved successful, Fruit Dispatch made similar arrangements with commercial organizations in other banana-market ports—the Boston Chamber of Commerce, the Mobile Business League, and the Galveston Cotton Exchange, to name only a few. At the time such ventures were considered "radical." But without doubt they were establishing a new era of public dealing on the part of a corporation, and they were making possible the survival of the nation-wide commerce in bananas.

As the new methods of banana selling became generally accepted, Preston began a patient search for more and better banana dealers. As the roster of United States banana jobbers grew to 300, then to 500, 1200, and eventually nearly 3000, the sales volumes grew by the tens of millions of bunches and Fruit Dispatch was presently distributing half or slightly more than half of the United States banana supply. United Fruit then doubled the number of Fruit Dispatch agencies and appointed resident messengers to inspect all banana cars passing through the principal railway terminals. A special department was created for the design and construction of refrigerated banana cars, and a claims department was established for the investigation of all complaints and the reimbursement of customers for losses for which the importer was responsible.

By ship and by rail, by truck, wagon, and pushcart, banana harvests were moving to market and becoming more or less familiar items on the counters of American groceries. William McFee, the former ship's engineer, described the scope and drama of the process:

It was a day of snow and wind last winter in Chicago, when . . . he saw the familiar yellow of a refrigerator car on the track beside the sleeper. . . . The present writer knew how far that thing had come, and he saw it all. He saw the elevators at New Orleans and the lines of cars in the echoing, cavernous sheds. He saw the Great River forever gnawing at his levees, forever churning up his shoals and mud banks and losing himself in the desolate multitude of his bayous. He saw the white ships afar on the blue

Gulf and still bluer Caribbean, the mountains of Cuba, and the loom of Mount Hope above the lush Jamaica valleys. He saw the islets of the Chiriquei Lagoon, the narrow white beaches where the jungle crowds to the very surf on the shores of Guatemala. He saw the swell lifting the vessels at the quays behind Grape Cay, and he heard the boom and crash of the sea on the black rocks of Santa Marta. He saw the long green alleys of the plantations, the piles of moving fruit covered from the dazzling tropical sun with great panoplies of leaves. . . . He saw the vistas of tropical rivers, the brilliant plumage of strange birds flashing like jewels in the sunlight as the boat thrusts onward between the lofty banks of living green. He saw the whole of that long romantic pathway leading down into the heart of the Americas from that yellow snow-covered refrigerator car. He saw it . . . as something beyond the mere delivery of a commodity and the earning of a dividend. It was indeed to his mind a symbol of the new theory of civilization, whereby the nations are joined in the effort to augment the fruitfulness of the earth.

Throughout most of the United States, on thousands of roadside stands and in tens of thousands of shops and stores, bananas were finding buyers most or all of the year. While temperate-zone fruits were being sold only during their proper seasons, bananas were being sold continuously—and at low prices. Andrew Preston was convinced that the banana trade could thrive on low prices and low profits so long as its volume remained large and steady.

Persistently and shrewdly Preston and his associates in United Fruit strove to keep the supply of the fruit abreast of domestic demands. To expedite the loading and discharge of banana ships, United Fruit developed and installed giant endless-chain belt conveyors to carry the green bunches in canvas pockets from loading piers to shipholds and from shipholds to car lines in domestic ports. Workers, however, were still needed—thousands of stevedores to carry the fruit and deposit it carefully in the conveyor pockets. The mechanical con-

veyor increased the rate of loading and discharging to 5000
bunches an hour and made possible the clearance of some
40,000 carloads per year through New Orleans alone.

During the First World War and the inflationary times that
followed, bananas remained among the cheapest of the staple
fruits. "It would be quite easy," Andrew Preston said, "to
raise the price of bananas now that there is an acute shortage
of the fruit. We do not choose to raise the price."

In the tropics, as in the States, warehouses were jammed
with goods for shipment and there were not enough ships, for
the largest vessels in the banana fleet were carrying troops
and supplies to France. Hurricanes ripped through the banana
plantations, and floods followed repeatedly in their wake.
Railroad strikes snarled traffic in the United States. But the
green-and-gold tide of tropical fruit continued to rise.

The banana trade was leaping from infancy to prime with
almost the magical lushness of banana plants plunging to maturity in the fertile wet tropics. Persistently and shrewdly
Andrew Preston strove to keep plantations and fleet abreast
of market demands. He reinstated Charleston as a banana-
receiving port and approved the dispatching of entire shiploads of bananas to Canada, where by rail, truck, and occasionally by horse cart the fruit found its way throughout most
of the Dominion. In 1916 the Canadian Banana Company,
Ltd., was founded as United Fruit's Canadian affiliate, with
Saint John, New Brunswick, as receiving port for Canadian
banana supplies.

Bananas grown in the Americas were now on the stands
throughout England and western Europe. England's first
bananas had come from Madeira. The first shipment of yellow bananas from the Canary Islands reached London in
1882. In 1884, when United States banana imports amounted
to more than 10 million bunches, England's totaled a mere ten

thousand. British shippers remained generally uninterested until 1892, when the London shipping firm of Elder and Dempster and Company began importing bananas from the Canaries. A competitor, Fyffes, Hudson and Company, followed suit.

But the fruit was expensive. Although the individual bunches were elaborately cased and insulated before the camel-back trip to Canary Island ports, the sea journey was usually rough, and too often the fruit arrived overripe or rotten. For ten years London's banana trade seemed certain to fail. It survived principally because of the efforts of two young men, A. Roger Ackerley and A. H. Stockley, both Liverpool youths who worked for Elder and Dempster.

Stockley was the salesman; Ackerley, so he said, was the office boy. They began their banana-vending partnership in 1882 with a first shipment of 500 bunches of Canary Islands bananas which Covent Garden hucksters eyed doubtfully. Stockley went to the Canaries to direct purchases and shipments of the fruit, while Ackerley remained in London to sell it. Sometimes Ackerley succeeded, but more frequently he failed. After ten unprofitable years, Stockley returned from the Canaries and the two young hucksters formed a partnership to import West Indian bananas from Jamaica.

The yellow Gros Michel bananas from Jamaica are about twice as big as the Canary Islands fruit and are of quite different flavor. The British market was slow to give its approval. Nevertheless, England's banana trade grew and, although the prices remained high and the selling season was limited to summer and autumn, the annual imports climbed to 20,000 bunches, to 30,000, and presently to 50,000.

During April, 1895, an affable gentleman with a peculiar rolling accent that was by no means Etonian called at a Covent Garden warehouse and introduced himself as Minor Keith of Costa Rica. With customary fervor Minor Keith proposed that Messrs. Stockley and Ackerley try their hands at marketing occasional shipments of Central American bananas, with the understanding that Keith would assume all risks for safe delivery and share half the profits. Stockley and Ackerley promptly agreed.

The first sample shipments of Keith-grown bananas began arriving at Avonsmouth in the spring of 1896. The stem tips were smeared with asphaltum, and the bunches were packed carefully in dried banana leaves and crated in heavy wooden boxes. A few were salable and at Covent Garden auctions the giant Costa Rican fruit sold for almost fifteen dollars a bunch—probably the highest in the history of the banana trade. But for every bunch that was salable five had to be discarded as hopelessly overripe. After two seasons of experimenting with shipments of 1000 to 2000 bunches a month, Minor Keith found himself the loser by at least $15,000. The impulsive Costa Rican withdrew temporarily from the English market. For six more years Stockley and Ackerley continued to ship and sell Jamaican bananas. Then in May, 1901, Elder and Fyffes, a limited-liability corporation, was organized in London. Sir Alfred Jones was chairman of the board, and Stockley and Ackerley became resident managers and salesmen for the new firm.

But the British banana trade needed more fruit and more ships. The two young hucksters from Liverpool knew who had the most bananas and the most ships. They went directly to Boston and to Andrew W. Preston. Out of the conversations that followed there grew an "association" between Elder and Fyffes and United Fruit—a supply-and-sales affiliation which after eight years found Elder and Fyffes, Ltd., the English subsidiary of United Fruit.

"The British children," as Andrew Preston called them, began with three ships, capable of delivering a total of 40,000 bunches a month. The next move of the team of Stockley and Ackerley was to cut the bananas into hands and pack them in boxes or baskets—ten dozen bananas to the box—so that the fruit could be sold by the dozen. Then they established banana "agencies" in various English cities and eventually founded the Fruit Distributing Company to parallel the work of Fruit Dispatch in the United States.

As the trade grew so did the fleet. At the beginning of the First World War Elder and Fyffes had twenty-two refrigerated ships with cargo space for 13 million bunches of bananas a year, 12 million of which were being loaded from United Fruit or citizen-owned plantations in Jamaica, Costa Rica, Panama, and Colombia. In addition to its interests in the Caribbean, Elder and Fyffes bought an 8000-acre area in the Canary Islands and latticed the farms with irrigation canals.

Shortly before the merger with United Fruit, R. H. Rhys, the Elder and Fyffes agency manager at Hull, began selling Jamaican bananas in Holland. The first shipment in 1909 was a crate of five bunches directed to a fruit merchant in Amsterdam. The next order was for ten bunches. Caribbean-grown bananas thereafter entered Western Europe by way of England. Holland had been the first country to import the fruit. Sweden was next, and Carl Matthiesson of Stockholm became the first Swedish banana dealer.

During the four busy years that preceded the First World War, Elder and Fyffes established forty European and Scandinavian branches. Bananas grown on Caribbean shore lines were being sold in Germany, Denmark, Sweden, Norway, Switzerland, Austria, France, Russia, and countries of the Mediterranean. Vienna had one of the world's best banana-ripening houses. To St. Petersburg of czarist Russia, Jamaica-grown bananas, wrapped in heavy blankets, were being shouldered through six-foot snowdrifts. Trial shipments of bananas had traveled from Stockholm to Spitzbergen, north of the Arctic Circle. Thus the most perishable of tropical fruits became one of the most widely distributed of New World crops.

Despite the ruthless effectiveness of the Kaiser's U-boats, despite shipping strikes and widespread conscription of merchant ships, England's banana trade continued during the first years of the First World War. When exports to Europe were abruptly blocked in 1914, banana prices in England fell to an all-time low of four for a penny and for economy's sake the hastily recruited home army was fed in large part on ripe bananas.

A hard-pressed Admiralty conscripted the banana fleet in December, 1916. During the following fifteen months, eleven of Elder and Fyffes twenty-two banana ships were lost to enemy action. During 1917 the Food Ministry restricted banana imports to one-fourth the level of the previous year, then lowered the quota still more until only one ship remained to carry all of England's banana supply. Though London fruiterers were bidding $250 a ton for bananas, which they could easily have retailed at ten shillings a dozen, Messrs. Stockley and Ackerley repeated Andrew Preston's phrase that bananas are a poor man's food, and they held banana prices at shipside within fifteen percent of prewar levels.

After the Armistice the European banana trade awaited the overhauling of war-worn ships and railroads. But European dealers took the initiative with plans and blueprints for improved storage and ripening rooms and electrically heated delivery vans.

Mr. Stockley predicted that the British and West European banana trade would quickly recover its losses. The prediction was soon proved in fact.

Premier David Lloyd George, reflecting on his immediate and distinguished past, said: "When I was Cabinet-making I had sandwiches as my nourishment. What a better job I might have made of it on bananas!"

England was again ripe for "ba-nah-nas."

Rotterdam became Europe's leading banana port, and boatloads of Caribbean-grown fruit glided along the placid Maas.

Although currencies were distressingly unstable and profiteering had been standard practice throughout most of the continent, the fruit trade grew until its volume in 1922 was twice that of 1912. In scores of European towns bananas were being displayed in electrically heated glass cases, and the tropical fruit was being sold even in remote Denmark.

Since Lorenzo Dow Baker had loaded a first deckload, bananas had traveled far—Captain Baker might have said, "too dadblamed far." On three continents the banana trade was active. Bananas had become a major commercial enterprise.

As more and more bananas went out to the world, more and more publicized personalities helped publicize the foremost tropical fruit. From the better watering places of the Riviera and South Spain, His Royal Highness Edward, Prince of Wales, revealed his favorite breakfast: "At breakfast time peel a banana. Lay it on a plate of ample size and ladle over it thick orange marmalade. Eat with a spoon, munching at the same time hot buttered toast. Sip coffee."

Among the best evidences of their popularity was the increasing frequency of bananas in song, whimsy, vaudeville, and humor columns. To most audiences bananas are more or less inherently funny. Banana peels are what people skid and fall down on. The very shape of a banana was beginning to induce laughter.

In his *Indianapolis Star* column called "Everyday Wisdom" Don Herold viewed bananas comprehensively:

. . . Bananas grow in boxcars and are very easy to pick. Compare the banana to the cherry, for instance. The cherry grows very far apart, and it is necessary to risk life and limb, and waste a great deal of time in gathering it; but, as for bananas, a whole bushel may be gathered with one well-directed stroke of a pair of scissors. . . . It is not necessary to husk a banana a half-day, as is the case with an ear of corn. No special husking mittens or paring knife or hammer or hatchet are required. In this connection, compare the banana to the walnut. Think of cracking the banana as we crack the walnut. The banana is even easier to get at than an egg, though, we will admit, there are points of ingenuity about the egg. Nature was very thoughtful and provident when she gave us that most convenient of all herbs, the banana.

Since the early 1890's "polite" jokes about bananas have cluttered the pages and columns of the growing ranks of periodicals. And the gain-weight-to-enlist stories have fluttered through news columns during our past three wars:

Lloyd Nickerson, who was sworn in last night, lacked seven pounds of making the weight when first examined, but he made the deficit up by eating seventeen bananas and drinking large quantities of water and was accepted.

—*Indianapolis Star* 1917.

There was, and is, the inevitable parade of helpful hints:

"While riding this morning on a Yazoo train from Bayou Bara," explained Mr. Gruenstein, "I discovered a new use for banana peelings. I wanted to get my shoes shined, but the porter had no tan polish. He bought two bananas from the 'news butcher' and ate them for breakfast. Then he rubbed the mud off my shoes and used the banana peelings in lieu of shoe polish. With the aid of a red rag he polished my shoes to a point of perfection never before attained by any bootblack."

—New Orleans *Item,* 1922

Then came the *New Yorker* entry:

THE PRESIDENT AGAIN

The latest story about Calvin Coolidge—and our present favorite —concerns a visit he made to the estate of the Du Pont family in Delaware. During the afternoon he spent an hour in the great greenhouses, rich in a thousand varieties of exotic growths. He walked in silence through aisles of rare orchids, strange fruits, and colorful blooms, as the chief gardener pointed out fragile and

flaring wonders. It was not until near the end of the tour that the
party reached a room where grew certain familiar fruit-bearing
tropical plants. The President stopped short, looked upon them
with evident interest, and spoke for the first and only time that
afternoon. "Bananas," he said.

Significantly, banana jokes and whimsies grew without the
effort of any banana company to sponsor them.

Unpredictably, the all-time high of banana comedy was
fomented by the fabulously giddy and world-circling song
hit of the middle 'twenties, "Yes, We Have No Bananas!"—a
playfully wacky lyric that took five continents by storm. The
phenomenon began when a jazz-band drummer, Frank Silver,
who was temporarily leading a New York theater orchestra,
chanced to notice a Greek peddler who drove a battered
produce wagon and a dreary old horse through tenement
streets of upper Manhattan. When a customer called out from
a high window for bananas, the son of classic Athens shouted
back, "Yes, we have no bananas!"

Silver thought that funny. He described it to Sam Cohn, a
fellow musician, and the two young men joined in a first
venture as popular song writers. Drummer Silver devised the
gay and bouncy tune, and Silver and Cohn collaborated on
the almost endless verses:

> Yes, we have no bananas,
> We have no bananas today.
> We just killed a pony so try our bologny
> It's flavored with oats and hay . . .
> And you can take home for the wimmens,
> Nice juicy per-simmons . . .
> But yes, we have no bananas,
> We have no bananas today. . . .

The two creative artists carried their effort to a succession
of thirteen music publishers, all of whom rejected it. Though
dubious, the fourteenth publisher accepted the "novelty" and

to the profound surprise of its authors and publisher the number began to "take." Within a year the sheet music was selling at the rate of 25,000 copies a day. Cautious Boston alone had accounted for 100,000 copies and 50,000 phonograph records.

In most American towns and cities dance bands pounded and protracted the ditty, which promptly swept to unprecedented popularity in England, France, Germany, and Italy. The verses were translated into eleven languages, including Swedish, Chinese, and Russian, and throughout a score of nations the title became standard repartee. Fruit dealers and restaurateurs crowded their windows with signs reading "Yes, We Have Bananas!"

The Boston *Herald* lamented editorially, "Boston is in the clutches of a musical crime wave. . . ." But the banana song also recruited distinguished supporters. The *Detroit News* reported from Battle Creek:

Professor Irving Fisher, of the political science department of Yale University, insists that "Yes, We Have No Bananas Today" as diction is admirably stated and that it does not merit the scorn it has received from our mental mandarins and privileged purists. Professor Fisher, a guest at a sanitarium in Battle Creek, Mich, was asked by a *Detroit News* correspondent whether the sentence was correct English. The professor stroked his academic beard, ruminated in a scholarly manner for a little while, then smilingly said, "Yes, it is correct—on a certain hypothesis."

The reporter, strangely enough, was eager for more information. "Well," said Professor Fisher, "it is technically correct in answer to the question: 'Do you have no bananas?'"

In New York and London night clubs, drummers were beating away with bananas, band men were sitting on bunches of bananas, dance floors were being strewn with banana peels. Even in China "Yes, We Have No Bananas" spread like Standard kerosene. Dr. Charles Dwight Reid, an

American physician at St. James Hospital of Anking, with
the help of some native collaboration, made a Chinese translation. Mr. George Allan England, of Boston, took Dr. Reid's
version to his friendly laundryman to seek an impartial
critique. The laundryman read over the translation in a low
hum, then indignantly declaimed:

It say, today, yes, banana, have not got. It say, bean, onion,
have got. Everything, cabbage, little onions, have got. . . . Red
melon, potato from Kow Wow, have got. It say, but, today, yes,
banana, have not got. Who write damn fool Chinese? Where you
get 'em? Crazy mans! Yes, sir. No good!

Meanwhile Frank Silver had organized a ten-piece "Banana
Band" which packed theaters and dance halls throughout the
United States. Each musician was seated before a large bunch
of real bananas, with a pictured field of bananas as backdrop.
"I know when I'm lucky," said the smiling Mr. Silver.

After twenty years the fabulously popular daffiness of "Yes,
We Have No Bananas!" found its counterpart in another
banana song, "Chiquita Banana." The latter began in 1944 as
a radio advertising jingle.

The objective was not that of selling more bananas, since
war shipping restrictions were holding the supplies immeas-
urably below the demand. John Werner, head of Fruit Dispatch, favored an effort to "educate" the consuming public
in the proper care of bananas—when, if, and as the fruit
became available. That involved adequate ripening—out of
refrigerators.

Radio advertisers were obsessed with rhyming jingles. Bob
Foreman, handling advertising for Batten, Barton, Durstine
and Osborn, Inc., and two members of his department, Gerth
Montgomery and Len Mackenzie, produced the ditty, Mackenzie "roughing" the music and Montgomery the words for
sixty seconds of jingling on hard-used ether waves. The lyric,
sung to a complicated rhumba rhythm, ran:

I'm Chiquita Banana and I've come to say
Bananas have to ripen in a certain way,
When they are fleck'd with brown and have a golden hue,
Bananas taste the best and are the best for you.
You can put them in a salad,
You can put them in a pie-aye—
Anyway you want to eat them
It's impossible to beat them.
But bananas like the climate of the very, very tropical equator
So you should never put bananas in the refrigerator . . .
No, no, no, no.

First broadcasts included phonograph recordings distributed to a long list of local stations. Patti Clayton, professionally described as a "good, swingy voice with perfect clarity of diction," sang the "vocal." The first recording remained in circulation for eight months. It brought anguished protests from harried listeners, but it also won avid supporters. *Time* called Chiquita "Number one on the jingle-jangle hit parade." Navy students at a Midwestern university voted Chiquita "the girl they'd most like to get in a refrigerator with." United Fruit raised the appropriation. John Werner taunted Samuel Zemurray and his "brain trust" and happily quoted the latter's earlier and highly derisive comments about Chiquita. The company began to print and make gratis distribution of the sheet music.

Apparently for the first time, a lowly radio jingle was rising to the ranks of hit songs. Name bands began playing the somewhat expanded lyric on major broadcasts that were in no way related to United Fruit. Fred Allen took up the ditty, ragged it murderously, and added enormously to its popularity. United Fruit arranged for recording and broadcasting a patois version for the French-Canadian banana trade and a Spanish version for broadcast to and in the tropics. In addition the company began to develop "wacky" recordings in swing and operatic styles to ridicule the jingle itself.

Significantly, United Fruit's eager exploitation of the un-anticipated bonanza of Chiquita demonstrated an impressive awakening to the strategies of mass propaganda or, more politely, public relations.

CHAPTER TEN

THE FIRST
QUARTER CENTURY

ANDREW PRESTON of Boston, on rounding his seventy-second birthday, remarked that he declined to be an old man at the head of a young trade. To portly Bill Newsome, his senior vice-president, the United Fruit president admitted that Father Time is a tough old rascal to fool. Bill Newsome, well past sixty, had to agree.

The banana trade was still young. But its leaders had grown old. Practically speaking, United Fruit remained a one-man company. In the tropics, as in Boston, New York, New Orleans, London, and elsewhere, the boss had competent assistants and junior officers. The directors were capable financiers and businessmen, but the directors met infrequently and were in no position to exercise direct control. Moreover, Andrew Preston's "boys" were not as yet senior executives, and senior executives were badly needed.

Many people referred to United Fruit as "the Banana

Trust." Mr. Preston still defined his company as only one of a group of produce firms with widely spread holdings of tropical farms. At any rate, there was no monopoly of bananas, sugar, cocoa, or any other produce grown, shipped, or sold by United Fruit. The company was growing approximately one-third of the bananas that it sold and buying the rest from independent farmers. It was growing less than half of the sugar cane it milled and buying the rest. Some of the farmers were well pleased at the prices paid them for their produce. Others were not. That, Mr. Preston said, is life and the produce business.

Nevertheless, United Fruit was paying "at par or above" for produce which it graded meticulously and sold competitively. Preston invited anyone who doubted this to visit the rail yards of Cleveland, Cincinnati, Chicago, Pittsburgh, or any one of the several dozen other cities on a summer week-end when carloads of bananas from Standard Fruit, Cuyamel, and probably Di Giorgio, as well as United, jammed all storage areas and railroad sidings; when jobbers were swearing or sulking, banana salesmen were pleading, and still more carloads were rolling in without specific destinations.

At seventy-two, Andrew Preston was likewise convinced that in many businesses, including the banana trade and international trade generally, a proprietor is damned if he does and damned if he does not. Had there been no banana railroads or hospitals, the old man of 131 State Street was certain that from many quarters there would be bitter denunciation of selfish gringo interference in Central American affairs. Now that there really was a big and prosperous banana trade with a network of affiliated services, many citizens of the United States were indignant at what they called "Yankee imperialism and paternalism among our southern neighbors."

Mr. Preston listened attentively and puffed at his medium-priced cigars.

People in 1916 were disturbed about "the High Cost of Living." The *Boston Post* offered but slight encouragement in its editorial of July 26 of that year. It discovered that prices of four Hub City staples—beans, moth balls, collars, and corncob pipes—had risen outrageously. "Yesterday," the paper commented, "a reporter went scouting for some good news in the way of something, the price of which had gone down. Bananas proved the best bet. . . . So far as can be predicted, bananas, the staple food of tropical lands, is on the verge of ousting the bean and the beefsteak in Boston. . . ."

But the banana trade was making other contributions. At Tulane University the United Fruit Company was giving financial backing to the establishment of a department for the study of diseases of the Caribbean coast lands. And in several Central American areas United Fruit was offering money and credit to banana farmers to facilitate the purchase by the company of a still larger proportion of fruit grown by local residents.

That there were solid business reasons behind such grants became obvious when, during September, 1916, the entire Jamaican crop, then leading the world in banana exports, was wiped out by hurricane. Hundreds of the island's banana growers were ruined. At Port Antonio and Kingston, public meetings were held for the purpose of founding emergency credit pools from which small sums of money could be borrowed by farmers anxious to replant their devastated lands. All fruit ships arriving at Jamaican ports left without cargo. For more than two months not one bunch of bananas could be found on the island. Many of the large exporters closed up shop, but United Fruit retained its Jamaican branch and even enlarged its credit facilities. When, after a period of readjustment, trade was resumed, United Fruit found both its advantages and its reputation greatly strengthened among the Jamaica farmers.

In several of the American countries the banana trade had begun to experiment with by-products of the harvest. Inventive *hombres* were trying to extract the purplish-brown stain from the stem (a stain which is almost impossible to remove from cloth) for making dyes and writing fluids. Others were making cloth from the fibers of banana stalks and grinding the stalks for paper and pulpwood. All these experiments were successful, but they had limited practical application.

A few other by-products of bananas seemed more promising. A syrupy confection was produced simply by drying the ripe fruit. Even before the First World War, dehydrated foods had been successfully marketed in Germany and Austria, and it was almost inevitable that the process would be applied to bananas. United Fruit founded the Banana Specialty Company, which in 1919 began large-scale experiments with "banana flour" at Puerto Limon, Costa Rica. The dehydration plant had a daily capacity for two tons of ripe peeled bananas, from which some 3000 pounds of water were removed and about 1000 pounds of powdered banana reduced to a bulk of twenty-five cubic feet.

Before the First World War, "experimental agriculture" had been a rather haphazard occupation. But the banana trade is also a farming trade, and the banana companies were in a mood to consider supplementary crops. There was, for example, the uniquely American tropical orchard crop called cacao or cocoa—a smallish tree, native to the warmer Americas, which produces squash-sized pods filled with seed from which chocolate, cocoa, cocoa butter, and other edibles are made. A good banana climate is usually a good cacao climate, and the tree flourishes on lands which the root fungus called Panama Disease makes unsuitable for growing Gros Michel bananas.

Andrew Preston decided to grow cacao in some 20,000

acres of Costa Rican and Panamanian banana lands which were being withered by the root fungus.

Cacao is one of the oldest crops of the hemisphere. Cacao beans were used centuries ago as the nickels and dimes of the Mayans, and less than a century ago they were the common rural currency in Costa Rica and Panama. Nobody could deny that the crop had been long tried and well proved. But the actual value of cacao depends on its market grade, which in turn depends on the locality in which the cacao is grown. Thus Venezuelan cacao is graded Caracas, Puerto Cabello, or Maracaibo; Ecuadorean cacao is Guayaquil, Bala, or Arriba; Brazilian cacao is Bahia or Para; African cacao is Accrass; Dominican cacao is Sanchez. The different grades have various distinctive qualities—Java cacao is noted for its attractive light-brown color; Arriba for its high aroma; Puerto Cabello for its distinguished flavor; and Panama and Costa Rican cacaos for their exceptionally high content of cocoa butter, sometimes as much as fifty-six percent of the weight of the cured pods.

After a great deal of planning, United Fruit Company men located fertile, well-drained valley lands, selected cacao seed for nursery planting and, when the seedlings were big enough for transplanting, set them about fifteen feet apart, and provided them with a temporary shade from banana plants. The small trees bloom about twice yearly. The blossoms break through the bark of the trunk and larger limbs and soon give way to soft pods which presently swell to six inches or a foot in length and three to five inches in diameter. Inside the pod, surrounded by a mass of fiber, are twenty to forty cacao "beans." Harvesting is a simple matter of cutting the pods from the trunk and limbs with a sharp knife or machete, splitting open the pod, scooping out the beans, and putting them to dry in the sun or leaving them to ferment in water, until they are free of fiber and bark particles.

Since the low valleys of Panana and Costa Rica are usually

too rainy for successful sun drying, the erstwhile banana chasers devised a curing process in the course of which several tons of the wet beans were placed in bins, left a few days to heat and ferment, then shoveled on an endless belt which carried them into heated revolving drums, each drum with a capacity of five tons. The drums turned slowly and after some thirty-six hours delivered the dry and highly polished beans in marketable condition.

United Fruit in 1919 harvested in Panama and Costa Rica almost 2 million pounds of cacao. Two years later the harvest was doubled, and in 1923 it amounted to more than 7 million pounds. In a very short time the world's largest banana company had become the world's largest cocoa raiser.

United Fruit, as we have already seen, had likewise made a major crop of Cuban sugar. In 1901, when Andrew Preston had finally agreed that the proposed Cuban banana lands were best planted to sugar, the United States had some seventy-three million people, whose yearly consumption of sugar averaged seventy-three pounds per person. The United States population was growing rapidly and so was the public sweet tooth. By 1916 each of our 100 million people was consuming about ninety pounds of sugar a year. By 1922 about 110 million were consuming 111 pounds per capita. There were no imports of sugar from the Philippines and practically none from Hawaii or Puerto Rico. Cuba was the sugar bowl for the world.

In Cuba, United Fruit had bought uninhabited wilderness land and had set about planting sugar cane. Workers cleared the land, cut down all trees and bushes, and saved the hardwood for building farmhouses and shelters. They burned the remaining brush and limb wood, then lined out the sugar-cane fields in squares of twenty acres each. After this they plowed the land with stout teams of bulls or oxen, two or three yokes to the plow, and planted the cane in shallow furrows. If the soil was damp and well tended, tiny cane shoots appeared about three weeks after planting.

Even today most sugar cane is harvested by hand with the bolo, or cane knife. First the harvester strips the leaves from the stalk, using the back of the knife as a stripping tool. Then he whacks off the green tops, cuts off the stalks flush with the ground (the richest sugar deposit is at the butt of the stalk), chops the stalks in three- or four-foot lengths, and tosses them into convenient piles.

The cane crop requires twelve to fifteen months to mature. After harvest new cane rises from the old roots. In Louisiana and Florida, annual or biannual planting of cane is the rule. In Cuba one planting, properly cultivated and tended, produces eight or ten crops and, sometimes, on heavy and rich soils, twenty or even thirty.

The cane is planted in the spring and fall. The Cuban harvest usually begins shortly after Christmas and, export quotas permitting, continues far into the summer. It is a wild and pell-mell sort of harvest, complete with cockfights, singing, dancing, rum drinking, and spontaneous visits to near-by communities. It has, however, its days of exacting labor when the cane is loaded into oversized two-wheeled carts and drawn by oxen to the railroad sidings, where field cranes swing it aboard especially designed cane cars, which in incredibly rapid succession are pulled away to the mills.

The Cubans call a cane-grinding mill a "central." Trainloads of cane cars pull into its portals like parades of ants. Huge electric cranes weigh the cars and spill their contents into hoppers, where link-chain conveyors carry the cane into massive crushers and feed into the grinding units or tandems. The corrugated crusher rolls prepare the cane for the final squeeze by batteries of horizontal steel rollers. Then the dry or almost dry cane waste, *bagasse*, is moved by mechanical carrier to the furnace to "fire the mill."

The raw juice is channeled into riverlike spillways and

through giant sieves, pumped to tanks high up in the building, and there treated with milk of lime to neutralize the acids. The "limed" juice is pumped into heating tanks, brought to boiling temperature, then discharged into settling tanks. The clear juice is drawn off the layers of impurities and boiled in a series of vats until its water content is reduced from its normal eighty to eighty-five percent to around fifty percent, and the juice then becomes sugar syrup, or *meladura*. This is boiled in vacuum pans until the sugar grains begin to form.

Raw sugar, the final product of the grinding mill, is sandy brown in color and about ninety percent pure. Its final preparation is accomplished at the refinery, which is usually located in the United States—in the case of United Fruit, the Revere Refinery of South Boston. Here the cargoes of raw sugar from the Cuban "centrals" are received and the brewing begins again. The raw sugar is washed with water in centrifugal machines, then dissolved in hot water, treated with a filtering medium, and passed through bone-charcoal filters which leave the syrup as clear as spring water. According to a precise and elaborate chemical formula the syrup is then finished off into commercial sugars.

The First World War found United Fruit with two giant sugar mills, a refinery, a sugar port, and about a hundred square miles of growing cane. In fertile lowland Honduras, Samuel Zemurray, whose name was being spoken more frequently in the banana world, was viewing sugar cane as a number-two crop for his renovated Cuyamel Company. But United Fruit was far and away the biggest farming concern of the Americas, and despite war forfeitures and losses of ships and men its farms in the deep tropics continued to supply United States markets with about 38 million pounds of bananas a week in addition to all the output of the largest sugar property in the hemisphere and many tons of cocoa and coconuts.

As war losses stripped the company's fleet of its better refrigerated ships, cargo after cargo of bananas arrived too late and too ripe. But the trade carried on. New Orleans was holding its place as the principal banana port. Messenger service and temperature control of railway cars were being perfected.

Central America was proving its place as the world stronghold for bananas. Standard Fruit and Cuyamel Fruit had centered their key banana farms in Honduras. United Fruit's new Honduran division was also in heavy bearing. Its first Guatemalan division was nearing completion as the International Railway edged along toward the sea. Costa Rica was producing magnificently, and the old Panama lands about Almirante were still contributing to the tide of green-and-gold fruit.

Fruit Dispatch maintained its leadership in banana selling, and about 2000 banana jobbers were still in trade. Head baskets and shoulder pads were now replaced by mechanical conveyors for unloading banana ships. At entry ports all bananas were being sold by the hundredweight and the ton, and most of the sales were made at shipside auction. On long hauls temperature conditions were checked and corrected at "fruit houses" located in railroad terminals.

More and more hurricanes swept over Jamaica and Cuba, and Central America was plagued alternately by droughts and violent rains. Banana losses often amounted to 6 million bunches a month, but the trade was not interrupted.

Minor Cooper Keith remained a director of United Fruit and worked in a small Battery Place office in New York. But he was principally occupied as president of the International Railway of Central America and spent most of his time away from New York in Central America, and not in Boston. Andrew Preston worked quietly at his roll-top desk, which contained, among many other documents, a lengthy manifesto from the office of Herbert C. Hoover, United States Food Administrator.

This paper was one of the numerous solemn warnings for which the "Great Co-ordinator" was destined to become still better known. The people of the United States were warned to continue conserving food; the United States would ship half again as much food to Europe during 1919 as it had during the final year of the war; food was the essence of the "material aid" which President Wilson asked for a badly blasted Europe; food would be short again; food producers could be of great help in the emergency; United Fruit was the largest grower of foods in the Americas; its continued co-operation would be gratefully anticipated by the undersigned.

As the year 1918 ended, the largest banana company studied its own records. In ten years its tropical farmers had produced and sold nearly a third of a billion bunches of bananas, and about one-sixth of them had gone to England and Europe. The Great White Fleet still had about ninety ships. United Fruit now owned or leased one and a quarter million acres of tropical or subtropical lands and operated about 1000 miles of railroad. The company had also completed twelve tropical hospitals, into which 90,000 patients were being admitted annually—among this number some 18,000 sick *tropicos* who were not employees. Though the annual medical deficits had grown enormously in the Panama, Costa Rican, and Cuban divisions, new hospitals were under construction and more than half a million dollars was being spent for new waterworks in the banana-growing tropics.

Throughout most of Central America safe drinking water was scarce. When United Fruit, through its Honduran subsidiary, the Truxillo Railroad Company, began to build Puerto Castilla, the work colony there had been obliged to drink rain water and to take "washing water" from the brackish rivers or the still more brackish lagoons and swamps.

Andrew Preston directed the banana engineers to build a waterworks. The nearest source was the Rio Negro, on the low hills thirteen miles from Castilla, the proposed banana port. There the engineers found a site for a dam—at the head of a picturesque but inaccessible waterfall. Only one steep, tortuous footpath led to the location. The engineers hired local Indians as workers and loaded all the necessary sand, stone, and cement into one-hundred-pound bags, which the Indians carried up the trail on their shoulders.

The work began in October, 1921. The diligent Indians carried hundreds of tons of sand and cement to the area of the waterfall, broke up a veritable mountain of building stone, and stacked the materials well above the highest known watermark of the Rio Negro. Then fifteen inches of rain fell within two days. During the second night of rain the river rose thirty feet and swept away all the precious sacks of sand, cement, and wall rock.

After the flood, the *Yanquis*, *Hondureños*, and Indians began again. They put up wooden frames for concrete abutments, dug the dam's foundation deep, and strengthened the basic cement work with reinforcing steel. Then, working waist-deep, at times neck-deep, in cold water, the Indian masons built the dam, while another work crew blasted out a first road to the location, and used oxen—three yokes to the wooden sled—to drag hundreds of tons of eight-inch steel pipe to the location. Then back at the banana port thirteen miles away they built a 100,000-gallon storage tank and laid a first water system and sewer works.

Equally difficult building was in progress throughout a thousand miles of banana farms—farms which had come to include big and little fields and Indian farmers as well as white men and Negroes. The supply of plantation-grown fruit was being supplemented by "pickups" from out-of-the-way independent farms. Typical of the "pickup" system was the run from Livingston Harbor in British Honduras to the Indian

farms along the Golfete Estuary and Lake Izabal. Bob
Jackson, fruit inspector for United's Guatemalan division, had
described his weekly pilgrimage on this route:

At six o'clock Wednesday morning the little motorboat *Riva*
nudges a lighter alongside the dock. . . . Our Carib crew loads
the cargo we are to carry to the private farmers on the Golfete
and Lake Izabal. Tarpaulins are lashed, food for the trip is put
aboard, and at seven o'clock we have three lighters on our towline and are headed for the Rio Dulce.

It is only half a mile from the wharf to the mouth of the Dulce,
and in a few minutes we are between the towering banks of this
picturesque river. The heavy, impenetrable vegetation grows
down almost to the water's edge except where an occasional lime-
stone cliff breaks through the jungle, struggling to hold its white
head above the sea of green. . . .

It is ten miles from the mouth of the Rio Dulce to the Golfete.
. . . On the way across we pass many beautiful little islands, too
low and swampy to be inhabitable. At the end of the Golfete we
pass San Felipe, the entrance to Lake Izabal. Five short blasts
from the whistle and the *Riva* slows down for the canoes coming
out from shore to meet us. They make fast to one of the lighters
and are towed slowly alongside as they discharge their cargoes of
bananas. . . .

We pick up a mere two or three hundred bunches at the town
of Izabal, but we unload a considerable quantity of merchandise
for the native farmers. Izabal was once a port, and at the height of
its prosperity as many as seven hundred mules a week were pack-
loaded for the interior of Guatemala, Honduras, and El Salvador.
Anchors of old sailing ships still lie on the shore at Izabal, but
parts of the sea wall, the ruins of an old Spanish church, and a few
cannon half buried in the ground are all that remain to indicate
the past glories.

We are soon on our way to Caxlampon five miles away, arriving there at dawn the following morning. As soon as our lights
are seen, lanterns appear on shore and by the time our anchor is
over, fifty or sixty canoes are racing out to meet us, each loaded
with green bananas, and each anxious to be received first. More

than half of all the lake-front planters are Indians. . . . The Indians speak practically no Spanish, and the Caribs speak very little Indian. . . . But once the Indian farmer has delivered his fruit, and watched it stowed on the pick-up barge, we give him a pay slip. He stuffs this into his shirt, then paddles alongside the *Riva*, where the purser redeems the slip with silver coins. . . . The Indians frequently bring along plantains, oranges, alligator pears, eggs, chickens, and fresh-water turtles to sell or barter to our crew. . . .

In from six to ten hours the fruit is all on board and . . . we cruise along to the other Indian villages of Murcielago, Socola, La Buena, Esperanza, and San Felipe, then head back to Livingston, where we arrive early Friday morning and with 6000 or so bunches aboard. From there we head for the coast boat that is lying about a mile off shore. Another motorboat and lighter are already alongside unloading. Late in the afternoon our turn for unloading comes. The work is done with a will, for all hands are thinking of the rest coming to them after almost sixty hours of continuous work. Our cargo is soon on the mother ship and then we turn toward Livingston and bed.

Boston, Massachusetts, is many hundreds of miles from Lake Izabal and the Indian farmers who were delivering bananas by canoe to United Fruit pickup boats. In sprawling, sunny New Orleans, in Mobile, or in palm-shaded Tampa, the temperature, humidity, and casual scenery are at least vaguely reminiscent of Central America. But many a *tropico* coming to Boston, particularly during the winter, has pointed out that running a banana company from Boston is like managing a Moroccan harem from a hermit's shanty in upper Alaska.

Andrew Preston regarded such comments as "normal exaggeration." Nor would he believe the jungle engineer who insisted that the only way he kept from getting lost in Boston was by carrying the office cat wherever he went. At the end of the day he would release the cat and follow it back to the United Fruit office. But Andrew Preston confessed that he still marveled at how a plain Yankee peddler like himself had

become the head of one of the world's largest tropical enterprises.

He found stimulation in the fact that he was not the only
leader in the banana trade. There was, for example, a tall and
brawny young man, Samuel Zemurray, who was still in his
early forties. As Samuel Zmuri, a Bessarabian immigrant who
had Americanized his name to Zemurray, he had watched the
arrival of cargo after cargo of bananas in Mobile, Alabama,
in the early days of the trade and he had done his best to sell
them.

Mobile port records showed such entries as "336,000
bunches sold by S. Zemurray in 1903," 574,500 sold in 1904,
408,900 sold in 1905, and so on to "1,773,212 sold by S. Zemurray in 1910." He had begun by selling bananas, frequently the ripe fruit which had to be disposed of quickly or
not at all, to Gulf-front peddlers and small dealers inland in a
fast, highly informal trade wherein man trusted man and
hoped for the best while preparing as effectively as possible
for the worst.

The energetic Zemurray plunged through profits and losses,
became an importer of Central American bananas, made
friends among his fellow immigrants and other fruit dealers,
and persuaded them to buy fruit, sell it quickly, and buy more.
The young man from Bessarabia eventually found a partner,
a conservative Mobiler, Ashbell Hubbard, who urged care
and caution and helped his alert colleague to establish the
Hubbard-Zemurray Company, with a capital of $30,000,
mainly on the cuff. That was in 1903.

On his first pilgrimage to Mobile, Andrew Preston, the
number-one banana seller of the United States, had met Zemurray, who was already well on his way toward becoming the number-one banana seller of Greater Mobile. On
August 5, 1905, United Fruit, on Andrew Preston's recommendation, bought for $4500 a sixty-percent interest in the
Thatcher Brothers Steamship Company, which had chartered

ships to bring bananas from Honduras to Mobile but was now in bad shape financially. Hubbard and Zemurray bought the remaining 40 percent. Preston declined to name a director. He preferred that Hubbard and Zemurray "use their own judgment." Time was soon to tell the correctness of the partners' judgment and the wisdom of Preston's request.

Zemurray was a perennial independent—"a risker, a thinker, and a doer"—and Preston respected him as an enormously effective banana seller, an exceptionally capable ship operator, and a crackerjack farmer. These convictions were based on personal acquaintance as well as authoritative hearsay. Through more than twenty busy years Preston had watched with interest the remarkable career of this young six-footer who, first from Mobile and later from New Orleans, directed the activities of his expanding organizations.

Zemurray's newest banana company was named Cuyamel, after the Honduran river whose brackish waters have supplied and replenished thousands of acres of superb banana lands. Shortly after the First World War, the astonishing Samuel Zemurray had been joined by an almost equally astonishing New Orleans banker, Dr. Paul V. Saunders, formerly professor of Greek at the University of Mississippi. By hobby an educator of Negro schoolteachers and a diligent student of early Greek architecture and sculpture, the studious Mississippian, on rounding forty, had become interested in credit and money and so ventured into banking.

After reviving an apparently irresuscitable country bank in Mississippi, Paul Saunders went to New Orleans, the banking capital of the deep South, and from there began refinancing many other small-town banks. In New Orleans, Saunders met Samuel Zemurray. Thereupon the scholar-turned-banker was bold enough to enter the banana business and became banking director of the renovated Cuyamel Fruit Company.

Once more his intentions were those of self-education, which proceeded fortissimo, like his previous studies of cattle farming and classical languages, his journeys to Greece, and his lectures to college classes and clubs. As banking director he facilitated the sale of 5 million dollars' worth of Cuyamel stock at par (17,000 shares of this were purchased by United Fruit) and established Cuyamel credit lines in Mobile, New Orleans, New York, Chicago, and other important cities. Paul Saunders traveled as an observant student with Samuel Zemurray to the source of banana production, the Honduran north coast.

The particular mission of the Saunders-Zemurray team was to acquire a strategic 5000 acres of land in the vicinity of a jungle outpost called Guanchita. This plot was and still is the very best of banana lands—smooth, fertile, and, as Samuel Zemurray had previously pointed out, well situated for irrigation from the rivers.

United Fruit had failed to get that particular 5000 acres. Two citizen owners claimed the land. United Fruit's legal department had pondered the intricacies of title and withdrawn from the dispute. Zemurray and Saunders bought the land from both of the alleged owners, paying each his asking price, and took possession of what was shortly to become a group of the world's finest banana farms.

The winter of 1924 had been especially severe in Boston. Preston, who ordinarily liked sharp winters, had not greatly enjoyed that one. He had not been feeling well—"a bit of a shade under par." To his intimates he complained of being tired, of having been born rather too many years before. He was seventy-four years old.

Though many times over a millionaire, he had retained a great deal of an earlier humility. He was still soft-spoken, kindly, and engrossed in his work. A half-century before, Captain Lorenzo Baker had paid Andrew Preston one of the latter's most cherished compliments when he said: "That young feller works so dadblamed hard he never knows that he's busy." Now, in 1924, Preston was so busy that he did not realize he had become an important man.

Repeatedly he pointed out in his "bulletins" that United Fruit was approaching its quarter-century mark. Privately he recalled that he had been selling bananas for fifty-three years.

At any rate, on the morning of March 29, 1924, Andrew Preston was not surprised to find at his office doorway a three-man committee. First came the gifts: from general office employees at Boston, a giant silver vase "affectionately inscribed"; from employees at New York and Philadelphia, two silver humidors; from an unnamed "old friend," a silver model of an old sailing ship. Mr. Preston smiled and shook hands with each member of the waiting committee—Bill Newsome, senior vice-president; Philip Reynolds, Preston's secretary and assistant; and Victor Cutter, a big and solemn young Yankee who had just returned to Boston from the banana tropics.

When the committee had left, Andrew Preston stood for a long time at the windows and watched the gray skies and the occasional flurries of snow. Philip Reynolds brought in a wire basket piled high with telegrams, cablegrams, and letters of congratulation. The old man loosened his collar and began reading some of the messages.

Naturally the silver anniversary of United Fruit called for a banquet. The dining room of Boston's Algonquin Club was bright with the flags of the twenty-four nations with which United Fruit carried on trade. It was a man's party, with the president of United Fruit in the place of honor. Bill Newsome made the opening speech: "Naturally we feel that we are a success, and we want Mr. Preston to know that we appreciate the fact that such success is due to his untiring efforts and business ability. That is why we are giving him this dinner."

The *Boston Transcript* publicized the event rather more fulsomely:

The United Fruit Company has made history . . . in twenty-five years. It owns and operates more territory than many a king. It is one of the biggest factors in transportation. . . . Sixty-seven thousand employees are listed under its flag. . . . In the "Great White Fleet" are scores of modern vessels, nearly all oil-burning steamers, which maintain a passenger and freight service to the tropics the year round. . . . In Mr. Preston's office is a list of forty-one ships that served the Allies in the Great War, and opposite the names of ten is the Gold Star which indicates that they went down fighting. . . . It is not generally known that the United Fruit Company is the largest self-contained sugar enterprise in the world. . . .

But neither Bill Newsome nor the *Transcript* had mentioned that United Fruit was lending substantial aid in keeping Boston on the map of international trade and, since a preponderant share of the company's ownership remained in the hands of New Englanders, contributed enormously to the deposits and over-all solvency of Yankee banks.

When it was Preston's turn to speak, he recalled that for half a century he had been working to save the banana trade from sudden death. He had sought to run a produce business, not a monopoly or a succession of governments. He had chosen to deal with existing governments or reasonable facsimiles thereof. Of necessity he had dealt in lands without bona fide governments or agencies for law enforcement. His men had made the best of it. He had directed the purchase of lands when such lands were owned and for sale. He bought concessions when concessions were available. He had believed in producing goods, in selling goods, and in relying on volume for his profits. He had never sought political subsidies from Washington or any other capital. He had never solicited protection from any country and had never composed any statements of political policy.

He had directed a banana trade to make money, and he had made a great deal of money. He had met competition, eliminated some of it, and endured the rest. Without professing any particular labor policy, he had authorized his companies to pay wages consistently higher than the established average of any given locale and to pay for all services rendered. He was proud that he had defined and established standards of quality which had profoundly influenced the growth of the banana trade and the produce trade generally.

Rounding seventy-four, Andrew Preston remained a plain, hard-working Yankee who made no boasts and few apologies. He saw himself as usually right.

But Andrew was tired and he admitted it. He continued to get into his office before ten each morning. Sometimes he carried little bottles of pills or vials of medicines. As a rule he placed the medicines on his window ledge, and frequently he left them there unopened. One day when a maternally inclined typist exclaimed, "But, Mr. Preston, you just aren't taking your medicine!" the old man smiled wryly and whispered, "Thanks, Letty—but I have decided to forget it this morning." Then he added for Phil Reynold's benefit, "The medicine I really need would be nice cold water from that fountain that the Spanish gent Mister de León kept looking for."

When spring came Andrew Preston said that he felt better, adding that no real Yankee can afford to be sick in June. But the evidence remained that Andrew Preston was sick or, at any rate, excessively tired. He did not come to his office at all during the last week of June. During July he appeared only at board meetings, but even there he had little to say and invariably left early. He died at his home on September 20, 1924.

CHAPTER ELEVEN

NEW LEADERS
AND NEW VENTURES

ON OCTOBER 1, 1924, less than a fortnight after Andrew Preston's death, the following notice appeared in the financial pages of the *Transcript* and other Boston newspapers:

"The Directors of the United Fruit Company take pleasure in announcing that Victor M. Cutter, vice-president, has been elected president of the company."

No newspaper in Boston had a file on Victor MacComber Cutter. There was no listing of the name in *Who's Who in America* or any similar directory. The Boston press had written at some length of the passing of Andrew Preston, but it had not given much notice to the matter of his successor. After receiving the short announcement, the newspapers began telephoning the general offices of United Fruit.

Those who answered the phones gave the reporters what information was available . . . "Sure, practically everybody around United Fruit knew Victor Cutter. He was one of the newer and younger vice-presidents; for several years the number-three boy at General Office. . . . Had his office next door to Mr. Preston's. Only forty-three years old. A big guy —over six feet; weighs about 200 pounds. Reddish-brown hair. Not too handsome, but big. . . . A tropics man, had been vice-president in charge of Central and South American operations."

The personnel office gave further details . . . "Sure, the company had the new president's records, because he had never worked anywhere except for United Fruit. Born at Dracut, a crossroads village near Lowell, Massachusetts, September 2, 1881. Went to Lowell public schools. Went to Dartmouth College in 1899. Graduated in 1903 with Bachelor of Letters degree. Spent one year at Dartmouth's Tuck School of Administration and Finance. Got an M.C.S. degree, whatever that means. Studied Spanish-American trade, Spanish language, and commercial geography. Joined United Fruit in 1904, as timekeeper in the old Costa Rican division. Salary $68 a month. Made overseer of Luisa East Farm in 1905 and took charge of the Costa Rican division experiment station. Appointed superintendent of Minor Keith's old Zent district in Costa Rica. In 1907 he was sent to Nicaragua to explore banana lands. After that he helped organize the new banana division in Guatemala. . . . We got a picture of him there in 1909. . . . Yep! Sitting in front of a *manaca* shack sipping a beer and listening to an old Beulah phonograph with a morning-glory horn. . . . No, you can't have the picture. It's company property!

"Then in 1914 he headed up the new Honduran divisions, the Tela Railroad, and the Truxillo Railroad. Started 165 miles of railroad and mapped 106,000 acres of land his first year. In September, 1915, they made him general manager of the Central and South American department—a big job—dealing with all the tropical investments except in Jamaica. . . . Yep, and in 1916 Mister Cutter got the post of general man-

ager of tropical banana divisions. That gave him supervision
of United Fruit's Jamaican division, too. He came to the
General Office in Boston in May, 1917, and has been here
since. Appointed vice-president in charge of all tropical divisions in October, 1917. That put him in the room with a
door that opened into Andrew Preston's own private sanctum.
That's all, mister!"

The press continued to call. An unknown new president
for the most colorful American business firm was tantalizing
news, at least for Bostonians. Up to this time the story of
United Fruit had been essentially the story of Captain
Lorenzo Dow Baker, Andrew Woodberry Preston, and the
impetuous but now very much quieter and no longer wealthy
Minor Cooper Keith. Keith was still among the best liked
men in the American tropics, but he had never been one of
Boston's own and was no longer a decisive force in the banana
trade, though he remained the head of the International
Railways of Central America. The successes and failures of
United Fruit had been substantially those of the three men,
but now a second generation of leadership had taken over
management of the company.

What about the new leader—this barrel-chested redhead
named Cutter? He was taking over a job even more demand-
ing than Andrew Preston's had been. His would be the
responsibility for long-term social and commercial planning
and international diplomacy; for an improved technical
agronomy; for research in tropical medicine, and practical
colonization; for fleet administration and an educational system in large areas of twelve American nations. Could the big
youngster from Dracut fill the Old Man's boots? Banana men
were wondering. Either overexpansion or ultraconservatism
could prove fatal to the trade.

Victor Cutter was heading a rich company with far-scattered properties and colonies. Its Fruit Dispatch was the most
effective sales and distribution agency in the fruit merchandis-

ing field. Bananas remained the decisive crop for United Fruit, and it was only natural that banana men in particular would review the past and guess at the future of Victor MacComber Cutter, the farm-bred timekeeper who had made good. Most of the older *tropicos* knew Cutter. Many outranked him in seniority. A few liked him; others did not; but the majority were waiting to make up their minds.

The old-timers around the general office recalled that Victor Cutter had first appeared there early in April, 1904. He had been preceded by one of the most enthusiastic letters of recommendation ever perused by Andrew Preston, who said to his secretary, Philip Reynolds, that any man who could give the Tuck School of Dartmouth such a head of steam as that might be worth looking at.

A couple of days later, the phenomenon strolled into Andrew Preston's office, a burly youngster, rough-handed and sunburned. Philip Reynolds listened to the young man's story . . . Raised in a poor home. Helped his father run a market garden. Used to drive wagonloads of beets, carrots, cucumbers, early potatoes, and tomatoes into the towns and peddle them. Started to college with nothing. Swept floors and fired furnaces. Continued to help his father in spring planting time, on summer vacations, and during fall harvests. Graduated from college and went an extra year. Made good grades. Phi Beta Kappa. . . .

Philip Reynolds then began his routine of discouragement. The tropics are lonely and uncomfortable for a *Yanqui*. There is little or no law, but there are leaky roofs, bad food, and hard work. When Reynolds had finished Cutter merely said that he had brought along his luggage and was ready to start for Central America that day. Andrew Preston strolled in, smiled weakly, hired the young man, and ordered him a one-way steamship ticket to Costa Rica.

Twenty years later Victor Cutter, as the second president of the world's largest banana company, had come up against some very great difficulties. One of the greatest was that of meeting the growing competition from another man who, at forty-seven, was the leader of the formidable Cuyamel Fruit Company of New Orleans, Honduras, Nicaragua, and Mexico. This was Samuel Zemurray.

United Fruit was also suffering from growing pains. As Victor Cutter said, "There is not sufficient knowledge by any one department of the policies and needs of other departments. He said further that "the increasing amounts of legislation, enactment of new laws, and increasing complexity of doing business make it essential that our executives shall be well informed in the general relations of our company to outside entities. . . . We are sadly deficient in general knowledge of the value of advertising and publicity. Our growth has been so rapid and our success so great that our needs in this direction have never yet been felt. It is not safe to assume that this will be the case in future. . . ."

All this was fairly obvious. So was the necessity for economy. Andrew Preston, who had known better than anyone else the vast potential earning power of his company, had said that United Fruit's greatest future problem would be that of intelligently conserving its wealth. Victor Cutter therefore spoke as he believed his predecessor would have spoken: "[Mr. Preston] realized fully that many of our houses and buildings went beyond mere utility and approached luxury, that many of our people were traveling in suites on boats and staterooms on trains, that luxury easily gets in the blood. Economy is the watchword for the coming year. . . ."

But an ever expanding working association in tropical farming and transportation cannot function on thrift alone. Andrew Preston, who had appraised multi-million-dollar investments with much the ease and assurance of a capable Yankee housewife going over her shopping list, had with few exceptions been able to pay wages proportionate to each wage earner's contribution to the enterprise. For example, in hiring workers he had effected wage scales considerably higher than the existing averages, for it was his opinion that workmen in the banana fields had to be stronger and more experienced than other laborers in the tropics. He would also boast that he paid as much for good fruit as "sound marketing" would permit.

Victor Cutter was speaking with the record in front of him when he said: "The founders of my company had the vision and wisdom to establish their business on a basis which would be as profitable to the people of the countries in which they operated as to the company itself. United Fruit has paid a total of 126 million dollars in dividends. And as against this sum which the company has paid to stockholders, it has now an annual expenditure for labor pay rolls of 25 million dollars a year in Latin America, or two and a half times the current [1925] annual dividend."

But he was also speaking of a time when the banana trade was a great deal simpler than it was in the late 1920's. In the earlier trade all contenders had struggled to take care of themselves first and last. During the previous generation banana lands had been among the most primitive of American frontiers and, appropriately, many rough and tough men had come to open them. But by 1924 and the elevation of Victor M. Cutter, the primitive simplicity of the banana frontiers had gone. If the sturdy young men from Jones Crossing, Iowa, or Springdale, Arkansas, were to perpetuate the banana trade, they and their associates would need a great deal more preparation than their New England predecessors had required.

The second-generation banana men would have to deal with a new profession, a new language, and a new society. Most of the banana lands had populations representing many racial and national groups. Indians, Negroes, Chinese, Turks, Syrians, Englishmen, Germans, Frenchmen, and Americans had intermarried or otherwise come together in a forthright if temporized society. Over the course of many years the banana farms had assumed a peculiar agrarian pattern.

By 1925, the average farm was about 1000 acres—roughly one and one-third square miles—and had a working force of 140 to 220 men. These men bring along their families and relatives and populate the *barracone* or labor camp, which becomes by virtue of this fact a permanent village, with store, school and church, *cantinas*, and a public market. Andrew Preston had provided the farms with bungalows and company clubs, game rooms, baseball fields, golf course, tennis courts, and rugby fields.

A good and satisfying life was possible on the banana fronts in 1925. But it was far from inevitable. Like new second lieutenants in the peacetime United States Army, employees of the banana companies usually found promotion slow; often more than five years elapsed before the first advancement. However, fewer than half of the fledgling timekeepers served out their first year, and only about one in five stayed long enough to qualify for promotion. These facts alone were sufficient evidence that the new generation of banana leadership was face to face with important problems in tropical personnel.

These, however, were not the only problems for Victor Cutter and his men. For some time they had been aware that United Fruit depended rather too exclusively on bananas. They were all the more conscious of this dependence when revenues from Caribbean sugar cane and cacao fell abruptly and unexpectedly. Cutter was in favor of developing supplementary crops.

At Colombiana, in Costa Rica, United Fruit started a pineapple farm. There was plenty of land available, and the banana ships had refrigerated space for carrying the plant-ripened fruit to market. Pineapples are native to the American tropics and someday they may still become an important export of the Caribbean countries. But for one reason or another, United Fruit's first experiment in pineapple farming did not prove profitable as a "company crop," however successful it might have been as a crop for citizen farmers.

Next the big banana company turned to mahogany. Most banana lands are heavily forested with timbers which cannot be used economically for fencing or building. From time to time banana growers had sought to check the waste of wood which might have some commercial value. In the Cuyamel valley of Honduras, Samuel Zemurray had established a creosoting plant to process native timbers for use as railroad ties and bridge structures. Both Standard Fruit and Cuyamel had for some time been experimenting with log houses for tropical homes. At the beginning of Victor Cutter's regime, United Fruit had a good opportunity to try native mahogany as a supplementary crop, for, as the Truxillo Railroad was being laid in the Black River Valley of Honduras, banana men found themselves working in lands overgrown with virgin mahogany.

Late in 1924 United Fruit jungle busters undertook the formidable job of dragging out the mahogany. They recruited a force of native woodsmen—Miskito and Sambo Indians—who began by blazing trails for the mahogany hunters and widening the trails over which ox teams could draw the logs to the *embarcaderos*, or shipping places. After the trails were opened Indian axmen built pole platforms from which to chop. When the trees were down, jungle "snakers" hitched teams of oxen to each log and dragged it to the *embarcadero*. It was hard work. Sometimes during the rainy season oxen and logs sank out of sight in the mud.

According to jungle folklore, the destinies of mahogany harvest are decided by the phases of the moon. Natives say that the sap rises in the light of the moon and that insects and diseases follow the flow of the sap. The Honduran moon may not have been exactly right, or the mahogany forests may not have been conveniently located. At any rate, after a year of incredibly difficult work the venture in mahogany hunting was also discontinued.

Nevertheless, as Victor Cutter continued to point out, United Fruit had become the largest farming company of the American tropics and was much more than a banana company. The cacao plantings in Costa Rica and Panama now amounted to 30,000 acres. However, British African interests had begun to plant the crop along the Gold Coast of West Africa, and cacao prices dropped precipitously. United Fruit investments in Cuban sugar cane had also depreciated in value, but company officials hoped the slump would be only a temporary one.

In supporting research in tropical agriculture in spite of several setbacks, the second president of United Fruit was showing both wisdom and courage. Tropical research had been lagging badly. Some twenty-one years earlier United Fruit had instituted what Andrew Preston had optimistically termed "scientific investigation in the tropics." But in 1903 such investigation usually followed the English country-gentleman tradition of bringing together all manner of plants and trees, planting them in a common garden, assigning a boy to water the vegetation, and leaving the rest to time and to God. The British government had previously established experimental gardens along the Caribbean at Georgetown, Demerara; Port-of-Spain, Trinidad; and Castleton and Hope, in Jamaica. These were "herbatariums" in which fruits, spices, fiber crops, herbs, and other botanical species from the tropical world were planted in small fields. It was all quite beautiful, but it proved extremely little, if it proved anything at all.

The first profitable research in the agronomy of the American tropics began about 1910, when sugar cane, then the most promising money crop for many of the Caribbean islands, was ravaged by insects and fungi. In a determined effort to save the Caribbean sugar industry, British government agencies began large-scale experiments to develop hardier and more resistant varieties of cane. Now banana companies had both the opportunity and the motive for carrying on the work. Victor Cutter, who nearly twenty years earlier had helped develop one of the first experimental farms in Central America, decided to go on with the work. He approved appropriations and plans for an experimental farm center at Lancetilla, a few miles inland from the port of Tela, Honduras.

Cutter employed one of the most able of tropical botanists to take charge of the project. This was Wilson Popenoe, a slender and energetic young man from Topeka, Kansas. Like his Huguenot forebears, young Dr. Popenoe was an inveterate world traveler. Born in 1892, he had attended school at Pasadena, California, was graduated from Pomona College, and was later honored with a doctorate of science from the ancient University of San Marcos at Lima, Peru.

The plant-hunting Kansan was thirty-four when he quit the United States Department of Agriculture to join United Fruit. Fifteen years earlier he had carried on investigations of fruit growing in Japan, Malaya, and India and had journeyed into Arabia and North Africa to collect date palms for transplanting to the Indio area of Southern California. In 1913, at the age of twenty-one, the young man, then with the Department of Agriculture, went on a prolonged botanical exploration of Brazil. That finished, he spent a year with the United States Plant Introduction Garden, at Miami, studying conditions of tropical fruit production in Florida. In 1916 the Secretary of Agriculture authorized him to conduct a detailed investigation of avocado growing in Guatemala and to secure varieties suitable for areas of California and Florida.

After sixteen months of tracking down promising avocado varieties in Mexico and Guatemala, the young scientist began a general botanical exploration of western South America, with a view to securing little-known crop plants from the remote Andes for trial planting in the United States. Then he returned to Washington and spent four years as supervisor of the Department of Agriculture's Office of Foreign Seed and Plant Introduction. In 1924 he was a United States delegate to the Third Pan-American Scientific Congress at Lima and a winner of official citations for distinguished service to Chile and Ecuador.

In support of the new tropical research establishments, Victor Cutter proceeded to establish a general research department at Boston. This division was headed by Hartley Rowe, United Fruit's chief engineer, a Hoosier with fifteen years of experience as design engineer for the Panama Canal and six more as a patent and industrial engineer. Other research heads included Dr. John F. Johnston, from the United States Department of Agriculture; F. S. Dellenbaugh, from the engineering faculty of Massachusetts Institute of Technology; and George L. Poland, a Pratt Institute chemist. Dr. V. C. Dunlap, of Maine and Cornell, now a preeminent tropical agronomist and pathologist, was general supervisor of tropical agronomy and pathology.

Cutter was also determined to maintain and improve United Fruit's already outstanding place in American tropical medicine. He had known and suffered tropical malarias, and as head of the largest of American tropical companies he was resolved to carry forward the outstanding and unrivaled work in tropical health which Minor Keith had started and Andrew Preston had continued.

We have already remarked that banana medicine in Costa Rica began with the efforts of old Jack Marti, former tender of the Fourth of July Bar in frontier Puerto Limon. Jack Marti's practical nursing, combined with his honest liquor, probably had much to do with Victor Cutter's own survival during his first year in the tropics. It was only reasonable that Cutter thought of banana medicine as the most distinguished contribution of the trade and industry.

Six years before Dr. William Clark Gorgas had undertaken the epoch-making cleanup of the Isthmus of Panama, United Fruit's banana men, already in charge of about 20,000 tropical workers and nearly 500 square miles of tropical lands, were beginning to eliminate mosquito-borne diseases in adjacent areas of Panama by laboriously filling, draining, and oiling standing waters and otherwise destroying mosquito breeding places, and by screening dwellings so that mosquitoes could not take infected blood from malaria or yellow-fever sufferers and inject the deadly parasites into the blood streams of healthy men.

Through the years banana medicine had carried on. The costs were enormous, but an advanced medicine was essential to the survival of the banana trade and immensely beneficial to the Panama Canal builders, as it was indeed to all citizens of the American tropics.

United Fruit had built its first field hospital during 1899, the birth year of the firm, at Bocas del Toro in Panama, a notorious center for tropical fevers not far from the festering isthmus lands where Ferdinand de Lesseps and his company had failed so tragically at building a Panama Canal. De Lesseps had struggled unsuccessfully against swamps and fevers in a mere thirty or forty miles of jungle and jungle edges. United Fruit had successfully fought disease throughout several thousand square miles of Central America. In their schools and churches United Fruit men were able to teach elementary sanitation and disease control to tropical citizens, young and old. In providing homes and barracks for banana farm workers, the company saw to it that screening was supplied and that sewage facilities were available for its employees. Garden plots and poultry were also arranged for so that the farm worker's diet could better sustain his health. That, too, was highly effective, since good food is the best of all medicines.

In 1903, three years before Dr. William C. Gorgas and Joseph Le Prince, his sanitation engineer, first ventured into the isthmus of Panama, an epidemic of smallpox swept over the Bocas del Toro banana front of Panama. For the immigrant Jamaicans and their families, as well as for the Indians, epidemic smallpox was the final black depth of tragedy. Smallpox vaccination, which in 1903 was still in its experimental stage and had been bitterly condemned in many quarters of the United States and Europe, was entirely unknown to the coastal lowlands of Central America.

When the epidemic struck, United Fruit doctors and their lay helpers hastily improvised field hospitals and sick camps in which they attended the sick and from which they buried the dead. Carrying back packs and burro loads of vaccine, they traveled through the adjacent valleys and within a few days vaccinated 7000 tropical citizens who had never before heard of vaccination. They kept this up until virtually all the residents of the jungle edge had been vaccinated. It was the last smallpox epidemic the Almirante region experienced.

There have been many similar instances of free public vaccination by banana company medicos in Guatemala, Colombia, Jamaica, Costa Rica, Nicaragua, Cuba, and other tropical lands. But the experiment at Bocas was the first of its sort. It predated by twelve years the highly publicized mass vaccination experiments of the Rockefeller Foundation; by fourteen years, the United States Public Health Service's heroic work in rescuing Haiti from smallpox. Bocas del Toro and dozens of other ports and villages on Central America's Caribbean coast had been for years endemic centers of yellow fever. But by 1905, the year in which New Orleans was scourged by yellow jack, United Fruit's medical men had succeeded in freeing the banana countries from the disease. The last case of yellow fever reliably reported from the banana fronts was in 1906.

The pioneer banana hospital at Bocas del Toro was merely the first in a chain of banana hospital bases. There were links at Limon, Costa Rica; Banes and Preston in Cuba; Quirigua, Guatemala; Tela and Truxillo, Honduras; Kingston, Jamaica; and Santa Marta, Colombia. More were to follow. Andrew Preston had found deep and quiet satisfaction in the great work. As the yearly total of patients admitted passed the 200,000 mark, and the company's roster of physicians increased to sixty-five and hospital staffs grew to 1300; as the annual medical deficit (far in excess of the two percent of wages regularly collected from tropical employees and their families for medical care) climbed from a quarter of a million dollars a year to a third of a million and shortly thereafter to half a million, Andrew Preston approved the payment as "fair pay for fair goods. . . . Never expected it to come free, nohow!"

Significantly, Mr. Preston had lived to see the death rate among United Fruit's tropical employees dwindle to the astonishingly low average of 7.44 deaths per thousand employees per year, ranging by locale from a minimum of 2.75 to a maximum of 12.62. During the last ten years of Andrew Preston's life, Boston's annual death rate averaged 16.97 per thousand, while the annual death rate of the Panama Canal Zone had fallen to 12.49.

"When you doctor a sick child in the jungle," Preston often said, "you have made a lifelong friend of that child and lifelong friends of its mother and its pa."

CHAPTER TWELVE

SOUTHWARD AND WESTWARD

IN THE BANANA INDUSTRY the United Fruit Company had been pre-eminently successful not because it had achieved a monopoly but because several thousand banana jobbers, wholesalers, importers, and distributors in the United States, Canada, the British Isles, and Western Europe had found it to be a dependable organization with reliable products.

United Fruit had consistently striven to satisfy the markets steadily and efficiently with carefully graded high-quality fruit. A steady flow of northbound banana cargo from widely divergent sources enabled the Great White Fleet to prosper and to serve its noncompany clients well. Bananas remained United Fruit's meal ticket. Sugar production had proved profitable only part of the time. Incidental crops had rarely earned dividends. Year-round banana traffic had permitted the company to live and prosper.

Repeatedly during the 1920's United Fruit had been

charged with banana monopoly. The company could readily have disproved the charge by pointing to Mr. Samuel Zemurray, whose Cuyamel Fruit Company, supported by its Honduran farming division, the Cortes Development Company, and other near-by tropical properties, was consistently raising and marketing millions of bunches of the best bananas sold in the United States—fruit which averaged rather better than United Fruit's best.

The banana trade was becoming increasingly aware of Samuel Zemurray. Victor Cutter realized that an increasing minority of banana jobbers were buying bananas from Cuyamel in preference to United Fruit. At sales conferences and directors' meetings Victor Cutter had referred to the colorful Mr. Zemurray as "that little fellow." Compared with United Fruit the Cuyamel Company was small. But matched with any one tropical division of United Fruit it was decidedly impressive even by 1924, and it had proved to be, as Victor Cutter knew, one of the best managed farm enterprises anywhere. Moreover, Cuyamel was hiring, almost invariably at better salaries, a number of United Fruit's most experienced tropical men along with many other colorful characters who somehow seemed to gravitate about Samuel Zemurray. In this, as in several other respects, Cuyamel was benefiting by being smaller and far more maneuverable than United Fruit. As Mr. Zemurray recalls: "It was fun to poke the giant's knees with my own little shovel . . ."

Students of the conquistadors will recall that, after his first expedition into Mexico, Hernando Cortes had marched over the hills and valleys of Honduras and had placed a shore garrison at Omao, about eight miles from the present Honduran port of Cortes. Later in the sixteenth century, when Omoa and its farming lands were suffering a great plague of locusts, the Spaniards moved their garrison and colony to a sheltered spot called Cuyamel, where the water "was clean and pure" and the lands better protected from storms. Two centuries after Spain had completed the Omoa fortress, the countryside of Cuyamel was beginning to grow bananas and many *Yanquis* were eager to buy them. Even before 1880, New Orleans banana importers were buying fruit grown in fertile clearings back of the ancient river port.

During 1914, after the original Cuyamel Company organized in 1905 had failed, Samuel Zemurray acquired and revived it. Zemurray's company began by exporting bananas from the open roadstead of Vera Cruz; then from the little lighter port of Omoa. Cuyamel Village had been the first headquarters of the company, and with passing time and growing earnings under Zemurray leadership the Honduran town of Cortes became its port, and La Lima, some forty miles inland, its farming headquarters.

The refurbished Cuyamel Fruit from first to last was Samuel Zemurray's work and playground. Cuyamel's ships comprised a "little" banana fleet which shipping experts respected and in which New Orleans, the world's largest banana port, took pride.

Every efficient banana division requires a good seaport, and Cortes, Honduras, is one of the best in the Caribbean. During 1918, Zemurray's Cuyamel built an excellent wharf at Cortes and equipped it with electrically driven belt conveyors and superb railroad facilities. After the port was ready the Zemurray men extended the railroads and tramlines, opened new farms, and made ready for banana irrigation to assure more regular supplies of better fruit. The irrigation project was particularly important for, regardless of annual rainfall, all banana areas have their dry or comparatively dry seasons, in the course of which fruit harvests fall sharply.

Cuyamel grew rapidly during the 1920's, and sugar cane joined bananas as a principal crop. La Lima was made the headquarters of the two banana districts, and each district had a complete management staff of about fifty men. La Lima was also the headquarters of the Cuyamel engineering staff, headed by Pat Myers, a Georgia Tech graduate who had

become one of the more renowned jungle blazers south of the
Rio Grande. The roster of Zemurray men read like an international telephone directory—Turnbull, Montgomery, Kelleher, Sunseri, Schultz, Funez, Hacket, Inestroza, Sinners,
Gauer, Ott, etc.

The first banana district had thirteen farms with about
15,500 acres planted to fruit, all in the rich silt valley between
the Ulua and Chamelecon rivers. All these plantings were
carefully drained and irrigated by open cement-lined canals
filled by a series of electric pumps which took water from
the near-by rivers. Cuyamel's second district had eight banana
farms, each averaging slightly more than a thousand acres. In
this lot were the five Guanchita farms which Sam Zemurray
had paid for twice in a title dispute—simply because they
occupied "the best damn banana land anywhere."

The Cuyamel banana farms were as good as any in the
tropics and better than most. Each had a well-screened, carefully policed labor camp and homes for the resident managers,
a good many of whom were Hondurans or other Central
Americans. Each farm had a livestock complement of about
a hundred mules and a dozen or so plow animals, principally
oxen. Wherever terrain permitted, mules and bulls were replaced by tractors and tractor-drawn carts, which frequently
permitted new banana lands to be planted at the rate of a
hundred acres per day.

The best test of any farming venture is the quality of its
harvests. About 1925 Cuyamel's yearly banana harvests were
totaling 5 million bunches. They were exceptionally large
bunches and frequently weighed more than a hundred pounds.
This was hard for the mules, hard for the stevedores, and
perhaps even harder for Cuyamel's competitors.

Cuyamel also harvested about 2000 acres of sugar cane.
This undertaking was supported by a sugar-cane experiment
station, the services of 700 cane cutters and some 230 oversize cane carts, as well as by mechanical loaders, special rail-

road cars, a grinding mill, warehouses, a power plant, and many other costly facilities.

Though impressive enough, Cuyamel's milling of sugar was distinctly a secondary enterprise, carried on chiefly to supply sugar for Honduras. Bananas were the financial mainstay of Cuyamel's tropical holdings, and banana cultivation requirements determined building plans and farm layouts. Cuyamel's railroads were primarily banana railroads with a traffic arithmetic of 225 bunches of bananas per car, forty cars to the train. Five to seven trainloads filled a ship. The fifteen locomotives were banana pullers. The big machine shop at La Lima; the roundhouse at Cortes where the rolling stock was built; the fleets of automobiles that raced on flanged wheels along the railroad tracks; the work force of fifty-five heavy tractors; the heavy dragline earth movers that scooped out deep drainage ditches and canals—all were there to produce bigger and better bananas.

Teamwork between Zemurray farmers and Zemurray engineers had produced what several experts said was the most effective drainage system ever installed in the American tropics. Cuyamel's next step had been to develop suitable irrigation. United Fruit engineers had likewise developed highly effective deep drainage. Normally the Ulua Basin has heavy rainfall, but each year has at least one rather dry season. Any tropical farmer knows that bananas require much rainfall, but the older school of farmers had assumed that in the tropics irrigation should be limited to the tonsils.

In 1924, however, Cuyamel had inaugurated a system for the regular irrigation of banana farms. The "radical" venture was immediately successful. Cuyamel farms flourished, and the Zemurray establishment increased its incidental facilities. A merchandising department was organized and an up-to-date telephone system was installed together with an electrical department with networks of power lines. Soon there were two company-owned hotels, playgrounds, parks, a new hospital, and a field dispensary.

But the strength of Cuyamel was not only in its physical properties. It was also due to a certain working fraternity which had been established between *Yanquis, Hondureños,* and nationals of many other countries. Zemurray men were of all kinds—some tough, most of them resourceful and rugged; men whose complexions, ancestries, and social backgrounds were not deemed to be of any great importance.

The hospitality of Cuyamel was far famed. Jungle prowlers and casual visitors were treated graciously, and Cuyamel Saturday-night get-togethers were far renowned.

The Cuyamel men knew their side of the river well, and they knew United Fruit's side fully as well. There were good reasons why United Fruit banana men crossed the river to better paying jobs and more ebullient company. Cuyamel Fruit's tropical division was better managed and more productive than United Fruit's best.

The Zemurray development indicated clearly the several distinct formative trends current along the banana fronts during the 1920's. The over-all picture of banana production was changing rather abruptly from a brightly colored but modest-sized canvas of tropical pioneering and highly individualistic, sometimes antisocial enterprise to a vast panorama of highly technical agriculture supported by far-flung corporate railroading, ship operations, and colonization in a dozen different nations of the American tropics. Though United Fruit continued to grow as the colossus of the trade, smaller and more youthful concerns were also hard at work. Among them Zemurray's company was by far the most impressive.

The remarkably successful emergence of Cuyamel following the earlier failures of more than a hundred American, English, French, Dutch, and German banana companies plainly suggested that effective competition in the maturing industry was not only still possible but could, indeed, prove to be revolutionary. Plainly too, various social and political aspects of banana production were still in a state of flux. The obvious truth was that in the course of a mere quarter century the banana industry had become so big that its responsibilities were outstripping the imaginations of most banana men. This development was further accentuated by the fact that by the 1920's a second generation of leaders was obliged to take over as inevitable replacements for the original banana pioneers now superannuated or deceased.

Yet granting that individual leaders were and are important to the trade, the banana industry was also at grips with powerful forces that no man or group of men could control, or even surely predict. Blind luck, vicissitudes of weather, epidemics, plant diseases, and uncontrollable and often unpredictable trends of consumer markets were likewise decisive factors. So were the complex and ever changing railroading and shipping industries.

The banana industry could no longer be viewed from a single vantage point. It was no longer measurable with any one yardstick. That was one reason why the annual reports of the United Fruit Company appeared to change their subjects almost as frequently as a page of a daily newspaper.

Bananas had become a world crop, and the American tropics—particularly lowland Central America, lower Mexico, Jamaica, and the northern fringes of Colombia—were supplying bananas for three continents. Canary Islands banana growing was severely limited by the scarcity of water for irrigation. The African crop, grown largely in the Cameroons, Nigeria, and scattered areas of French West Africa, had proved generally unsuccessful because of the scarcity of suitable soils and the failure of white colonials and native chiefs to develop plantations sufficiently big and efficient to make the export of bananas profitable. More valuable products, such as ivory, gold, palm oils, and palm fibers could be taken from the jungle far more easily and profitably than bananas.

Because bananas will spoil during voyages of more than twenty-five to twenty-seven days, South Pacific banana lands such as Malaya, the East Indies, the Fijis, and northeastern Australia were not contenders for the English and Western European markets. The Far East bananas, most of which are less palatable and more difficult to ship than the big yellow Gros Michels, remained local food crops, of importance and value only to near-by cities and ports. Moreover, about 1920 banana plantings in the South Pacific were attacked by a strange and fast-traveling leaf blight, a round-spore fungus (*Cercospera musae zimm.*) called sigatoka, or more accurately singatoka, disease. The name came from a once bountiful banana-growing valley of the Fijis, where the blight was first identified. The blight spots the banana leaves with grayish flecks and presently causes the foliage to wither and blacken as if burned by fire. As more and more of the leaf surface dies, the fruit stem gradually starves.

As early as 1910 sigatoka was destroying Fiji bananas, and by 1925 it had spread over most of the banana plantings of Malaya, New Guinea, and Sumatra and was even appearing as far away as India and the African Cameroons. Nothing of importance was being done about it. Local papers and a few scientific journals in French, Dutch, and British colonies mentioned the peculiar blight with well-justified alarm. But the Far East banana trade was of little concern to the home governments and, besides, the ominous leaf blight apparently did not destroy the principal varieties of plantains or cooking bananas, which in most areas of the Oriental tropics are more important to the local diets than the sweet bananas.

It may be significant, incidentally, that the paper "occupation" money with which the conquering Japanese flooded Malaya during 1942 bore a central steel engraving of a banana plant with a heavy stem of fruit ready for harvest. What the engraving actually shows is a type of banana which singatoka disease had completely destroyed throughout the Malaya peninsula prior to 1930—twelve years before the phony currency was distributed. The Nipponese artistic eye may have erred—or this detail may indicate how long and how minutely the Japanese had been planning their Greater East Asia Co-prosperity Scheme.

On the other side of the globe American banana growers had enough to do without worrying about the botanical mysteries of the peculiar South Pacific. The United States market continued to take at least three-fourths of all Caribbean banana exports. United Fruit was distributing roughly half of this volume (the annual percentages varied from 38.3 to 63.2). Cuyamel, Standard Fruit, and numerous Mexican growers, the latter working as individuals or co-operative associations, were supplying most of the remainder. Honduras was the number-one banana-producing country of Central America, since from this one country, no larger than Pennsylvania, Cuyamel and Standard Fruit together were exporting about one-fourth of the total United States banana supply, while the two Honduran divisions of United Fruit accounted for slightly more than one-fifth of the United States total.

The Dominican Republic made occasional exports. Martinique was shipping bananas to France, and Cuban growers were exporting several million bunches yearly, principally to independent dealers along the East Coast of the United States. Colombia's trade remained strong, with roughly half of its fruit exports grown by United Fruit and the rest by citizen farmers. Faraway Ecuador was also growing the fruit, and Brazilian exports were increasing. Jamaica continued to rival Honduras as one of the greatest centers for banana cultivation.

Inevitably, the mounting demands for bananas called for more ships, more railroads, and more ports. Late in 1928 the old steamship *Limon*, carrying the first full cargo of bananas ever to enter a West Coast port, steamed through the Golden Gate to open United Fruit's San Francisco division.

Four more United Fruit ships, the *San Mateo, Esparta, San José,* and *La Perla,* all refrigerated and with capacities of approximately 40,000 bunches, switched from the East Coast to the California run. At the end of 1928 a total of 224 banana ships, operated by eight shipping companies, were calling regularly at eleven United States ports, three Canadian ports, four ports in England, two in Scotland, and five in Western Europe.

Newer and bigger banana ships were under construction. During 1929, under the official "encouragement" of the Jones-White Merchant Marine Act, United Fruit agreed to build six new ships in American yards. More ships and more bananas were at sea, and more were coming.

Ships are an important item in a banana company's inventory, but it takes railroads, trains, and millions of bunches of bananas to load the ships. Before the First World War, there had been barely 500 miles of maintained paved roads in all of Central and South America. Immediately after the war more auto roads began to appear, at first in smaller countries, such as Venezuela, Panama, Haiti, El Salvador, and the Dominican Republic, and shortly afterward in Cuba, Mexico, Peru, Chile, Argentina, and Brazil. The road building was costly and slow. Railroads remained the important commercial carriers, and in Central America bananas were the chief commercial item.

By 1925 banana companies were operating enough railroad mileage in Central America and the Antilles to reach from Boston to San Francisco. Except in Jamaica, which was becoming latticed with narrow but fairly serviceable highways, the banana lands were still almost completely dependent on the rails that linked farms with seaports. Miles of railroads had to be built before new banana plantations could be opened. The Central American banana fronts became, therefore, a last haven of railroad location engineers, the Daniel Boones of an age of steam—tough old trail blazers who guided construction gangs into the wilderness, computed grades, bridge sites, fills, tunnels, and hazards of landslides and flood by eyesight and past experience, shot the through ways, put workmen at spreading ties and linking rails, and left the ballasting and fancy work until the bananas were planted. Under such leadership miles of crossties and rails would be laid in a single day. The next day work trains would ride through, despite sagging ties, dipping rails, and oceans of mud.

In the United States, as in much of Europe, railroads were puffing hard in an apparently hopeless rivalry with a rambunctious automotive age. But in the banana lands, in addition to the essential task of hauling fruit, the railroad remained the one reliable thoroughfare of the region. Many years earlier Minor Keith had predicted that as the banana trade grew its dependence on railroads would likewise grow, and through wealth and poverty, sturdy maturity and failing old age, Minor Keith went right on building railroads that were pivotal to the banana trade and indeed to much of Central America.

His biggest venture after the Costa Rican line was the Guatemala-Salvador railway system, which he incorporated as the International Railways of Central America. This ambitious project, joining the two countries with 800 miles of strategic main line and making possible the shipping of bananas as well as other important freight to Puerto Barrios and the sea, was not completed until six months after Minor Keith's death in 1929. But the success of his I.R.C.A. in maintaining rail transportation across the highest spines of the Central American mountains encouraged a number of banana men to consider the possibilities of new farming bases west of those mountains. But for the time being the Caribbean coastal plains remained the great source of banana supplies.

United Fruit's colony of Almirante, Panama, with its yellow buildings and its flowering hibiscus hedges, remained the capital of a banana division that included four main centers: Changuinola, Sixaola South, Sixaola North, and Talamanca—

in all, thirty-one plantations that grew a record number of bananas. Through the early 1920's Almirante's harvests had averaged about 8000 bunches or 275 tons a day. Rich, wet lands, an experienced work force of Jamaican Negroes and the division's outstandingly efficient 275-mile system of narrow-gauge railroad and tramlines contributed to the success of the enterprise. Two dozen locomotives hauled the fruit to port and provided passenger service to the inland villages. But offsetting the bountiful advantages of Almirante was the ominous fact that hundreds of acres of banana plantings had begun to wither and die of the root fungus called Panama Disease. The plague had first appeared in the Almirante area. About 1920 the fields worst stricken had been abandoned and diseased plants had been isolated, but the disease was gaining in Panama and spreading into the lowlands of Costa Rica.

Nevertheless the Costa Rican division remained in the trade. The Keith-built Northern Railway was operating continuous schedules on its 116 miles of main line between Puerto Limon and San José and its 215 miles of branches, spurs, and sidings which reached deep into the lowlands. United Fruit operated the entire system under lease and kept forty-three locomotives, fifty passenger coaches, and more than a thousand banana cars productively busy.

But Costa Rica, which had succeeded Panama as the mightiest country in the Central American banana industry, was now taking second place to Honduras. The Tela area that fronted the Caribbean and the Cuyamel lands was producing at lower costs more bananas than any other region in United Fruit's tropical empire. In addition to more than 10 million bunches of bananas per year, the Tela division was also producing beef and dairy cattle, developing vast pasture lands and small-scale plantings of such fruits as mandarins, limes, tangerines, avocados, mangoes, breadfruit, mangosteens, papayas, and coconuts.

United Fruit's newest Honduran division was the Truxillo

Railroad Company, at Puerto Castilla, where in 1502 Columbus had landed and claimed the shore lands for Spain before filling his water casks from the Rio Negro and continuing along the coast. As early as 1540 Truxillo had become a flourishing village of merchants and ship handlers whose trade with Spanish sailing ships enabled them to support a bishop, a royal governor, and a *capitan* of the port. But the jungle inevitably closed in and the village was abandoned.

United Fruit had become the railroad builder for the Truxillo coast about 1913, and by 1925 the banana company had completed 233 miles of main line and branches, equipped with twenty-two locomotives, some six hundred banana cars and fifteen passenger coaches—these last built of native mahogany. Banana trains were rumbling through the jungle, and about 43,000 acres of the rich countryside were growing bananas.

Hotels and clubhouses arose in the wilderness. Ice plants, electric plants, telephone and railway centers, waterworks, schools, and stores dotted the vast new forests of bananas.

The tremendous Castilla-Truxillo division grew like Jack's beanstalk and then, still in the 1920's, its banana plants began to curl and die from Panama Disease. As farm after farm was abandoned the banana railway ran fewer trains, and in time the jungle took back the stakes. The soil remains to this day rich and prolific—but not good for bananas. Here, again, bad luck and disease were deciding banana destinies.

Despite enormous costs and long-term investments the Central American banana fronts were showing signs of moving west. United Fruit's venture into the wilderness of Pacific Coast Panama was the first major demonstration. The scene was the Chiriqui Province, where Puerto Armuelles, then better known as Rabo de Puerco—Pig's Tail—became the outlet to the Pacific.

Panama's Department of Chiriqui was the very archetype of a tropical wilderness. In 1916 a colony of Mormons had moved into the dark coast land to found what they called the Panama Sugar Company. The Latter-day Saints planted several hundred acres of cane, built a grinding mill at Progreso, laid down a few miles of narrow-gauge railroad, and harvested one small crop before the 1920 collapse of the sugar market completely erased their experiment. The sugar fields reverted to bush and jungle. But there were other fringes of banana lands in the area from which hundreds of thousands of bunches of bananas grown by citizen farmers were shipped out to distant markets.

But the over-all trend was toward even larger banana farms and major growing centers. At Tela, which by 1929 had become its heaviest yielding division, United Fruit was following Cuyamel's lead in irrigating the crop. Work had begun in 1927, with the irrigation of 2718 acres. The experiment, according to its directors, had been "shot through with trials, tribulations, and profanity," but within two years the yields were almost doubled and the quality of the fruit had markedly improved.

In 1923 United Fruit banana farmers began to study the Chiriqui watersheds and soil chemists tested the qualities of the land. Three years later the newly established Chiriqui Land Company, a United Fruit subsidiary, bought lands from individual owners and, as the land buying continued, company soil chemists and engineers marked out prospective farm sites and possible sites for railroads, drainage canals, reservoirs, hydroelectric plants, commissaries, and medical and office centers.

The jungle fighting began in 1926 at Davíd, then the nearest railroad terminal. The government of Panama contracted with a New York construction firm to build thirty-five miles of new railway to link the port site with the government-owned Ferrocarril de Chiriqui. The banana company began to build a supplementary railroad to tie in outlying farms but first agreed that all banana trains and other rolling stock should pay the Chiriqui Nacional for main-line service.

Other crews of banana engineers were setting up a weather station, completing an aerial map of the proposed division, smoothing out an airfield clearing, fencing pastures, and buying oxen and cattle which would draw heavy machinery parts to the necessary assembly points. Then the builders set up a field hospital at Armuelles and assembled a medical staff, nurses, and laboratory technicians, who launched an effective attack against malaria.

At first about two-thirds of the employees had malaria. Within a year the incidence had fallen to about one-fifth of the work force; within another year to less than a tenth, even as the labor force climbed from 1200 to 5000. During the first thirty months of the development banana employees were obliged to leave their families behind—in Central America, the United States, England, or Europe.

The new port town sprawled over the hot sands of Armuelles. Screened sheds with zinc roofs afforded quarters for the workers and bosses alike, though in the beginning men were obliged to bunk in crowded barracks. Floods added to the discomfort. But after a rough-and-tumble year of pioneering, men were planting bananas—eventually 15,000 acres of them —and within another year fruit was in harvest and ships were loading green cargo for the Pacific Coast of the United States.

In the older divisions the workings of an improvised internationalism became more evident. Children of *Norteamericanos* were speaking both Spanish and English. Young men from the States were marrying Central American girls. Native children were eagerly absorbing English from the newfangled "talkies." In Jamaica, which was still exporting great quantities of bananas, a third generation of immigrant *vaqueros* was being born in banana-company hospitals.

More new employees, most of them men under twenty-five, were arriving from England, Holland, Germany, Rumania, Africa, and South America, and from all parts of the United States. Two decades earlier about a third of all employees from the States were from New England. Now the figure was one in fifteen as the Midwest and Southwest vied for first place. *Caballeros* from practically everywhere, eager college youths, jobless clerks, adventurous white-collar workers, refugees from city streets and country crossroads, teachers, soldiers, lawyers, engineers, storekeepers, cooks, road builders, swamp waders, bartenders, barbers, ousted politicians, soldiers of fortune, and impatient adventure seekers, peoples of all races and ages, were sprinkled over the ever expanding banana front, and in play, as in work, contrasting peoples were living the banana life as new plantations replaced verdant jungles and old plantations were returned to jungle.

At Truxillo, in Honduras, banana men organized and bet lustily on "lazy mule" races and devised community plays and home-talent minstrel shows. In Guatemala, in Cuba, and in Jamaica, banana men played polo. In many banana frontiers, as in the earlier frontiers of the United States, farmers staged their field days and get-togethers. In Cuba and Central America, as in the United States, farm people played and cherished the great American game, baseball.

National lotteries had long since become standard institutions throughout most of the American tropics, and peddlers of lottery tickets were about as omnipresent as the palm trees.

In timekeepers' houses from Guatemala to Ecuador, tinted pictures of Marilyn Miller were appearing above washstands or bureaus in bachelors' quarters. Honduran-born Don Carlos Mejia, farm overseer at Progreso, had been doubly commended locally as his country's most competent banana farmer and alligator hunter. In Honduras and Cuba, United Fruit pay cars were being bulletproofed with protective insulations of New York City telephone directories. In Honduras the company had bought a Fokker monoplane, named the craft the *Tela*, and put the plane to work carrying company mail and passengers between the port of Tela and Honduras' mountain capital, thus cutting the journey from four hard days by muleback to less than two hours. Statisticians were reporting that Central America was exporting enough bananas yearly to form a two-ply golden chain completely around the earth.

United Fruit pilots, engineers, and cartographers in 1929 completed aerial photographic maps of 2600 square miles of Central American wilds. Altogether more than 300,000 acres of bananas were under cultivation, and the total roster of all banana employees was passing the 150,000 mark. In eleven American nations banana companies were building or maintaining villages and colonies, hotels and clubs, general stores and commissaries, bakeries, laundries, bottling works, mills, machine shops, ship lines, piers, railroads, hydroelectric plants, schools, and churches.

Wages paid to banana workers south of the Rio Grande in 1929 totaled 50 million dollars, with half as much more spent for purchases of bananas grown by farmers of the American tropics. During 1929 United Fruit alone paid $4,974,800 for the purchase of bananas grown by independent farmers in Jamaica; $3,166,900 in Colombia; $2,008,300 in Costa Rica; $1,308,800 in Panama; $1,058,500 in Guatemala; and $1,004,300 in Honduras.

As the second and third generation of banana *vaqueros* took over in the tropics, a second generation of banana jobbers, dealers, and peddlers took over in the United States and other market countries. Fruit Dispatch, which Andrew Preston had launched so proudly thirty years before, remained the largest banana-selling organization of the United States. The closely associated Canadian Banana Company, Ltd., led the trade in Canada, while Elder and Fyffes and its subsidiary companies controlled most of the trade in the British Isles and Western Europe.

Many of the older men agreed that the banana trade was in better shape than ever, even though in the United States the trade was sharply competitive, with unit profits declining as total volumes rose. Yet the total picture was not entirely bright. During the 1920's death had taken the two great leaders of the trade, Andrew Preston and Minor Keith, and the new management was relatively inexperienced. A few of the more perceptive students of the trade asserted that the most likely contender for leadership was Samuel Zemurray, still being described by his mightiest competitor as "that little fellow in Honduras." However, that remained a minority opinion.

It was obvious too that the banana trade was not immune to the social and economic stupidities of the "Decade of Materialism." The trade had failed to define and publicize its work and aims. Repeatedly it had shrugged aside published or spoken censure without trying to separate the valid from the invalid criticisms. Though for the most part legitimate, its advertising too often exaggerated the therapeutic benefits of the fruit. Bananas are a good food, a superior fruit, and, ordinarily, a cheap fruit. But bananas are not a medicine, and if you have fallen arches, an ailing liver, a bad heart, or housemaid's knee, bananas will not cure you.

Even more serious was the fact that in Central America banana growing had become a one-crop agriculture. Efforts of the banana companies to effect crop diversification were still inadequate. This situation was being aggravated by the abandonment of banana lands as Panama Disease spread. When this underground root fungus blights a crop it is useless to replant Gros Michel, the staple market banana. But the disease does not poison the land for other products, and good banana land is capable of growing almost any other staple or subsistence crop. Nevertheless, banana companies, which had given value to tens of thousands of acres of previously value-less and untenable tropical lowlands and swamps, were missing the great opportunity to help citizen farmers help themselves to the lands no longer suitable for bananas. In some instances, too, major banana growers had scrapped or removed the rail-roads that should have been left as vital arteries to the abandoned areas. That point, virtually unnoticed by the U. S. press, was probably the gravest management fault of the banana industry.

In these respects several banana companies, including United Fruit, had erred grievously though not necessarily deliberately. Critics pounced on another conspicuous fault that was already being remedied in large part. As we have noticed, most banana centers are located in tropical wilder-nesses which have few or no inhabitants. As the clearing and building begins and as thousands of workers are recruited, the wage earners require goods for which they are willing to exchange a portion of their wages. Otherwise there is no particular point in working. In any country there are likely to be traders and shopkeepers to exploit the frontier and its ranks of newly arrived workers. That is the justification for the company or plantation commissary. The employer may feel obliged to supervise the quantity and quality of merchan-dise sold and thereby reduce the losses resulting from a work force pugnaciously drunk on cheap and ready liquors or poisoned by foul meats or spoiled flour, rice, and beans. But in earlier times, banana concerns had repeatedly abused the system of plantation commissaries. In some instances they refused to employ native storekeepers, imported the necessary merchandise, in many instances duty free, and sold the goods at outrageous prices to the workers—all too frequently on credit, making charges against wages not yet earned.

Such business was a straight road to peonage. Commissary managers, frequently rated according to the size of profits in hand, were inclined to squeeze harder and harder. By 1920 the banana commissary situation in frontier Central America was a wretched one. Its victims were complaining, "You pay us good wages and take it all back at the commissary!"

The situation was too corrupt to endure. United Fruit, under Andrew Preston, decided to "modify" commissary profits. Cuyamel and others followed suit. Samuel Zemurray gave native merchants trading space in Cuyamel towns. United Fruit cut commissary profits on staples such as rice, beans, cured pork, and work clothing to practically nothing, and often sold them below cost—leaving liquors, beer, tobaccos, and other such goods to earn the over-all profits. Repeatedly native merchants, who at first had wailed because they were not permitted to establish shops on the banana fronts, now complained even louder that the banana company "robbed them of a chance for fair profit."

Tropical merchandising remained a trying problem which, by 1929, all principal banana companies had striven to solve. But none had been entirely successful.

United Fruit had continued seeking new enterprises as well as new people. By 1926 its cacao plantations in Panama and Costa Rica covered about fifty square miles and the annual harvests of about 3 million pounds of the dried chocolate beans. On various borderlands company workers had planted about four square miles to balsa, a fast-growing, corklike wood which was supplying more than a million board feet yearly. In Greater Boston, United Fruit was operating a major sugar refinery, with seven acres of buildings, a special wharf, and an over-all daily capacity of 3500 barrels of sugar.

In Jamaica, Alfred Butler, a United Fruit soil chemist, was experimenting with mangosteen, "the queen of tropical fruits." In Costa Rica, at Siquirres, United Fruit had launched a supplementary experiment station to study reforestation, the improvement of cacao, and the cultivation of coffee—the latter for expediting the progress of the company's coffee plantation at Pejivalle. African oil palm, India mango, avocados, tung trees, nutmeg, tea, vanilla, Ceylon gooseberry, and various other tropical crops yet unproved in Central America were being planted experimentally.

The Lancetilla Experiment Station, which United Fruit had formally established near Tela, Honduras, early in 1926, was now the coming plant research station in all the Caribbean lands. There a number of able young plant researchers from Kansas, West Africa, Rumania, the British West Indies, Holland, Ecuador, England, Massachusetts, China, and many other distant places were investigating and making trial propagations of all manner of tropical crops.

In the fields of medicine and sanitation United Fruit was working effectively to treat about 35,000 malaria cases annually (about one-third were nonemployees) and the malaria deaths were reduced to about 160 a year. Smallpox had been swept off the banana fronts, and such diseases as cholera, hookworm, and bubonic plague were disappearing. Efforts to effect good water supply, sewage systems, food inspection, and wholesale vaccination were increased. By 1925 the death rate in Central American ports, estimated as 150 per thousand yearly as of 1900, was down to about fifteen per thousand.

Better farming practices, particularly the drainage of banana lands, were helping immensely in the struggle against malaria. Camp sites and villages were being leveled in order to eliminate the standing water which serves as breeding places for malaria-carrying mosquitoes. The remaining swamps and water holes were being poisoned in order to destroy at least part of the anopheline larvae.

By 1925 the sanitation squad was a basic institution of every well-managed banana or cane division. Next the foremost banana company had moved to wipe out the lingering though considerably exaggerated menace of poisonous snakes. United Fruit undertook this work in collaboration with the Museum of Comparative Zoology of Harvard and the Mulford Biological Laboratories of Glenolden, Pennsylvania. At Tela the banana company contributed a "serpentarium," complete with laboratory, observation building, and snake pits. Harvard named it the Neotropical Station of the Antivenom Institute of America. Here were developed antivenoms that presently obliterated practically all banana farm deaths from snake bite.

Nevertheless, the banana fronts continued to suffer from many other natural calamities. Leading among these inevitables were floods—resulting from the comparatively youthful to-pography, the steep and numerous mountains, heavy annual rainfalls and long rainy seasons. As banana fronts doubled in area, diaries of the 1920's abounded in stories of floods and flood fighting—frequently heroic stories.

From the Honduran banana front, where at least ten kilometers of the Truxillo Railroad were being navigated by *cayucos* or rowboats instead of trains, an observant young banana man reported the great Thanksgiving Flood of 1927:

Thanksgiving Day with Flood. Heavy rains have converted *quebradas* into rivers, and rivers are raging torrents. The Aguan, muddy and savage, sings and moans as it rushes forward to the Caribbean. Thousands of acres of land are inundated. Railroad bridges are going out; irrigation projects are badly washed and damaged; access to most plantations is impossible.

About 7:00 A.M. yesterday I talked to Mr. Veitch, superin-tendent of agriculture, who is at Maloa. Shortly thereafter the telephone service was disrupted. We have heard nothing since. Everyone anxiously awaits word. Several rescues were made with *cayucos* in Taujica and and Black River Districts. . . .

Early this morning, Lamoree, overseer, called from Colorado Farm house. He and his timekeeper have stored clothing, pay-roll records, etc., in the attic. Lamoree called again as they vacated the farmhouse for the shelter of Escaleras Commissary, where . . . they slept on rice bags on the floor. The water rose rapidly—one foot every fifteen minutes. . . .

Welsko, Grant, Spink, and myself started for Bonito in a small gasoline "scooter." The car had difficulty in getting through. At Kilo 47.0 we began to walk. In deep water we fell over a drowned mule. El Paso is an adobe house, the home of Don Pepe. . . . It was filled with water. Forlorn goats huddled together on top of boxes. When it became necessary to vacate the house Don Pepe's family swam to the bridge spanning the Bonito River. One woman clung to a small baby. All were wet, with the rain still pelting down, shivering, with neither a fire nor dry clothing a possibility. We pushed on, struggling for every foot. . . . At one place a beam of a bridge was exposed. On it were dozens of tarantulas, two snakes, a mouse, and numerous centipedes. In the water we saw small animals clinging for life upon the insecure footing of banana trunks. . . .

Banana-land floods come upon you with a sort of dream-like inevitability. Blackish gray clouds hover low and rain gushes down, sometimes at the rate of an inch every hour. Next morning you may note that the water is at porch level and you see floating gobs which you presently identify as your own chickens. Your telephone ceases to ring. The trains have stopped running. You are somewhat numbly aware that for the duration of the flood, food, medicine, and other necessary supplies will have to be delivered by motorboat, *cayuco*, or plane. You pull on your rubber boots, which are probably a foot or two too short for protection from the flood; you rescue the chickens, provide them temporary asylum in the attic, and wade to the nearest banana farm or village to join the flood fighters.

You are certain to find something to do; work that wets you, wears you, and washes you with slime. You will thirst for hot coffee and ache for food, as you toil all night to repair a boat, anchor a bridge, salvage a levee, safeguard commissary supplies, or push through a bogged supply train.

Whatever your flood adventures may be, you are likely to witness courage, fraternity, and ingenuity in a struggle that is worthy of any beachhead or battlefield.

It seems probable that there will always be destructive floods along the banana fronts. But during the 1920's, the banana companies, particularly United Fruit and Cuyamel, had demonstrated that improved engineering practices, more accurate location and drainage of banana farms, and constructive practices in land conservation can materially reduce flood hazards.

That was one of the more encouraging developments current during the 1920's. Consistent efforts to defend the banana lands from floods, plant diseases, human epidemics, and other natural liabilities had met with considerable success. But momentous liabilities remained. Nowhere is farming an easy or a simple trade. But in general as modern agriculture approaches the equator it becomes ever more laborious and complex. Banana companies, like all persistent banana growers, continued to learn this the hard and costly way.

This underscored the particular problems and toils of the young men who were struggling to operate banana plantations. Each successive death or retirement of an old hand added increased responsibility to the responsibilities of the newcomers. New tropical leaders, few of them fully tried, were feeling an ever-growing pressure of obligation which they sought variously to express and to shoulder. At Santa Marta, Texas-raised Arthur A. Pollan, manager of United Fruit's then mighty Colombian division and widely recognized as one of the more able young leaders of the banana trade, spoke to his department heads:

We must keep our fingers on the pulse of labor at all times. . . . The superintendents must be able to win the confidence of their men and hold it. . . .

One of the important questions confronting us today is the matter of developing men. Failure to do our part along this line will bring us to grief. Every official and department head in the entire organization should have first-class assistants who are capable and fully equipped to step into the position higher up at a moment's notice. . . .

All of our men must make a study of the Latin American peoples. We are living in their country, and it is up to us to adjust ourselves. Decent and honest diplomacy must be practiced at all times.

The banana trade was coming of age. In twenty years banana production had quadrupled along with consumer demands for the fruit. Its capital investments had soared to at least half a billion dollars, and though it remained a comparatively small part of the foreign investment of United States capital, its international position was outstandingly important. So was its place in international agriculture and shipping. The banana industry had long since ceased to be a venture in transient exploitation. It continued to create valuable farms from jungle wastes; to establish long-lived colonies; to merge tropical farming, transportation, and the international marketing of a perishable crop into a long-term, fast-motioned investment operation. Furthermore, the leadership and policy-molding of the maturing banana industry required specific and in some cases contrasting adaptations to the different nations in which bananas are grown—all small nations with limited abilities to absorb great chunks of foreign capital into their own particular national economics.

As the 1920's came to a close, the inter-American banana trade was a 3000-mile panorama of colorful but conflicting promises and dilemmas. It was swinging toward some sort of decisive climax without competent self-appraisal; without sufficient knowledge of its own strengths and weaknesses, and without any really clear definition of its vast load of responsibilities.

CHAPTER THIRTEEN

BIG MAN FROM THE ULUA

DURING DECEMBER, 1929, when business was still dazed after the previous October's Wall Street crash, United Fruit announced that it had acquired control of the Cuyamel Fruit Company, of New Orleans and Honduras.

A great many veterans of the trade were astonished at this development. Actually, negotiations had begun a considerable time before the crash. But late in 1929 two leaders of the banana trade had reached an agreement. One of them was Samuel Zemurray. The other was his respected acquaintance of long standing, Webster Bradley Palmer, the same "young whippersnapper" who many years before, in the company of Andrew Preston, had talked across the table with Zemurray at Mobile and New Orleans. This time Palmer, now the largest stockholder and a ranking director of United Fruit, was dealing not with an enterprising beginner but with the owner of United Fruit's most powerful and progressive competitor.

After much persuasion, Samuel Zemurray joined United

Fruit, which agreed to give 300,000 shares of its common stock for all the holdings of the Cuyamel Fruit Company, including approximately 35,000 acres of cultivated banana lands in Honduras, Nicaragua, and Mexico; fifteen banana ships (three of them newly built); railroads, livestock, land, and equipment—enough to produce and ship more than 6 million bunches of bananas yearly. Zemurray, already a wealthy man, was becoming at least 20 million dollars wealthier.

In its annual report, issued early in 1930, United Fruit announced from Boston:

In December of last year the directors authorized the purchase of the properties of the Cuyamel Fruit Company. . . . These assets will be added to the inventory of the United Fruit Company in 1930. This purchase was warranted by the growing demand for quality fruit by our customers throughout the United States and Canada. . . . The United Fruit Company, through its aggressive merchandising, selling, and advertising, has built up a demand for quality fruit in excess of its present supply and can market and distribute to great advantage the increased Cuyamel production.

Those who read the full report carefully noticed that Cuyamel was being merged with United Fruit. It had not been bought like a load of hay. The great Cuyamel farms were to continue in production, and Cuyamel ships were to remain in the Caribbean trade. Most of Zemurray's employees were keeping their jobs under the merged managements. And United Fruit's *tropicos*, particularly in Honduras, were delighted to welcome the Cuyamel men to their team and their side of the river.

The merger had made Zemurray a director and the largest stockholder in United Fruit, which remained preponderantly New England owned. He had agreed that he would not take over or otherwise operate a rival banana company, but there was not one word in the agreement to prevent him from taking over United Fruit.

He had at first intended to play an inactive part—to go to Boston only occasionally and to advise on matters when his help was needed, particularly in regard to Honduras. For few other men, not excepting Hondurans, knew that ever-remarkable, little-known country nearly so well as Zemurray knew it. The *"gran hombre* of the Chamelecon-Ulua Basin" had spent sodden weeks and months walking scores of jungle trails from Ceiba Point to Tegucigalpa. He knew and in general he liked the Honduran people, from the lowliest palm shack *mestizo* to the capital's aristocracy. He felt himself as one with Hondurans, and he felt toward the people and the country deep and wistful gratitude for their great part in making his success possible.

Certainly Zemurray had no driving urge to earn more money. His personal fortune—even apart from his banana company stock—was more than enough for his own needs. And he did not lack occupation. In New Orleans he had built or was planning a number of philanthropies, including a hospital for Negro women; and at Tulane University he had founded the Middle America Research Institute, an organization dedicated to the study of the archaeology and anthropology of Caribbean countries. Also, he had been contributing substantially to Tulane and its medical school.

All in all, at the age of fifty-two Zemurray found himself pleasantly unoccupied with the banana business. Near Hammond, Louisiana, about sixty-five miles inland from New Orleans, the self-made banana boss had bought a 25,000-acre plantation which he rescued from a lumbering concern. He had restored the aging plantation house and begun supervising the clearing of lands for planting several thousand acres of tung trees. Samuel Zemurray was happy and busy. He confided to friends: "All my life I've wanted to be a real season-to-season farmer. I've been wanting a farm of my own since

I was a little boy looking at the tall wheat fields back in the old country."

Out on Audubon Drive in New Orleans, the hero of this American success story had a town house, a four-story, somewhat palatial, late-Victorian mansion facing the Tulane campus. He had his big farm as his particular outlet for work and development. During his busy years he had earmarked many books. Now he proposed to read.

Samuel Zemurray, for the time being at least, had made his own personal decision. But the banana trade as a whole was riding the prevalent currents of indecision. United Fruit, now that it had absorbed Cuyamel, was still more conspicuously the dominant banana company. In thirty adventurous years this United Fruit had changed from what its founder-president had called a working association of banana firms to a quarter-billion-dollar corporation labeled by its enemies the spreading octopus from *Yanqui*-land and by its friends as the most colorful of American business enterprises. The fact remained, however, that United Fruit was come to its own particular hour of decision in rather obvious indecision.

As the great depression continued, United Fruit stock began to drop precipitously, from $163 to $117, down to $101 and on down to $72, $43, and $35. The market quotations reached still lower levels, although banana production and sales remained strong and although United Fruit kept paying regular yearly dividends of more than $4 per share. The banana trade was structurally sounder than it had ever been, but investors could not be persuaded of the fact. During 1930 United Fruit's volume touched an all-time high of nearly 65 million bunches of bananas for the United States and Canada, not including the British Isles and European trade. The capital reserve remained strong. But still the stock kept falling.

During these glum days of 1930, when lengthening breadlines were appearing in dozens of our cities, at least four

New York newspapers told how eight jobless young women in Manhattan had survived for more than a month on a diet of five bananas a day—for the eight girls.

The eight jobless girls had managed to raise a total of two dollars a week for their communal subsistence. After paying the rent of one shabby room (for all eight) in an east-side tenement they spent the rest for bananas. The girls cut the bananas into eight equal portions—about five inches of banana per day for each girl—to be eaten as one, two, or three meals as the recipient saw fit.

The spokesman for the eight girls who subsisted on five ripe bananas a day explained that there is more nutrition in a dime's worth of bananas than in a dime's worth of any other food. The story was confirmation of Andrew Preston's stubborn determination that bananas should remain cheap food for poor people. The delivery of bananas to a New York grocery involved an average of 3000 miles of exceptionally costly transportation; numerous hazards of weather and other natural enemies; and the painstaking handling and ripening of one of the most perishable of all foods. Even so, one of the more costly foods to produce was being cited as one of the cheapest to buy.

But the crisis of depression was becoming real to United Fruit as it was to the lesser banana firms. American agriculture generally was being pauperized. There were grim indications that banana farming could not long remain an exception.

In a time of such crisis it was natural that leaders of the trade should have re-examined the history and operations of the industry in an effort to establish a fixed position before planning future courses. For many years the trade had been guilty of a number of questionable practices in the conduct of its tropical affairs, though generally speaking the ethics of the trade had improved with the passing years.

The most obvious of the earlier transgressions had concerned that institution known as the "concession." Most of the development of the early banana industry in Central America had been based upon the concession, a legal instrument for contractual agreement between a government and a corporation or an individual. Invariably the contract specified that in return for a particular investment, building, or service the investor should receive certain "advantages, assurances, and/or rights" from the sovereign government in whose jurisdiction the investment was to be made. By no means all of the concessions were equitable, nor were they all in the common interest.

The 1930's were beginning as a decade of unusual political and economic stability for the banana countries. There had been some strikes and labor difficulties but none of extensive importance or great duration. In Colombia, Jamaica, and Mexico, as on shipboard, the banana companies were beginning to deal with union labor. Moreover, banana companies and Caribbean governments had been getting along reasonably well, though there had been several rifts in Mexico and Colombia and a few sharp words in Costa Rica. In spite of this, the companies had managed to grow and sell fruit in countries of varying political systems—from frontier anarchies to hyperconservative crown colonies; from Indian dictatorships and quasi-socialist states to republican democracies.

But by gradual stages United Fruit, Cuyamel, and Standard Fruit had instituted a great proportion of outright purchase of farms and lands that they deemed desirable for banana production. As the 1920's ended, the great majority of bananas in trade were being grown on lands that had been regularly purchased.

There had been specific instances, however, in which banana companies had interfered more or less directly in the affairs of Latin American governments. Although no banana firm had succeeded financially simply by the usurpation of civil authority, there had been enough meddling in local poli-

tics to earn the fruit companies something less than the collective good will of all the citizens of the countries concerned.

This reputation was offset to some extent by the banana
company hospitals, by the companies' development of tropical railroads, and by the contributions of the industry to the
cause of sanitation and public health. It was also true that
wages paid by the fruit companies averaged at least three
times those prevailing in near-by coffee *fincas* and other adjacent farm establishments. But the recitation of charitable and
virtuous acts (which were not altogether selfless in motive)
could not succeed in distracting attention from the injus-
tices.

For the most part, people not actually in the banana trade
knew remarkably little about it. For a variety of reasons, some
valid and others rather foolish, the trade as a whole had deliberately avoided the spotlights of publicity. Reports to
stockholders were uniformly perfunctory and unrevealing.
With extremely few exceptions, both the attacks against and
the praises of the trade were spoken and written with heated
fervor and appalling ignorance.

Year after year the opposition had charged and the companies or their friends or supporters had answered and coun-
tercharged. The facts, meanwhile, grew more and more involved and in many instances maddeningly obscured. Ironi-
cally, many of the more vocal commentators from Central
American and other Caribbean capitals knew no more, if as
much, about the actual ways and problems of the banana
trade than did the *Norteamericanos*. There were and are a
few exceptions that help prove the rule. Banana lowlands
have never been attractive to capital-city intellectuals or
high officials of Latin America, the great majority of whom
remain most fervently attached to the pavements, plazas, and
halls of their own or near-by cities and therefore lack specific
or intimate knowledge of the rural areas of their own coun-

tries. The best North American counterpart is the professional New Yorker, whose knowledge of rural conditions begins and ends with Central Park.

Most discussions of the pros and cons of the banana trade tended to emerge either as academic chitchat, exercise in political theory, or barroom soliloquies. Banana men traditionally began by pointing out that their trade consists of growing, shipping, and selling bananas; that bananas simply do not grow in legislative lobbies or capital buildings, and that politicians and talk-muches rarely grow the fruit and practically never buy it.

The opposition usually opened by charging that banana growers "exploit" labor and oppose unions. That charge was by no means pointless, but it was and is vulnerable to inquiry. For the Caribbean as a whole the 1920's and most of the 1930's were a period of national dictatorships. In most instances the dictators had opposed, sometimes fiercely, the advent of labor unions, mainly because labor unions are organized groups that may in time muster strengths to topple the dictators.

Those who opposed the banana companies stressed the fact that United Fruit, as the largest corporate employer in Central America, was in a position to dominate the labor markets along the banana fronts and to hold wages down, either by direct action or by checkmating local employment by way of "task" or contract work, thereby encouraging contractors and subcontractors to hold wages down for their own and the company's profit.

United Fruit's answer, if any, strongly supported by audited records, was somewhat as follows: The company consistently pays wages higher than the prevailing averages in the country in question. The company admittedly seeks the best available grades of workers because banana operations require superior labor. But the company's willingness to make equitable compensation is proved by the fact that the company con-

sistently raises wages to compensate for skills acquired by the
workers in the course of their employment. Banana men are
well aware that citizen planters usually oppose any moves by
outside employers to lure the best labor with wages too far
in excess of the accepted levels of the country in question.
They pointed out, too, that the actual worth of any wage
must be gauged in terms of local buying power—not of dollar
value in the United States or the Straits Colony; finally, that
in times of depression, labor markets were distinctly better
along the banana fronts than in most of the United States.

Strikes had occurred in banana lands—the most tragic one
in the Magdalena area of Colombia late in 1928. That particular strike had been led by the *Union Sindical de Trabajadores de Magdalena*, which demanded, among other gains,
a fifty-percent wage increase, weekly instead of fortnightly
wage payments, and more liberal collective insurance. In
time, United Fruit granted all the demands except the involved issue of collective insurance. But the strike began,
and on December 6, at Cienaja, an open clash occurred
between Colombian troops and the strikers. United Fruit
settled by paying all Colombian farm labor $1.20, $1.50,
and $2.00 a day as primary wages (substantially higher
than farm wages then current in the United States), plus
free houses, schools, and other facilities. The company also
built two additional hospitals, several additional schools for
workers' dependents, and better rent-free houses for workers, thereby establishing, incidentally, a rural housing standard much higher than that common to most of the United
States.

In Mexico, labor strife had not seriously molested the
banana fronts. In Costa Rica, labor agitation was preponderantly a case of banana labor, or elements thereof, versus the
citizen banana planters. United Fruit, until the later 1930's,
was buying from citizen farmers about three-fourths of all its
Costa Rican banana exports. Citizen farmers as a rule paid

lower wages and provided fewer accommodations for workers than did United Fruit or other North American banana companies. During 1931 the *Sindicato de Trabajadores del Atlantico* drew up a list of grievances and demands, presented the list to the planters' association, then solicited and won the help of railroad and harbor workers in launching a general strike. After eight stormy months, during which the Costa Rican banana trade sank to a faint trickle, the Costa Rican Secretary of Labor effected an agreement between planters and laborers, granting the latter improved transportation and medical facilities, and a compromise settlement of .7 to .8 colon per hour as the staple farm wage for banana workers.

In answer to charges of local tax evasion, the banana companies had receipts to prove that they were paying both farm land and other real property taxes and direct export taxes on all bananas in trade. Records showed that between 1.4 and 1.97 percent of the market value of the bananas in trade was being paid directly as export taxes to the governments within whose boundaries the fruit was grown. Banana men pointed out that no staple crop of the United States was obliged to pay anything like 1.4 to 1.97 percent of its market value in direct taxes.

A vocal minority of citizen planters in the banana lands continued to charge that United Fruit buyers were discarding too high a percentage of their fruit. But a still louder chorus of banana jobbers and dealers in the United States were prone to charge that United Fruit banana buyers were not discarding a sufficiently high percentage of banana purchases from tropical planters. Tropical managers kept on describing outloadings of "fine fruit" which the receivers in United States ports frequently decried as "mush" or "soup"—the strongest epithets of the banana trade. But that is part of life—and of trade in any perishable commodity where quick, frequently impromptu, sometimes arbitrary decisions must be made by fallible men.

At various times the banana trade and its leading member, United Fruit, had demonstrated faults that were big faults and merits (in resourcefulness, frontier courage, and administrative and marketing skills) that tended to counterbalance the faults. The real issue could no longer be presented in terms of rhetorical arguments, academic theory, personalized estimates, or individual instances.

The public, insofar as they noticed the banana industry at all, had every moral and constitutional right to hold and express their views or beliefs, and they did. Particularly in and around Boston, United Fruit, which by 1930 had about 42,000 stockholders in contrast to the original ten of Boston Fruit, remained a cherished institution. Local proverb said that every Bostonian who since 1899 had succeeded in saving, inheriting, winning, or otherwise acquiring as much as $200 owned at least one share of United Fruit stock. Home-town and other admirers continued to laud the company's every step at least as fervently as many probing critics condemned its every step. More perceptive onlookers were aware that the United Fruit Company, now bellwether of the inter-American banana trade and the only really big colonization company in the Americas, had inevitably grown into an international position shared by no other American company.

To millions of Middle American people United Fruit had become virtually or practically synonymous with the United States of America. Despite this and despite the fact that United Fruit in everyday business routines was and is a potent commercial ambassador to a dozen American nations, the company held no official status with the United States government. Other powers had long followed the expedient of formally, though sometimes secretly, sponsoring colonizing companies which were quasi-official in nature—which earned dividends and salaries for shareholders and employees but were founded and perpetuated, usually by subsidy, to serve in various capacities the nation or empire by which they were originated. Britain's East India, Hudson's Bay, Royal Niger, and United Africa companies, Holland's West Indies Company, and Bismarck's and Karl Peter's German Colonization companies are or have been typical examples. In some instances, after a period of business enterprise, home government had bodily converted the foreign companies to territories or colonies. For example, Britain's Royal Niger Company, operating in equatorial West Africa, became His Majesty's mandate of Nigeria, and the German Colonization Company became substantially the Hohenzollern empire in Africa.

But United Fruit, conceived and founded by a New England produce merchant, remained a widely spread farming and shipping organization, operating as an independent commercial enterprise with long-term basic properties in sixteen sovereign nations or colonies. Inevitably, United Fruit was "big business," with much more than the usual obligations of big business.

Therefore, the particular phenomenon of its bigness demanded renewed appraisal by its leadership. Policies and business practices that a smaller company or agency could effect with clear conscience and the best precedences—indeed policies and practices that United Fruit only a couple of decades before had followed lawfully and without qualms—were now entirely beyond the scope of feasible management. Now United Fruit was dealing not only with an extensive business clientele. It was dealing with the social structures, the basic economies, and the hopes for better lives of at least 30 million citizens of the Americas. The company could no longer meet obligations to its stockholders solely with small-caliber enterprises, however orthodox or sound—enterprises and tidbits of profits which a smaller company might have gained with complete decorum. United Fruit had schools, churches, roads, towns, ports, railroads, ships, and other transportation services to provide—along with bananas. Bigness had won advantages.

But it had also drawn obligations that few business leaderships are capable of understanding—much less fulfilling.

Though not nearly so badly off as many large companies in the 1930's, United Fruit was in need of immediate and careful attention. It was obvious that if the company failed the banana trade would be set back many years and would perhaps find itself faced with problems of reconstruction similar to the problems of organization it knew in 1880 or 1890.

Through 1931 and 1932 dividends were, respectively, $4.80 and $4.25 per share. A general wage cut of fifteen percent may have been at least partly responsible for even these returns. As the stock continued to fall, complaints from stockholders multiplied and the largest stockholder decided to do something about the situation.

In January, 1933, Samuel Zemurray walked into the dark-paneled directors' room at Number One Federal Street in Boston and without fanfare or dramatics advised his fellow directors that he was "ready to go to work." On that day his temper was mild. He did not lay proxies on the table. Though easily the largest stockholder in United Fruit, he actually owned barely one-tenth of the total shares. But that was a sufficient stake. Zemurray told the directors that he wished to assume the office of "managing director," that he did not seek the presidency. He explained that his decision was thoughtfully considered; that, speaking as one banana man who had learned the business the hard way, he had no intention of sitting quietly by while the greatest banana company in the world went to hell in a bucket. One man had made a final decision.

South of the Rio Grande the news spread like a cane fire. Down in rainy Honduras, several banana *hombres* wearing mud-splashed khaki, sodden boots, and rain-soaked sombreros gathered for a quick one at the La Lima bar. Bill Tyler from

the manager's office and Tony Martinez, *mandador* of one of
the old Cuyamel Guanchita banana farms, tipped glasses and
chanted *salud, pesates, amor*. Bill spilled the big news: "Cuyamel takes over United Fruit!"

Tony grinned to show at least twenty-four white teeth and
five gold ones. "*Sí, señor!* Feesh swallows w'ale!"

Samuel Zemurray's bold decision to take the wheel of
United Fruit necessitated a great many other bold decisions.
But first it called for a renewed appraisal of the company
properties that were scattered over a 3000-mile front of the
American tropics and subtropics, a study of the depression-
fogged business picture in the United States and other great
market centers, and also a new appraisal of certain chronic
symptoms of the banana industry's ailments, some of which
had lately become acute or desperate.

Victor Cutter, the somewhat perturbed president of United
Fruit, had made his own appraisal of the banana trade in
depression: "Our company is strong in its land reserves, is
well supplied with ship tonnage and equipment, and has a
sufficient volume of production to carry it through a severe
depression. Nevertheless under present world economic conditions there is no question but that we should conserve our
strong cash position and make every economy that is consistent with maintenance of our tropical properties and ships."

Victor Cutter was following his own advice and estimates.
As head of the big banana company he had maintained a strong
cash reserve. He had demanded maximum economy of his
employees. He had approved the slashing of wages ten percent, then an additional fifteen percent. That was severe prun-
ing, but the employees accepted the verdict with remarkably
little wailing. Cutter continued to remind his directors and
stockholders that as a crop bananas had kept an unusually
sound position in world agriculture. He had pointed out with
complete accuracy, too, that American investments in the

banana industry are not big—in fact, barely half as much as the little-noted United States investments in Far East rubber properties, less than one-sixth of United States investments in insular sugar properties, and less than one-twelfth of United States investments in foreign oil properties. Cutter also continued to point out that even as business generally bogged deeper into depression, bananas continued to sell in outstandingly strong volume.

On the banana fronts farm people continued to work and earn modestly, which was a great deal more than could be said of many other of the Americas. In Argentina corn was being burned in place of coal. The first recorded food riot in American history had occurred at England, Arkansas. In the corn belt grain elevators were glutted with old and unsalable wheat. Elsewhere in the United States the American Red Cross had distributed food, clothing, and medicines to millions of rural people in twenty-one states. Throughout the West and Middle West uncounted thousands of tons of fruits and other farm produces were being dumped or left to rot in fields because markets could not consume them. Eddie Cantor had written a book entitled *Yoo Hoo, Prosperity!* which his publishers had priced at ninety-nine cents or a carload of wheat. Milk strikes were breaking in Wisconsin and Minnesota. Farm foreclosure sales were everyday occurrences. Between New York and San Francisco about 9000 banks had failed, and the United States banking structure was facing strong prospects of collapse.

Victor Cutter's contention that the banana trade was not doing badly was not only plausible but specifically provable. But the bare statistics had failed to convince the stock-trading public or to brush away the dense clouds of timorous depression psychology. Furthermore, Victor Cutter did not see, and had never seen, the banana industry as Sam Zemurray saw it. Therefore Sam Zemurray, at fifty-five, was the no-salary boss of United Fruit and at fifty Victor Cutter, as big-salaried president of a big business, was on his way out.

Twice before in United Fruit's lifetime two strongly contrasting personalities had led together with marked success: first, Captain Lorenzo Baker, the sea frontiersman, and hardworking, deferent Andrew Preston, the Yankee produce merchant; then Preston, grown to be the master produce merchant, and Minor Keith, the daring railroader and empire builder. Successively, and for almost forty years, these two teams of strongly contrasting personalities had led successfully. But by 1933, for inevitable reasons, the banana trade was changed, and for good and sufficient administrative reasons, as well as for reasons of personal pride and prejudice, Zemurray's entrance meant Cutter's exit. Victor Cutter began cleaning his files and portfolios and seeking new fields of employment. For a few weeks at least, the general office staff had opportunity to ponder the case of the new boss versus the president.

At first their meditations involved considerable uncertainty. Except for a comparatively limited circle of friends and acquaintances in Honduras and Louisiana, few people actually knew Samuel Zemurray. Outside of the New Orleans telephone directory, where his residence and office addresses were listed, the new boss's name was not to be found in any widely used directory. For the most part Eastern financiers knew Zemurray only by name, if at all. During his occasional attendance of directors' meetings at Boston and New York, United Fruit men knew him only as an extremely tall, rather well-dressed man, who listened thoughtfully, spoke little, rarely wrote letters, occasionally argued vehemently and asked questions of devastating directness, then lapsed into deeply reflective silence. Observers also noted that the *hombre* from the far south had an amazingly good memory, that he knew Honduras like the contours of his hands, which he frequently studied thoughtfully while listening to others talk. In general, the Bostonians were deeply puzzled by Zemurray, and outside of Honduras few of United Fruit's tropical staff knew the man.

There were office legends to the effect that Zemurray and Cutter had been embittered enemies during their earlier years in Honduras. As with a great many office legends, the fabric of fact was decidedly thin. Some eighteen years before, Cutter had helped plan and direct the big United Fruit division on the right bank of the Ulua, while Zemurray was building Cuyamel's brilliantly successful banana farms and incidental properties on the Ulua's left bank. There the two *vaqueros* had met as pell-mell competitors. Both had sought and in some part won advantages. Each had committed lusty pranks on the other. There had been other frontier-style plays and counterplays which both leaders and their followers had taken as good, forthright sport. But the truth remained that Cutter had considerable respect and admiration for "that little fellow in Honduras." Samuel Zemurray has never been heard to make a disparaging remark about Victor Cutter. He has said, indeed, that he considered Cutter United Fruit's most logical choice of a successor to Andrew Preston. Evidently, however, the big *hombre* of the Ulua was referring to United Fruit without Zemurray.

The real conflict between the two outstanding leaders of the banana trade took root from inherent qualities of the men themselves. Both were and are American success stories, somewhat in the style of Horatio Alger: Cutter, the market gardener's son from Dracut crossroads, who had worked his way through college and thereafter worked and climbed to the presidency of a mighty international corporation; Zemurray, the penniless, observant immigrant boy who liked bananas and had succeeded in organizing fellow immigrants to sell them.

Though both had worked extraordinarily hard, Sam Zemurray had followed the rougher trail. From the beginning he had built on his own, and as an individualist and entrepreneur he had worked for himself. Cutter had worked and grown with a corporation, already big and successful. Cutter had learned at first hand how to plan, plant, and "tune up" a banana farm. But so had the newest boss of United Fruit. A natural-born farmer and farm lover, Zemurray had also learned by hard and frequently ingenious experience how to sell bananas from pushcart, dray, boxcar, platform, or ship-side. In the same way he had learned the fundamentals of ship operations, dockage, railroading, banking, communication, and auditing. He had founded and led a company for which he was qualified to fill personally every key job. Obviously neither Cutter nor any other living man could be qualified to fill competently every key position in a company fifteen to twenty times as big as Zemurray's Cuyamel.

Cutter had swung strongly toward prevailing credos and corpulences of big business. With each successive rung of the corporate ladder he had spent still more of his time in office suites and club rooms.

Zemurray, meanwhile, had literally kept in the sun, while putting to use personal experience, gargantuan enterprise, and what he terms "what little personality I got." He had not grown rusty or remote in his personal, vivid acquaintance with the everyday people—peasants, businessmen, banana jobbers, politicians, professors, and approximately all or any others, whether in Honduras, New Orleans, or Louisiana at large. He had instituted his lifelong and absolute rule of never addressing a public gathering and never permitting himself to be formally lionized. His vivid interest in specific people and specific works—the trait that had caused him, for example, to shun a bankers' banquet in New Orleans while talking trade and home problems with nondescript tung-nut gatherers at Hammond, or to avoid a special reception in his honor at Havana while sitting aboard ship discussing the handling of manifest documents with a lowly ship's purser—had engendered many advantages over the "big business man" in

Boston. So, too, had Zemurray's highly personal and exceptional quality of almost passionate modesty. However unique or baffling, the latter trait had dealt a great many signal advantages to the new managing director. For one thing, it had enabled him to keep in accurate touch with the farm workers, transportation laborers, and ultimate consumers who actually keep the banana industry ticking. Repeatedly, on inspection tours of tropical properties, Victor Cutter, because of unwieldy commitments of time, had been obliged to pass up invitations from the everyday *tropicos* who had actually done most to make possible his success story. Thus he found himself speaking (in excellent Spanish, to be sure) to the Rotary Club at the nearest capital while far out on Hernandez's banana farm a fried chicken dinner grew cold.

In a similar situation Zemurray invariably took the fried chicken dinner and let the Rotary Club get cold. At the chicken dinner, he would listen thoughtfully and sympathetically to all conversation, including lengthy descriptions of the baby's colic or the local news about catfish. Indeed, as required, he would view the baby, mix the drinks, and help clear away the dishes.

In the tropics, Cutter more or less of necessity traveled by private car or private train. Zemurray was as likely as not to travel by muleback, or to rise before dawn and walk over miles and miles of sodden banana plantings, setting a pace that few men could keep up with.

All in all, Cutter, like his Boston colleagues, did not comprehend Samuel Zemurray. He was considerably baffled by the latter's viewpoints. His bewilderment increased when he heard that Zemurray had been living for weeks at a time on nothing but figs; or that Zemurray was taking a "fast cure" for twenty days; or that Zemurray had been seen standing on his head beside a shade tree in the process of proving (or disproving) that inversion benefits the digestion. Victor Cutter considered such actions "queer." Samuel Zemurray

considered and committed them as rational experiments justified on the ground that you cannot know without trying.

Under Victor Cutter the company had lost its pioneer
spirit. As Andrew Preston would have said, it had lost its
"Git up an' git." Simply because he was the company's head,
Cutter embodied the softness and deterioration of the whole
company as it got more and more out of touch with the
real problems of the banana frontier.

Very probably Samuel Zemurray understood Victor Cutter
and the problems of United Fruit a great deal better than
Cutter understood Zemurray or the unique success of the
latter's enterprises. The *gran hombre* from the Ulua appraised
United Fruit and the banana trade generally as victims, at
least in considerable part, of curable and avoidable ailments.

One of these ailments was the evident fact that the great
banana company was beginning to circle and stumble in
corporate indirectness, not sufficiently mindful of the fact
that, however big it is, a banana company is still a succession
of farms tied by roads, railroads, and ship lines to specific and
exacting markets. Zemurray also believed that United Fruit
had suffered needlessly from the policy of sitting on the cash
and counting capital reserves while the vital productive assets
of the trade were left to flounder. Along with this conviction, Samuel Zemurray felt an urgent and personal obligation to his own trade and to Honduras. He contended that as
a big business and the decider of banana destinies, United
Fruit was obliged to shape and effect a sequence of actions
and a charter of principles revised to keep pace with the
times and the changing needs of an industry.

Specifically, as a big international corporation, United Fruit
was now obliged to face squarely and answer effectively two
principal challenges of the times. The first was the feat of
acknowledging in specific work as well as in words the sovereignty of the Caribbean governments that were directly concerned; to prove by specific and practical dealings that the

good of the banana trade and the good of the publics of the banana-growing countries are identical. The second challenge was vitally related to the first. In several countries, particularly Honduras, Costa Rica, and Jamaica, labor markets and national economies had become excessively dependent on the banana crop. Experience had clearly proved that only superior lands can produce bananas profitably and that there are not enough superior banana lands to go around; *i.e.*, to provide major farm populations the opportunities to grow the crop. Therefore, the big banana growers, particularly United Fruit, were squarely confronted with the obligation to support or to assist effectively in developing other sound crops in areas which bananas could no longer support.

These added up to a truly man-sized job, which the new managing director proposed to tackle in his own way and without Victor Cutter. But first there were specific organizational details to attend to. When Victor Cutter resigned after eight and one-half years as president of United Fruit, the aging Francis Russell Hart, son of Thomas Mandell Hart, and distinguished scholar of Boston, succeeded him. But the managing director proceeded as boss and conditioner to an ailing giant.

Zemurray set about to reorganize his management. He appointed as manager of the crucially important Honduran division his old Cuyamel associate and practical diplomat, Walter Turnbull, born in Mexico and seasoned in Brazil, Honduras, and points south. For executive vice-president he chose Arthur A. Pollan, a Texan still in his forties, who had spent a quarter of a century in the banana trade, beginning as a train dispatcher and graduating successively to port manager, assistant manager of two divisions, manager of the Guatemala division, manager of the Colombian division, and, finally, to supervisor of all of United Fruit's banana divisions.

Other Zemurray appointees included Joseph Kelleher, Cuyamel's expert on shipping and railroad operations; Joe

Montgomery, a lawyer from Louisiana; H. Harris Robson, Australian-born ship's engineer who had already served as United Fruit's supervisor of ship maintenance. There were also a number of promising young leaders: Reginald Hamer, a native of Mexico City, who succeeded Pollan as manager of the Colombian division; William Taillon, a Dakota agronomist who was experimenting with new techniques of banana farming; Jack Kansas, a youthful commissary expert and statistician; Martin Connolly, with a creditable past and promising future as a tropical administrator; Dr. V. C. Dunlap, a distinguished Cornell pathologist and soil expert; the scholarly Harry Laiser, Zemurray's assistant in earlier Cuyamel days; John Werner, east side New Yorker and the able young leader of Fruit Dispatch; and Robert Howley, Boston messenger boy who was working his way to the top of Tropical Radio.

These were some of the men on whom Zemurray relied for assistance in reorganizing United Fruit. The problems which faced them called for prompt action. The situation on the banana fronts was thought-provoking—for any banana man.

CHAPTER FOURTEEN

THE NEW REGIME

IN 1933 there had been a sharp reduction of banana acreage in harvest. Between 1930, the year of highest banana profits, and 1933, commonly reckoned as the depth of the depression, the total commercial plantings had fallen from 335,000 acres to 260,000. United Fruit's plantings alone had declined from 190,000 to 130,000.

During 1932 Honduras had far outdistanced all other banana-growing countries by exporting nearly 28 million bunches, and Jamaica held second place. By 1933, Panama's banana exports had dropped to an eighth of the Honduras output, and Nicaraguan exports had fallen even lower. Guatemala's production was also down, and Costa Rica's exports amounted to only 4,350,000 bunches. For the first time the Cuban banana crop led the once decisive Costa Rican crop.

The Mexican exports had risen to 4½ million bunches. Colombia remained the foremost banana-exporting nation of South America, but rather suddenly Brazil entered the trade with a 1932 tally of almost 7 million bunches, practically all of which were marketed by independent shippers.

Throughout the 1920's several United States companies had dealt in Mexican-grown bananas: Standard Fruit through its subsidiary, the Mexican-American Fruit and Steamship Corporation; Joseph Di Giorgio through direct purchases from Mexican planters; and Cuyamel Fruit, which for a time operated in Mexico, through the Ulua Development Company.

Most of Mexico's banana lands are in widely separated valleys. The railroads permit direct rail shipments to Mexico City and other domestic markets, as well as limited exports to the Southwest United States. Banana prices in Mexico had remained exceptionally low—from fifteen to twenty-five dollars a ton when shipside prices in the United States were forty to sixty dollars a ton.

Late in the 1920's local unions of farmers, principally those with small acreages, joined a central banana producers' league (*Liga de Productores de Roatan*). The co-operative association included a group of boatmen who were to transport the fruit down river to seaport and a group of stevedores who were to load it aboard ships. In the Oaxaca–Vera Cruz region two similar organizations were founded to grow and sell bananas for Mexican markets. Still another union, *La Nacional Plantera*, was established in 1931 to grow and export bananas from the Chiapas valley. Significantly, Mexican banana growers' co-operatives came back strongly during the last two years of the Second World War, and they continue to gain.

These and similar organizations had their ups and downs. In Jamaica a producers' co-operative was founded in 1929 but failed after three years. Late in the 1920's the *Cooperativa Bananera Costaricanse* was established. This association of 800 farmer members sold their harvests through the big banana companies.

Few of the newly established independent banana companies succeeded. The high mortality rates of earlier decades seemed to be returning. Much of the reason for this could be traced to depression price ranges, of which the 1933 average port price of graded fruit was typical. The average of $2.63 a hundredweight or $52.60 a ton was fourteen percent under the prevailing shipside prices of 1920. From this $2.63 per hundred pounds were subtractable all agricultural costs; losses from storm or plant diseases; depreciation of equipment; the cost of reaping, grading, and hauling to seaports; stowage charges; and the inevitable weight losses which refrigerated shipping causes.

It was obvious that greater efficiency was a life-or-death issue for the trade. Without any really convincing exceptions, all the early co-operatives had failed in their attempts at organization and had no trained merchandising representatives. Even the established companies, with the benefit of years of experience, were having serious difficulties.

Zemurray at United Fruit was confronted by many problems requiring immediate action. Ships needed overhauling, and the communications systems had to be co-ordinated. Rail shipment, truckage, and hauling of bananas called for a series of continuing improvements and required the services of skilled engineers, transportation agents, and "expediters."

Bananas also had to be sold. Jobbers remained the principal distributors, and increasing numbers of these were building costly ripening rooms with elaborate controls to regulate temperature and humidity so that green bananas purchased at port auction or delivered by railroad cars could be stored and ripened prior to delivery to the retailers. Since banana sales involved rapid and frequent turnovers, a regular replacement of supply was necessary. This in turn necessitated a well-co-ordinated system of farming and shipping.

After Zemurray had plunged into action, earnings began to increase. Even during 1933 United Fruit was able to pay a two-dollar dividend. Though conditions in the trade were far from completely satisfactory, there were enough indications of improvement to allow at least a cautious hopefulness.

During the early 1930's the unprecedented depression economy continued to focus the attention of fruit men on several unique characteristics of the banana trade. One of these was that there can be no such thing as mass production or assembly-line procedures applied to banana farms. For bananas are one of the most unpredictable and eccentric of all crops. They require extremely fertile, well-drained soil, with abundant, evenly distributed rainfall. They are a frail crop, easily destroyed by wind, flood, drought, or "cold snaps." The plants blacken and die at temperatures far above freezing. There have never been enough really suitable banana lands to maintain the trade as even a relatively permanent one-crop agriculture. An unfortunately large proportion of the earlier plantings had been placed in unsuitable soils or locations. That had resulted in short-lived plantings and premature abandonments, with the inevitable losses of both jobs and capital investments.

These risks had been heightened by the sudden ravages of Panama Disease, the virulent root fungus which had forced out of bearing thousands of acres of bananas. Many more thousands of acres of plantings that had borne salable bananas in earlier times were no longer able to bear fruit good enough to satisfy the ever more exacting market demands.

The need for more fertile and better protected sites for banana growing was more and more urgent. Samuel Zemurray and his men looked about for farther and better lands. In the far Chiriqui province of Panama the first major banana farm center on the Pacific shore of Central America was already in successful bearing. Now still more pioneering was in order. Soil chemists, location engineers, and experienced farmers roamed far inland from the eastern coast, crossed the central mountain ranges, and tested several areas on the Pacific slopes. It was rough, strenuous work and a prelude to one of the most expensive and ambitious ventures in the clearing and reclamation of jungle land.

This second pioneering period was still in the making when a major natural calamity intervened. Singatoka, the same ruining leaf blight which had nearly wiped out banana plantings in tropical Pacific islands a quarter of a century before, was discovered in the West Indies during 1934. Early in 1935 the devastating round spore, carried by the wind or air currents halfway around the equator, began to appear in the banana fields. It was first identified in Trinidad by Wardlaw of the island's Imperial College of Agriculture. Next the fungus was reported on the island of St. Kitts, then in coastal Jamaica, then in western Cuba. The important banana lands of Central America were obviously in its path.

Pathologists knew practically nothing about singatoka other than to rename it sigatoka. They had observed the cycle of the disease—the appearance of the first blotches on leaf surfaces of the plants and the spreading of the blight until soon the huge leaves began to twist and turn gray, as if burned by fire. They had noticed that certain species of plantains were resistant to the blight. The yellow Gros Michels, however, were most vulnerable to the fungus destroyer, and these were the standard commercial bananas.

Banana shippers were the first to learn the bad news. Although the diseased plants eventually wither and die, in the early stage of the blight they continue to nurture their fruit stems. Even to expert eyes, the fruit in green harvest seems to be quite normal. But the fungus destruction of leaf surfaces robs the fruit bunch of essential nutriment, which results in premature ripening or yellowing of the green cut bananas. When the fruit reached the market ports, shippers saw, to their consternation, that banana cargoes were arriving fully ripe and therefore in unmarketable condition.

The flight of the spores soon reached Central America, and in the important banana lands of Honduras sigatoka appeared and spread like wind-blown fire. At the end of 1935, United Fruit and, indeed, the entire banana industry were face to face with disaster. Samuel Zemurray, who had succeeded the ailing Mr. Hart as president of United Fruit, was facing the most formidable dilemma in all the dilemma-crowded history of the banana trade. He and his men were fighting for the life of a great industry.

Pathologists worked frantically to devise measures to curb the destroyer. Banana workers sprayed test plots of the stricken plants with all kinds of chemical solutions. They chopped down infected plantings only to see them replaced by new growths that yielded even more readily to the ruining blight.

Sigatoka swept on through the great banana valleys of Honduras, burning and twisting tens of thousands of acres of unexcelled plantings. Then from the lands of the Ulua the spores blew north into Guatemala and south into Costa Rica, ravaging large and small plantings, company and independent farms alike.

There was no known way of applying chemical spray quickly and uniformly to all of the huge and tangled leaf surfaces of banana plants. But this had to be done. The spores could not be kept out of the fields, for they traveled with the wind. Pathologists in airplanes had held treated slides out the plane windows. Even at 5000 feet the slides became coated with the floating spores of the *cercospera musae*.

From Honduras, where sigatoka had struck hardest, came the first small promise of a workable defense against the disease. At La Lima, Dr. V. C. Dunlap, of the United Fruit tropical staff, reported cautiously that he had tried out a spray solution that had evidenced some measure of effectiveness against the fungus. After several field tests Dunlap and his associates had reason to believe that the fungicide Bordeaux mixture, composed of copper sulphate, lime powder, and water, sprayed repeatedly on the foliage arrested the blight. Obviously the difficulty lay in the problems of devising and installing suitable spray equipment.

United Fruit engineers, headed by Hartley Rowe, joined the pathologists and farmers in their experiments with a new type of spray system for banana farms. This included elaborate, centrally located pumping centers which mixed the spray solution automatically and employed Diesel-driven pumps to force it at high pressure into metal pipes leading from the central plants to piping that girded the banana fields. At suitable intervals the pipes were provided with outlets or pet cocks to which workmen attached rubber hose. These hose were topped with spray guns which converted the liquid spray into a high-flung, soaking vapor bath.

After many failures, the spraying system, which at first resembled one of the more fanciful creations of Rube Goldberg, became workable. Permanent installations appeared on thousands of acres of blight-stricken banana farms. Spray teams composed of one nozzle man and one hose carrier, self-styled *chemicos*, began working the fields, treating an average of four or five acres in a day, and covering the leaf surface of every banana plant with a protective coating of the fungicide.

The experiment was saving banana crops. The directors of United Fruit hastily approved the appropriation of millions of dollars for installing permanent spray systems. This called for training additional thousands of farm workers, technical foremen, pipe fitters, and maintenance men and for purchasing millions of feet of galvanized piping and thousands of pumps and motors. One hundred or more spray "centrals," each serving from 400 to 1400 acres of plantings, were constructed, and crops were sprayed, according to the severity of the sigatoka blight, two or three times a month. Within a year, more than 40,000 acres of sigatoka-infected plantings were returned to bearing.

In the earlier stages of the sigatoka invasion United Fruit established an airfield at La Lima and instituted what was then the largest and most audacious venture in airplane dusting of a farm crop. Planes flew low over the banana fields, usually at dawn while the foliage was still wet with dew, and "gunned" powder mixtures of copper sulphate and lime over the fields, frequently scraping the tips of the plants and landing with running gears wrapped tightly with banana leaves. After the pipe-line spray systems were installed, however, plane dusting was abandoned.

But the plague was not entirely checked. It continued to spread into the valleys of Mexico; throughout much of Jamaica and other islands in the West Indies; into Guatemala, Nicaragua, and southward into Panama and Colombia.

The United Fruit Company carried on its far-flung and expensive fight against this powerful enemy of its principal crop. For a time it fought alone. Most other banana growers simply waited, like the fabulous man of Bombay who thought syphilis just went away. But sigatoka does not just go away, and many more banana farms withered. Some returned to jungle. A number of outlying farms, whose owners lacked the money or the necessary water supply for installing the expensive and bulky spray systems, experimented desperately but not very effectively with spraying banana plants by hand. Others tried pack or tractor spraying.

By 1937, however, United Fruit had substantially won its warfare against sigatoka. Spray systems were working on approximately 75,000 acres of the best plantings. But the company needed to do more than re-establish its own properties. First in Honduras, then in Guatemala and Costa Rica, it provided independent farmers with loans needed to restore their plantings and equip their fields with permanent spray systems. The citizen farmers were to repay the long-term and low-interest loans with specified deductions from the price of bananas sold to the company. Samuel Zemurray welcomed this opportunity for a practical expression of his belief that interdependence was a fundamental principle of the industry and for convincing proof that United Fruit was not seeking monopoly in banana production. By 1940 United Fruit had advanced loans, materials, and engineers for rehabilitating 13,000 acres of privately owned banana lands.

Though the press and radio had said little about it, the fact remained that United Fruit's conquest of sigatoka had been one of man's most successful struggles against a major fungus enemy. And it was, moreover, inaugurating a new era in banana technology. The mechanical spraying system requires about one ton of permanent installation and an additional capital investment of at least $150 for every acre of banana planting. It also necessitates a still greater development of drainage and irrigation. But United Fruit's stand against sigatoka had saved the American banana industry from certain ruin. It had brought about a working co-operation among banana men, who more convincingly than ever before had banded together against a common enemy that had very nearly succeeded in destroying a great industry.

Dry seasons in the banana countries are usually losing seasons. For fifty years or longer, surface irrigation had been used in such tropical dry lands as the Canary Islands, northern Colombia, and some of the arid valleys of Jamaica. During 1924, Zemurray, then head of Cuyamel, had begun a program of large-scale irrigation of Honduran banana lands which, despite their comparatively heavy annual rainfall, suffer from intermittent dry spells. Three years later, on the other side of the Ulua River, United Fruit had followed suit.

Experience had proved that because of its immense leaf structure, the banana plant benefits most from overhead irrigation, provided the irrigation can be made to resemble the tropical rainfall to which the plant is accustomed. Determinedly, the Zemurray command began to install systems for overhead irrigation in additional thousands of acres of plantings. This new departure involved a succession of slender steel towers, each twenty-five feet high, each an upright pipe into which water is pumped from a central main. The mains, in turn, are fed from pumping stations where batteries of Diesel-driven pumps maintain pipe-line pressures of about 200 pounds per square inch. Vast quantities of water are drawn up from artesian wells or taken from open rivers and distributed through networks of flumes and cement-lined surface canals. Atop each tower is a riser, resembling a fire-hose nozzle, which is rotated by a water-pressure motor. Turning slowly, the riser throws a spray over a three-acre circle. This drenches the crowded wilderness of leaves and fruit stems and practically assures uniform yields.

It is strange on cloudless days to see banana workers wearing raincoats or carrying umbrellas as hissing jets of water splinter in the sunlight and spray down on the jungle of leaves below, forming rainbows over the dark-green fields.

By 1939 the United Fruit Company had put into operation the most expensive and the most highly mechanized installation in agricultural history. Hundreds of horsepower and tons of equipment were allotted to each producing acre. The building of overhead irrigation and permanent spray systems proceeded apace until the Second World War made unavailable the necessary tonnages of metal pipe and other construction materials.

Bananas were no longer, as the early traders had thought, the manna of the jungle. No other major crop required so heavy a capital investment. And no other major crop repaid to those who cultivated it such rapid increases in average yields. In the earlier days when men simply slashed bush and jungle, planted banana roots, circled the first tender shoots with a machete, and left the rest to time and nature, market yields of 100 bunches per year were considered satisfactory, and yields of 150 bunches bountiful. Gradually, as methods of planting and drainage improved, yields of better lands had climbed to 200 bunches. However, with permanent spray installations in use, and with instantly controllable overhead

irrigation, average yields increased to 350 or 400 big bunches
("counts"), and bunch weights grew from averages of fifty
to seventy pounds to eighty or a hundred pounds.

Technology in banana farming changed accordingly. Virtually overnight, tens of thousands of machete swingers and
other primitive laborers became spray men, mechanics, pipe
fitters, tractor operators, shop workers, carpenters, plumbers,
welders, metal smiths, or workers in other skilled trades. From
these ranks, in turn, emerged an ever-growing number of
professional workers—pharmacists, laboratory technicians,
nurses, lawyers, engineers, and administrative executives.
Banana pay rolls in 1939 listed more than 250 professions and
trades, from surgeons and airline pilots to pipe fitters.

Banana wages were made proportionate to the rising levels
of skills. On lands that stretch from southern Mexico to Ecuador, more than 100,000 workers had proved a degree of
adaptability in work of which any nation or people could
well be proud. And contrary to the assumptions of a great
many economists, the mechanization of a once primitive agriculture had not replaced men with machines. Plantations that
had previously employed about 150 men per thousand acres
of producing land now employed to 200 or 220. The rosters
of the United Fruit Company showed an increase from about
55,000 before the installation of the new machinery to 70,000
after it had been accomplished, and the estimated total of all
banana employment had risen from 130,000 in 1930 to 165,000
in 1935.

The trade was earning again. Dividend rates and stock
quotations were once again rising. Samuel Zemurray's leadership of the United Fruit Company had been outstandingly
successful. Even as the number of unemployed increased in
the United States and as the WPA struggled to reduce the
length of bread lines, the banana lands of Central America
were substantially free from unemployment.

But there were other difficulties. Sigatoka continued to spread into the outlying areas of the banana companies' holdings. Mexico, Colombia, and Jamaica still suffered from the disease which had wiped out or was in the process of destroying at least 75,000 acres of citizen-owned banana plantings. In Central America, United Fruit extended its work in helping farmers re-establish banana plantings that sigatoka had laid waste.

In the United States, Canada, and the British Isles demands for bananas were increasing. Central America was being more and more clearly proved the banana stronghold of the world. But the need for new and better banana lands was obvious. After the first excitement of fighting the ruinous fungus had abated and sigatoka had been brought under at least partial control, Zemurray and his men continued the search for new territories.

During the late 1920's and again during the early 1930's, Henry T. Heyl, manager of Compania Agricola de Guatemala, United Fruit's Guatemala division, had exported small quantities of bananas grown in the western part of the country by independent farmers. This undertaking had defied one of the fundamental principles of the trade, for that section was comparatively dry. The fruit was reaped and hauled by mule pack or cart to the nearest station of the International Railways of Central America. Then the fruit was drawn by train over the steep spine of Guatemala 300 miles to Puerto Barrios, where it was loaded on banana ships and carried to market. Old-timers among banana men knew that such a fantastically roundabout system could never work, for it involved first of all planting the fruit on lands that everyone knew were far too dry to grow good bananas. It also involved an unreasonably long rail haul of the green fruit over one of the most heavily graded railroads in the hemisphere.

But the big banana firm was once more in a pioneering mood. Engineers and woodsmen prowled over sparsely settled hillsides and valleys of western Guatemala, testing the deep volcanic ash soils, measuring the rivers, creeks, and underground water sources. It was remote Indian country, dotted with occasional coffee *fincas* and marked with ancient roads and trails on which the surveying parties sometimes met pack trains of mules carrying bundles of merchandise bound for inland stores and cantinas. More frequently the group met Indian burden bearers plodding along—squat, powerfully muscled men who carried enormous back packs of pottery, baskets, produce, or wooden cages piled high with home-made pottery.

The banana pioneers established a colony at Tiquisate and enlisted Indian workers for their helpers. They marked out railroad sites and drew charts and blueprints for farm sites, reservoirs, canals, pump centers, commissaries, and airfields. Rapidly they began to build a new banana division with a work force of some 4000 local Indians, many of whom had never seen a banana. Company planes flew in men and supplies. A hospital and a clinic were completed, and sanitation squads went to work. Railroads, homes, clubs, stores, roads, farms, irrigation systems, schoolhouses, and playing fields appeared and multiplied.

The new Tiquisate division was unique in that its loose volcanic soil quickly absorbed the moisture provided by the new irrigation system and its 18,000 acres of banana fields came to bearing only ten months after the bits had been planted. Tiquisate became the first completely mechanized banana farm. Its lands were latticed by 400 miles of roadways, and tractors and tractor-drawn carts replaced the long caravans of banana mules.

Meanwhile United Fruit was building a still larger division on the remote Pacific shore of Costa Rica. For this work an entire railroad system (the Southern Railway of Costa Rica) had to be constructed and two seaports established. Once more location men pushed into the jungles. Experienced guides got lost in the thorny brush. The first engineering parties had to stay close to the river lines, for there were few trails and no easy route to the territory from either land or sea. The banana men sent thousands of tons of machinery and building supplies into the area by airplane. They dismantled tractors, motors, automobiles, and other heavy equipment to fit into the holds of the planes and reassembled the machinery in the far jungles.

At Quepos Point, a coastal Indian capital in pre-Columbian times, ships loaded with construction supplies were anchored far offshore and their cargoes were landed by lighters. Woodsmen from the hills of Nicaragua cleared valley forests. Planes carried workers to and from the locations, landing and taking off on narrow strips of beaches while tides were at ebb and wild hogs usually asleep in the forests beyond. When the tide came in pilots and passengers would sprint desperately to board and take off before the rising water caught the planes. Pilots, engineers, accountants, doctors, and clerks—all grimy and bearded—lived in screened shacks, worked all day, played poker and drank Scotch through the night, and departed at dawn to work again.

Within two years the hot wilderness was transformed into additional thousands of acres of banana farms. Now there were railroads and tramlines, hospitals and schools, stores and whole villages of well-built and attractive homes. During 1939 the Southern Railroad of Costa Rica threaded through wild lands to the new Pacific harbors.

In this modern development, however, many of the older ways persisted. Since the soil was too wet for the widespread use of tractors, mules were again being led into the fields. Dragline operators continued to swear and guzzle beer while scooping out huge irrigation canals and occasionally sinking almost out of sight in the blue mud. *Hombres* and their *mujeres* still gathered at the markets to watch the coming and going of the planes and to examine the outbound trainloads and shiploads of bananas. Wandering marimba players accompanied dancers on the village squares, and weary harvesters roused themselves from afternoon siestas to dance. Location engineers continued to sip Scotch, shake their graying heads, and marry young wives, while railroad foremen continued to demand that visiting celebrities keep the hell off the main lines so that the banana trains could get through. Farmers continued to boast of next month's or next year's yields.

There were the inevitable poker fests, the swimming-pool parties, the tennis matches, and the pell-mell rugby tussles that the *tropicos* call *futbol*. There was, finally, the inevitable talk of bananas: "fourteen-hand bunches . . . four hundred counts per acre . . . hand supplying . . . pick-up trains . . . number 19 loading spot . . . lottery tickets in sevens . . . another short one . . . iguanas in the riser nozzles . . . fruit's too big for the mules . . . fruit's too thin . . . fruit's too thick . . ." Years were hurrying by. The earth was shrinking. A globe-circling war was plainly brewing. But there were the bananas, and there always will be.

CHAPTER FIFTEEN

THE WAR AND AFTER

ON SUNNY JAMAICAN HILLSIDES Negro plowmen guided their worn wooden plows drawn by heavy Brahmin bulls through rows of green banana plants. Some five hundred miles away, in Guatemalan valleys, rawboned, khaki-dressed farm hands from the Dakotas, Iowa, and New York directed powerful caterpillar tractors across the sloping fields. Along hundreds of miles of Caribbean coast line, teams of native workers swung razor-sharp machetes or led rope-linked processions of banana mules from the fields toward the loading spots and the stacks of newly harvested green bananas. In Cuba, thousands of men and women cut and stacked segments of sugar cane, bundled them into the trains, and watched the locomotives rumble away to the mills. In almost every Central American nation, exploration parties of guides, mule men, and prospectors, loaded down with bedding rolls, fire-blackened skillets, and cumbersome surveying instruments, waded through swamps and pushed through brush and forest growth as they charted the slopes and the rivers and tested the soils.

The great majority of these people were employees of United Fruit. In only slightly more than a third of a century the company had become the largest farm enterprise in the Americas. Between 1930 and 1940 it had paid approximately 40 million dollars in taxes to the Caribbean governments, 200 million dollars in wages to citizens of those countries, and 140 million dollars for the purchase of bananas and other products of the Central American tropics. Other banana firms had added perhaps one-third to each of these totals. In this same period United Fruit had received from its combined operations an average return of five and a half percent on its direct capital investment. The figure was close to the average for the trade as a whole during the 1940's.

United Fruit had built and was maintaining eighty-one schools for more than 3000 children of its employees. North Americans and Central Americans were working together in the same offices, farms, and shops. There were at least ten citizen workers for every North American, and there were increasing numbers of native overseers and other executives.

In 1940 roughly one-half of the total national incomes of such countries as Honduras and Costa Rica came from the banana companies. Throughout much of Central America the financial dependence of entire nations on a mere 400 or 500 square miles of banana fields was a dangerously one-sided economy. Except for bananas and coffee practically all the exports of the lowland tropics had fallen off.

Indigo, once the leading crop of Central America, had been largely replaced by chemically derived dyes. Vanilla, though native to lower Mexico, had become the principal export of Madagascar. Most of the world's supplies of the staple tropical spices were being grown in the Netherlands Indies or in South Pacific colonies of Portugal and France and marketed by powerful cartels. Cuba remained the sugar bowl of half the earth, but Central America's sugar crops were not sufficient to meet even the small domestic needs. Coconut and many other valuable oil palms are indigenous to the Caribbean countries, but because of a cheaper labor supply and superior plantation establishments, the Netherlands Indies, French Indo-China, and other Pacific areas were supplying most of the billions of pounds of palm oils consumed in the United States. The Pacific tropics and India were supplying practically all of the 300 to 500 million prounds of tropical fibers which the United States was consuming yearly, and Malaya and the Netherlands Indies together were supplying somewhat more than 95 percent of all United States demands for natural rubber, by all odds our largest import, already exceeding 500,000 tons annually and rapidly growing as American factories continued to make about three-fourths of all rubber goods used in the world.

The cocoa situation was not much better. The United States is the great chocolate market, with its imports of about 620 million pounds yearly. But the greater part of this was coming from Africa, and, during a decade when at least twelve countries of the American tropics were struggling to set up minimum wage laws, cocoa production was booming in Nigeria, the Cameroons, Sierra Leone, the Ivory Coast, Ceylon, and Java—places where native labor was cheap.

These were only some of the problems which faced any entrepreneur who might have wished to grow other tropical crops which the American tropics could well have provided— bamboos, medicinal plants, citronella, lemon grass, volatile oils, cork, teak, rosewood, rotenone, and various tropical fruits.

Between 1920 and 1940 the principal imports of the United States came from tropical countries. Less than six percent of these imports, however, came from the American tropics. There were many reasons for this serious lack of balance, not the least of which were inadequate enterprise and insufficient research.

The countries of the American tropics are agrarian nations

with some of the richest soils in the world. They are also the homelands of at least 30 million people who live on lands unsuitable for growing bananas. The great majority of these people are farmers with small holdings on the mesas or along the jungle edge. There are many tropical crops that can be grown more effectively on small farms than on large plantations. It had been well proved that rubber, tropical fibers, volatile oils, palm oils, drug crops, spices, and other products could be grown economically on small farms. Such enterprises, however, usually necessitate a preliminary government-financed research, the distribution of free or cheap seed, some sort of technical instruction, and publicly owned or co-operatively owned processing centers.

Many Americans became aware in 1940 that essential United States industries were dependent for necessary tropical supplies on Far Eastern sources that were immediately threatened by Japan and separated from our shores by such vast distances that our Navy, or all other navies combined, could not defend the territories from a powerful aggressor.

The banana trade was in no position to remedy this situation singlehanded, but Samuel Zemurray and his men were determined to try. Zemurray explained his motive in such an effort as one of "enlightened selfishness."

During his first seven years as head of United Fruit, Samuel Zemurray had helped signally in the launching of what banana men from Guatemala to Ecuador were already terming the Zemurray era. There was no reasonable doubt that the social as well as the economic structure of the banana trade had been improved memorably under Zemurray's leadership. Because of natural enemies, the total commercial acreages of bananas had been decreased by about a fifth of the 1930 totals, but because of improved cultivation, extension of irrigation, and development of better banana lands, the over-all volume of banana exports had remained approximately staple and quality standards had improved markedly. United Fruit had

pioneered and brought to bearing three new banana-producing areas on the Pacific slope of Central America; one
at Tiquisate, Guatemala; one back of the Costa Rican Pacific
port of Capos; the third at Golfito, Costa Rica, far down
toward the South Panama frontiers—all long-term developments.

United Fruit had retired some 35,000 acres of older banana
plantings that had become hopelessly infested with Panama
Disease, the root fungus. But the lands so abandoned remained
usable for other crops, when and as desired. Practically all
United Fruit bananas were now being grown on lands regularly purchased from private owners. Research and crop
development experiments were again in progress. The company had adopted a retirement pension plan for career
employees. The tropical commissary system, so long a subject
for well-justified criticism, had been painstakingly overhauled
and was operating on profit margins lower than those
reported by any major department store, chain store, or
principal mail-order establishments in the United States.
United Fruit had taken and was holding the lead in saving
the banana crop from destruction by sigatoka, by now appropriately termed the green monster of the banana fields.

The company was dealing fairly amicably with growing
forces of union labor, and by logical processes of upgrading
wages in terms of required skills, *i.e.*, as spray men, pump
men, metal workers, pump tenders, tractor operators, carpenters, auto and Diesel mechanics, stevedores, etc., the
company had raised the average banana wage, as current in
1930, by at least forty percent. The company was permitting
native shops to compete with its commissaries. Throughout
most of its operating divisions it had substantially improved
housing standards for workers. Schools, hospitals, and medical
services had been extensively improved and modernized. Two
splendidly equipped new hospitals were being commissioned

in western Costa Rica. Distinguished progress was being made in field sanitation and preventive medicine.

Profit earnings and dividends were becoming conservative and staple. Bribery in tropical relations had been effectively banned. Without any noteworthy exception, over-all relations with Caribbean governments were improving.

But despite the progress and benefits of the enlightened selfishness, a number of faults remained. Though reasonably well chosen, some of the tropical managers persisted in various actions and attitudes that were not invariably enlightened. The home office administration remained considerably in advance of management policies current in some, though not all, of the tropical divisions. In the tropics there remained certain factors of snobbery, discrimination, and jungle-edge bureaucracy that impeded progress and required further remedies. In the tropics the ratio of citizen employees to *Norteamericanos* was approximately ten to one, but in some instances native workers were still being retarded in deserved promotions and the social habits in some of the company towns were not so democratic as they might and should have been. The Zemurray regime faced these facts.

All these were, of course, common human failings, and on the whole they were waning gradually as the new leadership kept trying to remedy them. Even the severest of company critics were obliged to admit that the advent of sigatoka and other natural calamities, including the tragic incubation of another world war, had impeded and delayed these and other phases of tropical house cleaning. In any case the Zemurray command had worked hard and for the most part effectively to keep a big company and an uniquely important industry apace with changing times. The most serious gap in the entire administration was the fact that United Fruit had not done enough about developing alternative crops to be grown by farm citizens of the banana fronts, particularly in those areas where bananas could no longer be a profitable crop. Bananas generally were still too much in the ever-perilous camp of a one-crop agriculture. But by 1940, as war clouds darkened over all tropical countries, greater needs and motivations for better diversified tropical agriculture were at last materializing. Unfortunately, a world conflagration was apparently required before government and policy leaders could discern a rudimentary need that Zemurray and other banana men had seen clearly for years. Unfortunately, too, the fortunes of war imposed gravest difficulties on all the banana-growing countries, along with most other countries.

During 1940 the United States government had begun to lease some of the larger and better equipped banana ships for emergency defense duty. Shipping shortages began to reduce the volume of Caribbean trade.

Costa Rica became the first Central American nation to declare war on Japan. In rapid succession all the countries of the Caribbean entered the war as allies of the United States against the Axis. From Washington the Maritime Commission and War Shipping Administration called to government service all important banana ships. These ships ferried troops, planes, and munitions to Hawaii, the imperiled Philippines, Australia, and other war fronts.

From its Great White Fleet and its British-charter Elder and Fyffes line, United Fruit sent a total of 113 ships to war, of which forty-two were lost to enemy action. Fast refrigerated ships were and are an imperative need of combat forces. Such craft could not be built quickly by the rapidly expanded war industries, and United Fruit had available more fast and refrigerated merchant tonnage than any other American shipping line.

After the American entry into the war banana imports fell to the lowest levels since 1899. Only a few of the older ships, principally those without refrigeration and with fuel capacities too small for convoy duty, remained to carry fruit. Runs were limited to the nearer Southern and Pacific ports. Of the approximately one hundred cargo ships which United Fruit continued to operate under contract with the United States government, only sixteen carried bananas.

Bananas soon became the scarcest of major food crops. During 1942, 1943, and most of 1944, when they were unobtainable throughout much of the United States, an average of 75,000 tons of bananas rotted in the fields of Central America every month. That was one of the greatest wastes of food in history. Under the circumstances it was unavoidable. The nation was fighting for its life, and ships were desperately needed for combat supply.

In the tropics, meanwhile, growers struggled to keep their best plantings alive in spite of shortages of copper spraying compounds, machinery, and other necessary equipment. But the bearing acreages of the banana fields dropped rapidly. Now those tropical crops which had been so long neglected became important products of the banana fronts.

During the first ninety days of 1942 the Japanese armies had swept over more than 2 million square miles of tropical or subtropical lands which held the world's decisive supplies of natural rubber, quinine, palm oils, tropical grass oils, abaca or Manila fiber, staple spices, and about twenty other important products. These indispensable crops were cut off from the United States and the other United Nations. The Pacific harbors were blockaded. After a half century of evasion of responsibilities for the lands and potential crops of the American tropics, the United States turned desperately to our nearest southern neighbors.

Shipping men knew that one ship in service between a Central American port and the United States can do the work of at least four or five ships in service between the United States and the Netherlands Indies. They also knew that in war the one ship is very much easier to protect. The theorists who had opposed the establishment of a better balanced agriculture for the American tropics as detrimental to the "economic balance of the Pacific" were silent now. The problem was no longer an academic one. It was a matter of waging and winning a war on which depended the destinies of scores of nations.

The banana trade entered the period of war-sponsored agriculture with a crop called abaca—*musa textilis*. On January 3, 1942, United Fruit signed a contract with the Defense Supplies Corporation whereby the banana company gave without charge to the United States government its Panama seedbed of this bananalike fiber bearer and agreed to plant without profit an initial 20,000 acres of the crop, most of which had previously been grown in the Philippines.

Early in 1942 it was evident that the Philippines could not be held. For the previous half century the Philippines, particularly Mindanao, had been producing about ninety-five percent of the annual quarter of a billion pounds of abaca ordinarily exported in international trade. Abaca fiber, commonly called Manila hemp, is used for making the strong and highly resilient ropes and hawsers that are essential to the operation of naval craft and merchant shipping. There is no substitute for the fiber, whose unique qualities, early recognized by mariners, had been influential in opening the Philippines to world trade.

This fibrous banana plant (which does not bear edible fruit) had been introduced into the American tropics by Harry T. Edwards, a plant explorer for the United States Department of Agriculture. During 1925 Edwards brought from Davao to Almirante, Panama, about 1000 abaca rhizomes and growing plants. These were set out on United Fruit Company lands in one of the many and little noticed early experiments with subsidiary crops. Through the years, the banana company maintained, recorded, and gradually increased the plantings as more rhizomes became available. When the Japanese bomb bays opened above Pearl Harbor, United Fruit had about

2100 acres of abaca in bearing—the only planting stock available in the Western Hemisphere.

This was a great new crop for the New World. Abaca culture is similar to that of bananas. In Panama, hundreds of Jamaican Negroes who had worked all their lives at growing bananas eagerly planted abaca, now that Gros Michel bananas no longer flourished on the old Almirante lands. United Fruit transferred thousands of its banana workers to abaca fields and began extensive plantings of the crop in Panama, Costa Rica, Guatemala, and Honduras.

At Almirante, United Fruit engineers designed a decortication mill for separating the fiber from the heavy stalks that are cut into four-foot "junks" with machetes and carried from field to mill by mule pack and flatcar. Before the Second World War abaca fiber grown in the Philippines by companies paying labor less than fifty cents a day had sold throughout the world at a price of about ten cents a pound. In Panama, where prevailing farm wages were perhaps three times those of the Philippines, mechanically processed Manila fiber proved to be of better quality (well above the exacting standards of the United States Navy) and no more expensive than the same fiber which had been removed and combed by hand in the Philippines and Java.

The accelerated shipbuilding program multiplied the demands for abaca fiber. Shipments of Panama-grown abaca to the United States early in 1942 checked the Japanese elation at having grabbed the original source of a material that had been so desperately needed by the United Nations' shipping.

There is good reason to believe that peacetime demands for abaca fiber may grow substantially, and there may be, consequently, a large market for Caribbean-grown abaca even after the Philippine and Javanese plantings have been restored. The Philippine yields had averaged 500 to 800 pounds of fiber per acre of planting each year. First harvests in Central America averaged over 1000 pounds of fiber per acre. Within one year this average had climbed to 1500 pounds to the acre.

Having accomplished the first mechanical processing of the crop, United Fruit began to build more decortication mills in Costa Rica, Honduras, and Guatemala and to increase the plantings of abaca. The banana countries were busy again. Steam shovels and draglines were scooping out giant irrigation canals. Workers were clearing away the jungle and burying rhizomes in shallow holes. New homes and *barricones* were rising, and rails once rusty were becoming shiny with use.

During 1945 and 1946 about 28,000 acres of the newly planted abaca were being harvested, and hundreds of tons of the strategic fibers were being shipped from tropical mills to Navy yards and busy factories. Planting stock of the crop had been distributed among the governments and several hundred citizen farmers of Central America. The world's largest banana company had transferred a world-important tropical crop halfway around the earth and established it not as a company crop but as a permanent and staple agriculture for farmers of the American tropics.

As the strongest and most experienced of tropical companies, United Fruit had men, lands, and capital with which to lead the most widespread crop-introduction program in Caribbean history. Now there was an opportunity to coordinate all the crop experiments of previous years and to build working agricultural exhibits which tropical citizens could judge for themselves and adapt to their fields.

Rubber plantations were also among the new ventures. Even though hevea and all other principal rubber-bearing plants are native to the American tropics, rubber production had for years been confined to Far Eastern lands of coolie labor. In 1923 Andrew Preston had authorized the planting of several hundred acres of native hevea on company lands near

Turrialba, Costa Rica. This project, however, was listed as a failure and discontinued. But other American firms persisted in their research with rubber plantings. In 1928 Henry Ford began to plant hevea trees in Brazil. At first the Ford experiment met with little success, but it began to show promise when its senior horticulturist, Dr. Claude Wier, grafted buds of high-yielding strains of hevea from Malaya and Sumatra to native hevea trees of the Amazon.

The Goodyear Rubber Company in 1936 established a hevea nursery at Gatun, Panama, took over the long-forsaken groves originally planted by United Fruit in Costa Rica, and began a cautious program of rubber planting. They made another planting in Guatemala.

As the threat of war grew, other companies joined in the effort to return the rubber crops to the Western Hemisphere. It became evident that the plan was a wise one when, shortly after Pearl Harbor, the Japanese seized some 8 million acres of hevea plantations in the Southwest Pacific which had been the source of more than ninety-five percent of all the rubber used in the world.

United Fruit, with its research base at La Lima, Honduras, began to establish nurseries with outputs sufficient for stocking several thousands of acres with bud-grafted and high-yielding hevea trees and supplemented these with extensive experimental plantings of castilla, the native rubber tree of Central America.

But since seven to fifteen years are required for rubber trees to reach profitable bearing, the Zemurray men thought of rubber principally as a small-farm crop which tropical citizens might eventually develop as a valuable home crop, in time providing rubber for the manufacture of heavy tires and other products for which natural rubber is still superior to synthetic. Crude rubber is not perishable, and its harvest is more or less continuous. Moreover, its cultivation does not involve a great deal of expensive machinery or equipment.

Once a small planting of the trees is in bearing, the latex can easily be harvested by a farmer and his family. With the war finished both Goodyear and Ford have moved to withdraw from Latin American rubber production. United Fruit keeps the great crop.

Just as it had experimented with rubber as a crop for independent farmers, United Fruit turned its attention to the planting and milling of rice in Honduras and Ecuador. These, like most countries of the American tropics, are rice-eating nations that had been importing most of their rice supplies from China, Burma, or Siam. In the Tenguel area of Ecuador, United Fruit assigned about 1800 acres of company-owned lands to independent farmers for rice plantings and purchased a central rice mill. Near Cortes, Honduras, the company established another mill and set aside 800 acres for plantings.

In Costa Rica and Honduras United Fruit planted derris, one of the better sources of rotenone, now the most valuable and widely used of vegetable insecticides. This root crop had been grown principally in British Malaya. The United States was importing annually more than 5 million pounds of it, and demands increased as man's struggle against insect enemies became more widespread.

In Guatemala and Honduras the banana company made trial plantings of castor beans, another important export crop of the tropics, and in Honduras the company supervised extensive plantings of tropical grasses such as citronella, lemon grass, and vetiver. These grasses, which were formerly grown in Ceylon, Java, Madagascar, and other Eastern tropics, are the sources of volatile oils used for making menthols, perfume bases, soaps, insect sprays, and numerous pharmaceutical products.

Then the banana company introduced several varieties of soybeans as local food and feed crops. Beginning with a supply of a few pounds of tropical soy seed brought from Siam,

Puerto Rico, and the Dominican Republic, United Fruit made experimental plantings of seven different species. As in most ventures of this kind, it was first necessary to build up a supply of locally grown seed. This work is still in progress.

Bamboo is still another crop offering some promise for independent farmers in the Caribbean countries. In similar latitudes of the Eastern tropics and subtropics, from Formosa and South China to Java, Siam, and India, bamboo has long been a principal crop. There are many varieties of bamboo and the various species of the giant grass can be used for building cheap but durable homes, for making roofs, fences, corrals, and livestock shelters, for landscaping, for soil anchorages, and as a ready source of pulpwood. Inexpensive and long-lasting furniture can be made of hard bamboo, and some types of the wood can be used as substitutes for iron rods in masonry and cement work and for metal pipe and tile in draining wet lands or installing makeshift waterworks. The United Fruit Company has begun to cultivate the more desirable types of bamboos and to distribute the culms to local farmers who may be interested in trying out the plantings.

During the war years the list of experimental crops grew longer and the plantings spread over 50,000 acres in Panama, Costa Rica, Honduras, Guatemala, Nicaragua, Ecuador, Colombia, and Cuba. In all these activities United Fruit had taken an introductory role. The company did not intend to grow or merchandise the new crops. It had simply prepared a series of exhibits for the benefit of tropical farmers, and early in 1943 it established a department of new crops to carry on the work. Atherton Lee, formerly director of the United States Department of Agriculture's Tropical Experiment Station at Mayaguez, Puerto Rico, and for many years a tropical crop administrator in Southern Pacific agricultural activities, was made head of this new department.

Tropical crops, even more than temperate-zone crops, require the unremitting work and planning of skilled geneticists, and the development of highly productive and resistant breeds, strains, and clones of field crops. Tropical farming continues to be threatened by flood, hurricane, and erosion far more severe than those calamities which interfere with agricultural activities in temperate zones. It must also fight against rust, rot, and disease. For these and other good reasons, tropical farming faces a difficult future. If the new crops are to endure and prosper, farmers must work with adequate tools on suitable lands and must have in addition a sound knowledge of agricultural techniques.

Some time before Pearl Harbor, Samuel Zemurray drew up plans for a technical agricultural school which might help young native farmers of Central America to qualify for leadership in the inevitable new era of tropical agriculture. He believed that it ought to be a work-and-learn school, with perhaps a plantation or large farm, centrally located in a section with a soil and climate typical of the American tropics. He also felt that the school should have a faculty of experienced geneticists and biologists from many countries and that the curriculum should include courses dealing with dairy farming, forestry, farm engineering, marketing, general health and sanitation, the cultivation of field, garden, and orchard crops, and the raising of livestock and poultry. It would have to be a free school, since many promising and deserving young men had no money for tuition. The school would prepare its students for farm work in the communities from which they came.

At Zemurray's request, the United Fruit Company adopted the plan as a corporate enterprise. The directors made an initial contribution of $500,000 for building such a school and promptly added $300,000 to the original grant. The School of Pan-American Agriculture (*Escuela Agricola Panamericana*) is the result of this action. The site chosen for the institution was a plantation, Finca Zamorana, in the high valley of the Yeguare River, about twenty-five miles from Tegucigalpa, the picturesque capital of Honduras. Here are 3500 acres of fields, pasture lands, and woodlands. The average temperatures in the region are low enough to encourage the growth of most of the staple grain and vegetable crops common to the temperate countries, yet high enough for almost all kinds of tropical crops.

The students are farm boys between the ages of sixteen and twenty-one, poor boys for the most part whose families could not otherwise have sent them to school. Entrance requirements are determined by the common school education provided by the pupil's home community. In rural Central America that is rarely more than the equivalent of the first four or five grades of public school in the United States. The prescribed course of study is for three years, with a fourth year of graduate or specialized study. The school pays all the expenses of the students, including those for medical and dental services, clothing, books, and other necessary supplies. Students spend each weekday morning observing or taking part in practical farm work and the afternoon in classrooms and laboratories. Spanish and English are the accredited languages of the school. Graduates are not encouraged to enter the service of the United Fruit Company or any other banana company, nor are they taught any of the details or problems of banana farming

In September, 1943, the *Escuela Agricola Panamericana* was opened for a preliminary or tryout year, with a student body of seventy-three young men from Mexico and the six nations of Central America. During this year the curriculum assumed a clearer definition. The morning *practica* or field demonstration was more closely related to classroom and laboratory study. Horticulture now includes a dirt-farming experience in planting the seed, tubers, rhizomes, or cuttings, and in budgrafting valuable plants. As a part of this training, each student plants, grafts, or buds a nursery collection of several hundred fruit trees which become his own property if he agrees to plant the trees on his family's farm or in his home community after his graduation. Gardening courses lead the student to the planting and management of home gardens, to the commercial production of vegetables, and to a study of their nutritive values.

In the course of each year the student works in nurseries, gardens, forests, livestock ranges, farm shops, orchards, dairy barns, and poultry pens and does further work with bridge building and road making. In a comparatively short time he becomes familiar with all the operations of a large farm.

On Columbus Day, 1944, the *Escuela Agricola Panamericana* was formally opened with a complement of about 140 students, most of them from farms of Honduras, Costa Rica, Panama, El Salvador, Mexico, Cuba, Nicaragua, Guatemala, the Dominican Republic, and Ecuador. The waiting list contained the names of thousands of young men from every country of the Americas.

In the United States, with our hundreds of colleges and universities and our millions of students, the founding of an agricultural school is not noteworthy. But in a part of the continent lacking in facilities for agricultural education, the foundation of the School of Pan-American Agriculture was a memorable event. It is, however, only one school, and dozens more are desperately needed in the American tropics.

The mere fact that the United Fruit Company started such a school was significant indication of changing policies in inter-American business, a concrete expression of the conviction that the present and future good of an industry depends upon the present and future good of the nations in which the industry operates. In founding the school, United Fruit had committed itself to just such a policy. It was a late beginning and would have been even more welcome in 1900 or 1910. It is regrettable that some part of the profits that helped to build fine homes on Beacon Hill could not have gone sooner to the citizens of the countries in which the profits were made.

The *Escuela Agricola Panamericana* is now well known, at least to Central Americans. Other recent activities of the banana trade have remained virtually unnoticed. One of the most important of these is a land-building operation in Honduras, one of the least developed American nations. There banana farmers and engineers are using a swift and violent river to transform large areas of tangled jungle swamps into highly productive farm land.

Rivers can destroy productive farm country by a displacement of soil, and many farmers in the tropics regard rivers as serious liabilities to a successful agriculture. Even in the United States, for every dollar or work hour spent toward making rivers produce something of value, we spend hundreds in efforts to prevent destruction by rivers. We have built thousands of miles of levees only to have the rivers rise even higher above the levels of the adjoining valley lands. We build the levees higher and cause still greater overflows. By and large, our techniques of river control are still defensive. We struggle to keep rivers from hurting us instead of devising ways to make them help us. The Ulua River project in Honduras may be studied with profit by those planners of the future who care to reverse the situation.

Long before the coming of white men, native Indians of Honduras had listed the Ulua as a "bad river." The early Spanish settlement at the headwaters of the Ulua had been abandoned, and for three centuries the swamp-infested valley bred nothing but mosquitoes and pestilence. In Honduras, as in most Latin American countries, the towns and villages were in the foothills and the mountains. Except for a few squatters who built shacks and tilled small garden fields along the river edge, the rich coastal valleys of the Ulua were uninhabited.

From late September to March is the season of heavy rain in Honduras. October usually finds the Ulua and its tributaries at flood stage. For an average of thirty days each year the river runs full channel and, as the rains continue, the

brown waters spill over into the broad valley and sweep away
or bury in mud all farms, fields, buildings, and bridges in the
path of the current. Eventually the flood waters spill farther
down into a huge crescent of pestilential swamplands.

That had been going on for centuries, but the Ulua's en-
croachments have grown with the passing years. As foot upon
foot of silt settled into its channel, the Ulua's bed rose above
the level of the valleys through which it raced. The chances
for an effective system of flood control seemed slim.

Ulua lands are exceptionally good for banana growing.
Hondurans knew this even before the turn of the century,
when the international banana trade was still in its infancy.
But it was not until 1919 that two important banana companies established divisions in the Ulua valley. On the east
bank, or Tela side, of the river were the farms of the United
Fruit Company. On the west bank, or Cortes side, were the
farms of Zemurray's Cuyamel Fruit Company. Both companies relied heavily on their engineering departments. Co-
incidentally two young civil engineers—Patrick Meyers of
Cuyamel and Tom J. Barnett of United Fruit—began separate
studies of the Ulua currents.

On both banks of the river big and little planters alike
watched the Ulua nervously. At first only fringes of river
banks and small areas of the valley lands could be cultivated.
The earliest fields were only strips of two or three rows of
banana plants parallel to the river's course.

Meyers and Barnett discovered that when the waters of
the Ulua were at their highest and the current velocity ranged
from two-and-a-half to five feet per second, the river carried
one-thirty-second of an inch of silt per cubic foot of water.
They estimated that during an average year the Ulua's waters
carry in suspension enough fertile soil to cover 25,000 acres
of valley land with a twelve-inch layer of rich new earth.

But how could the rapacious river be made to part with
the valuable soils? Late in 1919 Pat Meyers of Cuyamel, with

the encouragement and support of Samuel Zemurray, began an experiment on the west bank of the tributary Chamelecon River shortly above its confluence with the Ulua. Within twelve years he had succeeded in building 5000 acres of land with silt deposits of six inches to ten feet. These first river-built lands are now worth at least a million dollars.

Meyers and his men next began to experiment with building collapsible check dams or wide-crested weirs to facilitate the spreading of silt by waters drawn directly from the river channel. They used draglines and steam shovels to dig small surface canals or *boquerones* by means of which the river waters during the rainy season could be swept back and forth across the low stretches of valley at a controlled velocity. That allowed the silt to settle into the swamp sinks and the silt-bearing water to be distributed evenly. Then the engineers had to dig exits for the silt-free water.

The first results, though far from perfect, were successful enough to be encouraging. The *boquerones* and the swamplands between them were leveled and enriched by silt deposits ranging from six inches to twelve feet in depth. Several thousand acres of the reclaimed areas were bearing profitable crops of bananas by 1934. Fertile lands had actually been created by this controlled sedimentation.

In late 1929, when Cuyamel and United Fruit joined forces and properties, the land-building technique had been rather well proved. Since that time the banana men have kept at it. They have built about 9000 acres on the east bank and other banana farm sites on the west bank. Several privately owned plantations—among them Finca Oro and the Birichiche Estate —have joined the United Fruit Company in the project.

More than 15,000 acres had been reclaimed before the Second World War began and war shortages of machinery and ships delayed the work. But the Ulua land-building enterprise continues. Its completion depends, among other things, on the striation of the deep lower swamps with immense discharge canals which will lead sixty miles or more to the Caribbean Sea. The costs will be substantial—$100 an acre, at a conservative guess—but the returns will be well worth such an expense. Already these new lands are yielding 400 or more big bunches of marketable bananas per acre every year. That is almost nineteen tons. Only a few years ago banana yields of 125 bunches, or four tons an acre, were regarded as very good.

Banana growers have made the Ulua lands an international proving ground for land building by recovery of silt. Though it does not necessarily provide an inflexible formula for work in other river basins, the Ulua project is significant laboratory work for building rich new lands in other countries— for reclaiming at least a fragment of the loot that is collected and usually destroyed by the rivers.

Land building, however, is only one of the incidental achievements of the banana trade. The Honduran teak groves, most of the Ecuadorean and Honduran rice fields, the far-scattered groves of African oil palms in Central America, and the *Escuela Agricola Panamericana* are still others. All this is a far cry from the days—still remembered by some contemporaries—when Captain Lorenzo Dow Baker piled the first load of bananas on the splintery foredeck of the *Telegraph* and prayed loudly for a favoring wind.

It is a far cry, too, from the days when New Orleans waterfront gentry puffed fat Cuban cigars to ward off the miasmas of yellow fever while waving in the schooner loads of dead-ripe Bay Island bananas they had bought with whisky, calico, and Turkish medallions—or from the piloting days of old Ed Gill who gave the *Stillwater* a thirteen-degree list and spilled her deck load of green bananas into the blue Caribbean.

As purveyor of half, sometimes more than half, of all bananas in international trade, United Fruit has become an old company and a rich one, and bananas remain the productive work and sustaining life of United Fruit. Without bananas there could be no United Fruit, and, as many buyers have lately remarked, even with United Fruit there are not enough bananas.

Through the centuries banana agriculture has developed and there is no reason to believe that it should not continue for many more centuries. Bulbous rhizomes will be buried in shallow troughs of wet rich earth, fat buds will open, and broad-leafed *plantillas* climb skyward under the rain and the tropical sun. Then giant pink-purple blossoms will flower and dwarfish stems of fruit appear and grow until the weight of the fruit bends down the stalk and the clusters grow upside down. The long leaves will broaden and the brownish stalks grow thick as sun and rain join in the mysterious chemistry of plant creation. Then the cutters will come, driving tractors or leading strings of mules. They will notch the stalk, reap the fruit, and carry it to loading spots, sort it, wash it, and clean it. They will stack the bunches for the pickup trains that take on the green cargo and haul it to shipside. There the waiting files of stevedores will lift the heavy fruit to their shoulders and put it into canvas pockets of conveyors that will carry it into the holds of the ships.

That is how the trade begins and why it does not end. For after the ship sails, as before, on screened farm porches, in offices, in drowsy cantinas, or under the shade of giant banana leaves, men will continue to talk about rum, Scotch, women, and lotteries—but mainly about bananas.